P9-CPV-149

3 1611 00127 8321

780998

Penguin Education

Teaching School Mathematics
Edited by W. Servais and T. Varga

A Unesco Source Book

Teaching
School Mathematics

Edited by W. Servais and T. Varga

Penguin Books – Unesco

UNIVERSITY LIBRARY
GOVERNORS STATE UNIVERSITY
PARK FOREST SOUTH, ILL.

Penguin Books Ltd, Harmondsworth,
Middlesex, England
Penguin Books Inc., 7110 Ambassador Road,
Baltimore, Md 21207, USA
Penguin Books Australia Ltd,
Ringwood, Victoria, Australia
United Nations Educational, Scientific
and Cultural Organization,
Place de Fontenoy, 75 Paris 7-e, France

First published 1971
Copyright © Unesco, 1971

Set in Monophoto Times by
Oliver Burridge (Filmsetting) Ltd, Crawley
Made and printed in Great Britain by
Compton Printing Ltd, Aylesbury

This book is sold subject to the condition that
it shall not, by way of trade or otherwise, be lent,
re-sold, hired out, or otherwise circulated without
the publishers' prior consent in any form of
binding or cover other than that in which it is
published and without a similar condition
including this condition being imposed on the
subsequent purchaser

Contents

QA
11
.S46

Appendix 253

Some Notions of the Basic Structures of Mathematics 255

Bibliography   289

Index   299

Preface

Curriculum development considered in its widest sense has been recognized as the main generating force not only for quality in education but also for fostering the ability to assimilate changes, especially those due to the rapid scientific and technical evolution now in progress. This book is designed to assist those involved in curriculum planning and development by providing information on new approaches and experiences, on new methods and techniques in the teaching of mathematics – a subject of considerable concern in curriculum-reform programmes.

The introduction of a new curriculum involves a change in the very purposes of education and in teaching practices. Thus curriculum has different meanings in various contexts and at different working levels. What is offered here is a survey of new approaches to teaching mathematics, including both practice and theory – from examples of classroom application to the problems of identifying the processes by which mathematics learning takes place. For those readers on the operational level there is provided a selection of syllabuses, a survey of available teaching aids and materials, and a reference appendix to the fundamental concepts of the new mathematics. A comprehensive list for further reading is to be found in the bibliography. Thus it is hoped that the reader, whether working in mathematical education as a curriculum planner, teacher-educator or practising teacher, will find material of interest. Despite the increasing importance of the primary stage in the reform movement, the present book focuses on the secondary level where the mathematics curriculum reform started and has been more readily applicable.

As with the teaching of any science, the teaching of mathematics must necessarily keep pace with advances in the field of mathematics itself. Towards this end, various national and international professional organizations are making sustained efforts to promote the fundamental reforms necessary for the improvement of school mathematics teaching. Mention is made here of one of Unesco's activities in this field, a meeting of experts, the International Symposium on School Mathematics Teaching, convened in Budapest by the Hungarian National Commission for Unesco with the participation of the Organization. At this meeting recommendations were formulated concerning mathematics curricula and the furthering of mathematics teaching to serve as international guidelines. Reference to the Budapest recommendations – a valid and far-reaching statement of objectives for the reform – is made throughout the book.

To prepare this book Unesco approached two experts in the field of mathematics teaching: Willy Servais of the Institut Supérieur de Pédagogie and Préfet des Études at the Athenée Provincial du Centre in Morlanwelz, Belgium, and Tamas Varga, Research Officer of the National Institute of Education in Budapest. Mr Servais and Mr Varga served as consultant editors for this volume, but also wrote major portions of the text, contributing in the areas of their special interest and concern. They turned to the following leading mathematicians and mathematics educators for contributions: Matts Håstad, Secretary of the Nordic Committee for the Modernization of School Mathematics; Anna Zofia Krygowska, Professor of Mathematics and Mathematical Education, Teacher Training College, Cracow; Geoffrey Matthews, Project Organizer of the Nuffield Foundation Mathematics Teaching Project; E. A. Peel, Professor of Educational Psychology, Department of Education, University of Birmingham; and Angelo Pescarini, teacher of mathematics in the secondary schools of Ravenna. These contributions reflect the different experiences and approaches being tried in curricula and methods. To present adequately the current situation in mathematics teaching, the manuscript was submitted to other specialists and educators whose comments and suggestions were incorporated in the book.

Any opinions expressed herein are those of the editors and the authors and do not necessarily reflect the views of Unesco.

It is planned to follow this first title with other guides to the teaching of the basic sciences: biology, chemistry and physics. Science teaching has proved to be a field which most countries are anxious to develop and certainly it represents a marked priority within the national scheme of educational development.

General Introduction

Prepared by T. Varga

0.1 The reform of mathematics teaching

Towards the middle of this century a vast international movement emerged, aimed at making profound changes in mathematical education. Groups, centres, projects and societies were formed with the object of reshaping school mathematics. Research mathematicians, psychologists, teachers and education-ists all became active in the reform both of the content and of the methods of teaching. Individuals and centres joined forces, both within and between countries, and experimental courses were set up.

What are the motives underlying the reform?

One of the possible answers is the conflict between *demands* and *accomplish-ment.*

The science of mathematics is expanding rapidly; school mathematics lags behind by centuries. Social and technical progress depend more and more on up-to-date mathematics in an increasing range of professions. This is because mathematics is becoming a more flexible tool than it ever was in many fields of life and culture, old and new alike. Computers, as results and pro-moters of the progress in mathematics and technology, deserve a special mention. Their rapid spread is an important component of the process of mathematization.

Under the pressure of such factors, vocational training and higher education are overburdened with mathematical topics. This pressure is transmitted to schools which are required to modernize their mathematical training.

Yet there is an opposite pressure, resulting from the lack of ability. For the the majority of pupils even the present curriculum seems to be over full and too difficult. There is much evidence that the mathematical thinking of most pupils does not reach a very high level. Much of the effort these pupils would need to continue their mathematical studies could certainly be put to better use.

The contrast between demands and accomplishment appears to be irreconcilable. Those who meet different facets of the problem come to quite opposite conclusions: one would increase the subject matter, another would decrease it; one would move the teaching of certain topics to lower levels, another towards higher grades. Some recent curricular reforms seem to be the resultants of these two forces, without much attempt to find the roots of the problem.

The awareness that more thorough changes are needed, not just the insertion or exclusion or shift of topics, marks a crucial turning point. The whole curriculum, from the very beginning, is seen to need revision both in content and sequence. Teaching methods must also be re-examined. The reform stands or falls by the teachers; their training and re-training, at every level, is fundamental.

Knowing what is needed would not itself have led to the development of the reform movement. The recognition of new possibilities gave it momentum, and instilled the hope that real advances, not half measures, might be reached in the field of mathematics teaching. This optimism has been fostered both by an appreciation of recent developments in mathematics and psychology, and by actual teaching experience.

In this century mathematics moved away from what is generally called school mathematics. This is one fact. Another is that its core became in a sense more integrated, more coherent and thereby more suitable for building a new 'school mathematics'.

Psychology, too, has made its contribution. In particular, genetic child psychology and various learning theories have led to results that pay a dividend in the learning of mathematics, especially by young children.

It is not only the mere theoretical development in mathematics or in psychology which has given rise to optimism, but the experiences to which they have led. This has helped to dispel the sceptical view according to which understanding mathematics is the privilege of a select few endowed with peculiar innate abilities. This view is readily accepted by those who understand mathematics (for they are, then, an *élite*) and also by those who do not (for then they cannot be blamed for it). Most reformers are none the less convinced that the ability to attain a high level of mathematical culture is within the reach of human beings in general, not of only a select company. This conviction is rooted in the teaching experience mentioned above and has led to further experiment.

From these experiments new ideas and principles are now taking shape, related partly to a new system of school mathematics and its teaching, partly to the strategy of the reform movement, and partly to problems of realizing the reform in practice. Some of these ideas and principles are set out below.

0.2 New and old

In speaking of the reform of mathematics teaching the words 'new' or 'modern' are often used, in this work as elsewhere, as terms of praise. The words 'old' or 'traditional' are accordingly used in a pejorative sense. Such labels should not suggest that a topic is to be rejected solely because it is not recent, or another preferred because it is recent (or labelled as recent). No successful and durable reform may be conceived without a reasonable knowledge of both the old and the new in this field, their evaluation, the integration of what has been found valuable and the rejection of what has become worthless in them.

Here is an example. Comenius (Jan Amos Komensky) revolted centuries ago against the verbal, memorizing way of teaching that survived from the Middle Ages (when it was justified by lack of printing machines). Experience, said Comenius, should be the starting point. Yet because of the inertia of education his principles have not yet been put into practice: the exposition of ready-made knowledge and the overemphasis on verbal memory as opposed to experience and understanding are all too frequent today, even in mathematics teaching. In this respect the principles of Comenius are still 'new' and 'modern'.

0.3 The reform of content and teaching method

Every balanced reform project seeks to modernize both content and teaching methods. Under given conditions one or other may be more important or more urgent, yet 'both in mutual assistance' is usually considered as a better policy than 'either . . . or . . .'. Routine content automatically entails routine ways of presentation.

Content can be analysed into content proper ('What to teach?') and its inner organization, this latter being most closely related to teaching methods. Similarly, teaching methods can be analysed into presentation of the subject matter (e.g. the use of graphical devices or models) and the organization of classroom work, the former being most closely related to the content.

Table 1

Content		Teaching methods	
Content proper (What to teach?)	Organization of the content	Presentation of the content	Organization of classroom work

Some reform trends pay more attention to content and others to teaching methods. The view that the reform of the content is more important than that of the teaching methods is rarely stated explicitly. It is, however, implicit in many publications and schedules. Wherever the reform moves mainly from above (from authorities) downwards, there is a tendency to emphasize content. The content – what to teach – can easily be imposed upon the teacher. Less easy to control is the way it is organized into the curriculum, still less its presentation. Least susceptible of all is the most properly pedagogical activity of organizing children's work. But all of these can be communicated from person to person, like an epidemic. This is an indispensable counterpart, or a desirable alternative, to the introduction of new curricula by higher authorities. If new and more appropriate curricula have been introduced and they still do not pay the expected dividends, the trouble may lie with person-to-person communication of the ingredients.

0.4 Mathematics as a tool and as an autonomous science

In learning mathematics, as in learning a language, use is the best starting point. Few are interested in the structure (mathematical or grammatical) of what they have not experienced in use. If they have, the growing appreciation of the structure is fundamental in promoting correct and efficient use.

Some are anxious lest school mathematics should become by reform too theoretical instead of more practical, as if these two aspects exclude rather than strengthen each other.

Look at mathematical logic. Some decades ago this seemed to be one of the most remote mathematical disciplines to which the rest of mathematics was sometimes opposed as 'concrete mathematics'. Suddenly it has turned out that apart from being theoretical it is also extremely practical. A basic knowledge of logic is, for example, indispensable in understanding and using computers. Logic is now seen as fitting well into the school curriculum and adding much to its theoretical and practical value.

Other topics, elements of which may have a similar twin effect on school mathematics, include mathematical analysis, linear algebra, probability and statistics, information theory and game theory.

To produce this twin effect, it is not enough to have such topics represented in the curriculum. Teachers are needed who themselves think both in terms of applications and in terms of pure mathematics and who can transfer those ways of thinking and of doing to children.

The following example may help to bring home the point. If we, as teachers, suggest to children a useful heuristic rule such as: 'In order to determine three unknowns try to find three conditions', then we train them in the spirit of applications and, of course, heuristic applications. There is no theorem of pure mathematics to the effect that three conditions are either sufficient or necessary to determine three unknowns. Even if we restrict conditions to equations, there is none. Further strong restrictions are needed to guarantee absolute validity to such a statement. In mathematics the proper word for absolute validity is: validity – both in pure and in applied mathematics. Mathematics is a whole; only the aspects differ. From the point of view of applications our primary concern is not validity, at least not to the same extent as in pure mathematical thinking. The time element comes to the fore. We run a risk. But we must know we run a risk. Teachers and pupils, applied mathematicians and academic mathematicians alike must clearly distinguish between heuristic rule and theorem, plausible reasoning and proof.

The traditional teacher has a horror of speaking in inexact terms. But he is not always able to be exact. This makes him inclined to blur the frontier between what is a theorem or a proof and what is not. The clear distinction between these is not exclusive to pure mathematics. An awareness of this distinction enables us to treat the subject in both its theoretical and practical aspects.

In order to see clearly where exactness can or cannot be expected, the distinction between *physical systems* and their *mathematical models** is vital. The idea is old but its consequent realization in schools is a new and promising feature of the new trends.

Certain aspects of a physical system (e.g. a moving body or a statistical sample) can be more or less exactly characterized by mathematical models (e.g. functions). Usually one may choose between models that fit less well to the system but are simpler and more manageable, and others that fit better but are more complicated and more cumbersome. It is usually much harder to find (and harder still to invent) a mathematical model suitable for solving a problem about a physical system and to interpret the result obtained within the mathematical model in terms of the physical system, than to solve just that part of the problem which falls within the mathematical model. The translation from and to the physical system rarely – and then only partially – lends itself to algorithmization; it demands much of sound judgement and intuition. Every teacher of mathematics knows how much more difficult it is to teach the solution of 'word problems' by means of equations than solving the equations themselves, in spite of the fact that word problems in books usually lead to much simpler equations than those extracted from real-life situations and are often little more than straightforward translations of equations.

School mathematics is further detached from real life by an excessive use of simple whole numbers, in order to avoid long and tedious calculations. The best way to get rid of such time wasting is, however, not always by using simple numbers, nor by avoiding numerical data, but by using calculating machines and other devices such as the slide rule.

Such devices, applied in real-life situations, help to develop in children a feeling for order of magnitude and reasonable approximations, and skill in estimation or in the use of rapid rough calculations of numerical results.

All in all, a balance between numerical and non-numerical problems, of widely differing origins, is generally expected from new mathematics teaching.

*The word 'model' is used in mathematics in another, nearly opposite sense as a *mathematical model satisfying a system of axioms*. The point is that a system of axioms is more abstract than its model, but a physical system is less abstract than its mathematical model. If we insist on speaking about models of axiom systems then it would be more reasonable to speak of a physical *model* and a mathematical *system* describing it, than the other way round.

Where to put the emphasis is a matter for consideration and is to be answered according to the situation.

0.5   Mathematics as an art

Many students leave school without ever having felt the beauty of mathematics. More often than not they take the opposite view.

One of the fundamental aims of the present reforms is to help pupils enjoy mathematics, to make them realize its beauty. As a beginning, the fear and anxiety so often raised in them should be removed. Essential to this approach is freedom of expression, arising from playful activity. To realize and enjoy the beauty of mathematics, pupils must be given sufficient opportunity for free, playful, creative activity, where each can bring out his own measure of wit, taste, fantasy, and display thereby his personality.

Students who have a feeling for beauty realize more easily, for example, that mathematics gains in beauty if we put $3^0 = 1$ and $3^{-2} = \frac{1}{9}$ rather than accepting, say $3^0 = 0$ and $3^{-2} = -9$. They find this harmonious and they also find it useful because it fits into and extends the pattern of earlier knowledge. Such examples make them aware of how beauty can show the way towards utility.

An important type of problem developing (and making use of) the sense of beauty is the search for patterns.

Mathematical recreations also have a role in helping pupils to like mathematics. Puzzles in mathematics are somewhat similar to songs in music: short and self-contained, not too ambitious and accessible to many. Some are the personal inventions of creators of mathematics; others are of unknown origin, becoming polished through centuries, emerging here and there in different variants like folk songs. They are also like anecdotes, which often point to deep ideas. Think of their role in the development of topology, probability or logic. Puzzles can be excellent starting points and incentives for deep ideas in school mathematics as in creative mathematics itself.

0.6   Mathematics as a whole

One of the main disadvantages of traditional school mathematics is its piecemeal character; on this there is general agreement. In the new-style curricula, however different they are, unifying tendencies emerge. *Set, relation, function, group, vector* and many others are 'unifying concepts'. Their place in the curriculum is the object of much controversy and experiment.

Those who prefer later introduction, because these concepts are too abstract for children, think it is preferable first to meet a number of special cases in order to have a firm base for generalization. Those who are for an early introduction think that arriving at a reasonably general concept through concrete situations, and then applying the idea to special cases, has the advantage of giving a comprehensive view.

Those who hold the first view are influenced by attempts to introduce general concepts without adequate preparation, without sufficient motivation, in an uninspired way. Those who hold the second view contrast these cases with successful experiments, which they regard as existence theorems.

Typical of the piecemeal approach are courses of geometry in the Euclidean spirit. Krygowska (1962)* has written in this connexion:

Their illusions [i.e. those of the partisans of Euclid] have long hindered the enrichment and the modernization of the average pupil's education through mathematics teaching, given the piecemeal treatment of the general notions of classical geometry, often presented virtually in fragments. (For example, the pupils recite the definitions of a convex angle, of a convex polygon, of a convex polyhedron, but they have no idea that a circle is convex.) The general definitions based on the idea of sets of points were alien to the deductive system of Euclid's *Elements*. Yet such restrictions are inconceivable in a modern geometry course.

The new curricula, which are being tested in many variants, aim at not merely removing this fragmentation from *within* the various mathematical disciplines such as geometry, arithmetic and algebra. The disciplines themselves are gradually being integrated.

The separation of arithmetic and algebra in the school time-table is regarded today as anachronistic. It sounds indeed incredibly dull, although it is a fact, that in many schools after having studied arithmetic for five, six or seven years, the pupil moves to a so-called course of algebra which begins with equations such as $3x = 18$ and with statements such as: 'The commutative law of addition is valid not only in arithmetic but also in algebra: $a+b = b+a$.' (As if this identity did not express in a general way – at this informal level – the very fact known from arithmetic that the sum of any two *numbers* is the same whatever the order of the numbers is.)

Instead of this obsolete separation we now find it quite natural that the solution of equations as well as inequations is an integral part of learning arithmetic, or rather of mathematics, as early as grade one.

The integration of the mathematical curriculum does not stop here. Algebraic methods (this time not only in the sense of traditional school mathematics) penetrate into geometry. They abolish the division between 'synthetic' and 'analytic' geometry and contribute to the integration of geometry with the rest of mathematics.

There are concepts in mathematics having a unifying strength which goes beyond the scope of traditional mathematics. It might be said that those concepts extend mathematics by establishing patterns not previously envisaged.

An example of such a concept is a *set* (together with other pertinent concepts such as *element*, *subset*, *intersection*, *union*, *Cartesian product* and *relation*). If we regard grammatical notions such as *noun* and *adjective* as useful in

*References for the Introduction will be found on p. 32.

17   Mathematics as a whole

developing clear thinking, we should attach even more importance to the following ideas about sets. Given a fundamental set, for example that of human persons, some nouns and adjectives, such as 'sailor' or 'one-legged', each define a *set* within the larger set, that is a *subset* of the larger set (see Figure 1). Proper nouns and some other designations (such as 'G. B. Shaw', 'the first cosmonaut') identify *elements* of the fundamental set (Figure 1). Other words and phrases (such as 'is the son of', 'knows', 'is older than') express *relations* between elements of the fundamental set (Figure 2). An adjective together with a general noun, or two consecutive adjectives ('one-legged

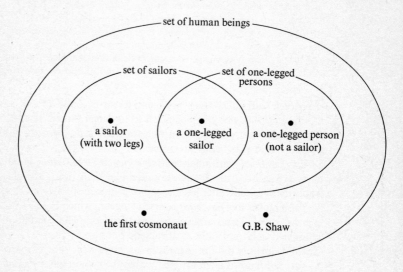

Figure 1 Subsets and elements of a fundamental set

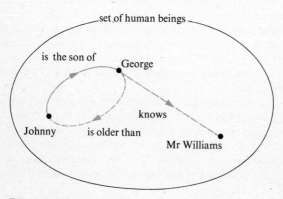

Figure 2 Relations between elements of a set

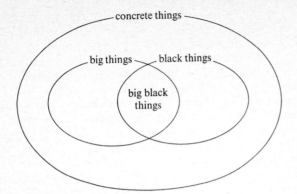

Figure 3 Intersection of sets

sailor', 'big black') usually determine the *intersection* of the two sets defined by them separately (Figure 3); and so on.

In the above examples concepts of set theory have been related to those of grammar, as the less familiar to the more familiar. This order is hardly natural. Such fundamental set-theoretical concepts as those listed above and the logical concepts closely linked with them, such as those of conjunction, disjunction, implication, etc., are simpler, deeper and more powerful than those of grammar and by no means assume a previous knowledge of grammatical notions. Their grasp at an age of, say, between six and twelve is a powerful aid to clear thinking.

In mathematics itself these concepts enable pupils to realize relationships between many notions that earlier emerged accidentally and were learned without apparent connexions. (For example, when we speak of the greatest divisor of two numbers, or of the solution of simultaneous equations, each time we look for the intersection of two sets.)

In a similar way, *equations* and *inequations* as special concepts are fitted into the more general concept of a *condition* or an *open sentence*. The following are all open sentences:

$$x+2 = 5, \qquad \square+2 < 5, \qquad \text{— divides 6,}$$

—was a sister of Branwell Brontë.

The *truth sets* of these sentences are, in the case of the first three, subsets of the set of natural numbers $\mathbb{N}$, and of the fourth, a subset of the set of human beings $\mathbb{H}$:

$$\{3\}, \qquad \{0, 1, 2\}, \qquad \{1, 2, 3, 6\},$$

{Anne Brontë, Charlotte Brontë, Emily Brontë}.

Each of the above is an open sentence in one variable; they determine *subsets* of a set (of $\mathbb{N}$, of H). Open sentences in more than one variable, such as '— divides —', define *relations*.

The concept of an open sentence is extremely simple, children of six to seven years old can easily grasp it through everyday examples. Yet it is just as deep as it is simple; it contains the germ of one of the most important concepts of modern logic: that of a propositional function.

An early knowledge of general unifying ideas does not mean a hunt for half-ripe abstractions alien to the mind of the child. Rather it amounts to what may be called a striving after 'globality': instead of starting from the parts and trying to fit them together to a whole, it means going from the whole to its parts. Learning is viewed by the reformers as an aspect of the development of an organism – a human being. Characteristic to the development of organisms is the start from a whole, a germ. Learning is much more similar to biological growth than to manufacture, where component parts are first produced, then fitted together.

Another aspect of mathematics as a whole is the balance between knowledge and technique. Without the latter the former is of little value. A wide view of very general concepts is not much use to a student if he cannot simplify an expression like

$$\frac{a^2-1}{1-a} \quad \text{or} \quad A \cup (A \cap B).$$

Yet formal skills are only a small part of technique in mathematics. A much more general view is expressed in the well-known memorandum of sixty-five American mathematicians published in the March 1962 issue of *Mathematics Teacher* and *American Mathematical Monthly*: 'To know mathematics means to be able to do mathematics: to use mathematical language with some fluency, to do problems, to criticize arguments, to find proofs, and, what may be the most important activity, to recognize a mathematical concept in, or to extract it from, a given concrete situation.'

0.7 **Familiarity and surprise**

An outstanding mathematician once said that one can teach anything to children, even false ideas, but only for a while. Nothing will become lasting and useful knowledge unless it is rooted in ideas familiar to children, connected with their range of thought. As Polya has put it, each step in a lesson should be of such a character that the student might have thought of it himself. . . . One might add: or such that he would *not* have thought of it at all. A surprising idea, one that shocks the child, one that he would have thought *differently*, is also connected with his range of thought.

'What are the neighbours of 1099?' This is a good question in grade 3 or 4, because some of the children will perhaps say 2000 for one neighbour. Traditional educationists are not fond of questions which may lead to a false answer.

'Children should not be confused,' they say. One of the most important means of new-style mathematics teaching is to puzzle children, indeed to confuse them, again and again.

'What are the neighbours of $\frac{2}{3}$?' – this question sounds bewildering. The new style teaching of mathematics does not refrain from raising such questions, nor from answering directly if the questions are raised by children.

To children accustomed to surprises and shocks, it is no longer easy to teach *anything*, especially not if it is false. Those who are often 'confused' in the above sense are more likely to think independently and less likely to accept an idea or a statement on mere authority. Keeping within the children's range of thought also means letting them express their ideas in their own language. Their struggle with words helps their thoughts to ripen; the need for successful communication improves their ways of expression.

A non-authoritarian approach is required to realize the possibilities of teaching young children more mathematics than before.

0.8 Levels

'In which grade should coordinate geometry be taught?' This is a question characteristic of the construction of traditional programmes. Now the question would be asked in the form: 'What ideas of coordinate geometry should be included in a particular grade?'

This change in the formulation of questions is connected with the shift of emphasis from imparting knowledge towards mental development. The same subject matter can be 'known' at different levels. We begin to see what these levels are and begin to consider them in planning curricula. This results in a much more intricate curriculum than in the past, much less describable in the usual terms.

In order to express the idea that we return to the same topic several times, each time at a higher level, the terms *spiral curriculum* and *concentric curriculum* are used. An instance of the latter is the two-level teaching of elementary synthetic geometry: a 'propaedeutic course' (for example from ten to twelve years of age) and a 'systematic course' (from thirteen to fifteen). In the spiral curriculum there are no such breaks; there is a gradual transition and the two levels coexist for a long time. Instead of a sharp change from one level to the other there is a back-and-forth traffic between the two. This is the best way of making the transition – if it can be so called – from arithmetic to algebra (in the traditional sense). One can never say, 'The course of arithmetic is over; the course of algebra begins.'

Good teachers have always adapted themselves, as far as the programmes allowed, to the natural developmental levels of mathematics learning. They were induced to do so perhaps by their need of contact with the students. Yet there is something new today in this respect: the conscious use of scientific knowledge about child development and the growth of human thinking in general. The reshaping of curricula based on this knowledge will do much to promote adaptation.

In the past much has been said about the psycho-pedagogical conditions governing the drawing up of the programmes, especially of where to begin. It has often been said that what was called 'deductive thinking' could not be started before an age of about twelve.

Recent psychological research and educational experience have considerably modified this view. Instead of waiting for the ripening, the idea of making ripe has come to the fore – an idea advocated earlier by such psychologists as Stern and Vygotsky. As we now see (Bruner, 1966):

... some capacities must be matured and nurtured before others can be called into being. The sequence of their appearance is highly constrained. But these steps or stages or spurts ... are not very clearly linked to age: some environments can slow the sequence down or bring it to a halt, others move it along faster. In the main, one can characterize these constrained sequences as a series of prerequisites. It is not until the child can hold in mind two features of a display at once, for example, that he can deal with their relationship, as in a ratio.... The steps or stages have been variously described by a variety of investigators working in centres as widespread as Geneva, Moscow, Paris, London, Montreal, Chicago and Cambridge, but they seem to have an interesting likeness.

Some of the researches into identifying the levels, or the series of prerequisites, in various fields of mathematics teaching are the following: Van Hiele and Van Hiele-Geldof (1958/9), Skemp (1962) and Pyshkalo (1965).

The five levels distinguished by Pyshkalo in the development of geometrical ideas may be summed up as follows:

1. The child sees the geometrical figure as a whole, without distinguishing its parts and without realizing relationships between them or between different figures.

2. Beginnings of analysis: through experience (observation, drawing, modelling) the child gets acquainted with constituent parts and properties of figures but he does not see relationships between properties; the idea of defining a figure by some of its properties is unknown to him.

3. Beginnings of deductive thinking: the insight that some properties imply other ones; appreciation of definitions; logical organization is local, the role of axioms is not yet grasped.

4. The view of geometry as a deductive system: defined and undefined concepts, proved theorems, axioms accepted without proof; the logical structure of a proof.

5. A system of axioms as the definition of an abstract structure: the possibility of different interpretations. The validity of a theory independent of its interpretations.

Pyshkalo has found by surveys made in five schools that before the usual systematic course started, at about eleven or twelve years of age, more than 90 per cent of the pupils had not moved beyond level 1. Yet the systematic course assumed a maturity corresponding to level 3. Similar considerations led much earlier in England to the end of the rigid systematic course of geometry in the Euclidean spirit and its replacement by what is known as the stage A, B, C approach to geometry.

Having regard to the prerequisites and adapting the curriculum to children's levels of thought allows them much quicker progress than the imposition of adult thinking. Those whose experiences are mostly related to the 'adult thinking' kind of teaching find alarming the idea of a curriculum in which children from six to fourteen years old acquire mathematical notions previously regarded as higher mathematics, belonging to the fields of sets and logic, modern algebra, probability, etc.

This would be alarming indeed if children mastered words only without the notions behind them; or only isolated notions not rooted in their own thinking which do not develop into useful tools. Producing such pseudo-results instead of looking for the optimal conditions of children's development in mathematical thinking is not rare. Yet behind sham results and half results it is impossible to see the real ones. Partial though they may be, they have modified our earlier view about the potentialities of young children. Those who have experienced the development of these potentialities in average children, even under unfavourable conditions, cannot help thinking that many other children are being deprived and wasting a mathematically receptive period that will never return. Quoting Bruner again:

In the last few years there have been reports showing the crippling effect of deprived human environments as well as indications that 'replacement therapies' can be of considerable success even at an age on the edge of adolescence. The principal deficiencies appear to be linguistic in the broadest sense – the lack of opportunity to share in dialogue, to have occasion for paraphrase, to internalize speech as a vehicle of thought.... Unless certain basic skills are mastered, later, more elaborate ones become increasingly out of reach. . . .

As we see today, the traditional teaching of mathematics can be looked upon even when successful as a sort of 'replacement therapy' – some kind of special education for retarded children (the majority of school children today). 'Better late than never', we try to save what we can. This is extremely important. But it is even more important to make the best of the years which are the most receptive for mathematical growth.

0.9 Cycles in learning mathematics

0.9.1 In the learning of mathematics, research workers have identified a certain cyclic structure. In the formation of a concept or in the learning of an item of knowledge, stages or phases have been distinguished which together constitute a cycle. When it is complete, or while it is still growing, a new cycle, consisting of similar stages, may begin.

Two descriptions of such cycles, due to Dienes (1960, p. 39) and Polya (1963, p. 605), are worthy of comparison:

Dienes	*Polya*
The preliminary or play stage corresponds to rather undirected, seemingly purposeless activity usually described as play. In order to make play possible, freedom to experiment is necessary.	A first, exploratory phase which is close to action and perception and moves on an intuitive, heuristic level.
The second stage is more directed and purposeful. At this stage a certain degree of structured activity is desirable.	A second, formalizing phase ascends to a more conceptual level, introducing terminology, definitions and proofs.
The next stage really has two aspects: one is having a look at what has been done and seeing how it is really put together (logical analysis); the other is making use of what we have done (practice). In either case this stage completes the cycle, the concept is now safely anchored with the rest of experience and can be used as a new toy with which to play new games.	The phase of assimilation comes last: there should be an attempt to perceive the 'inner grounds' of things; the material learnt should be mentally digested, absorbed into the system of knowledge, into the whole mental outlook of the learner. This phase paves the way to applications on one hand, to higher generalizations on the other.

The growing appreciation of the value of beginning with lightly structured, guided, explorative activity is one of the most conspicuous and most promising features in reform work the world over.

0.9.2   Another remarkable characteristic in the new mathematics teaching, closely related to the cyclic course of learning, is the almost total absence of drill in developing skills or in memorizing facts, as an independent activity. Skills in formal arithmetic, for instance, are not developed by doing sums mechanically, but by activities which lead to interesting new concepts and knowledge. In terms of the above, while completing the last stage, a new cycle is being started. The new activity may be the solution of equations or of inequations, first by simply guessing, then by consecutive approximation, in each case by substituting the supposed roots and testing whether they satisfy or not.

The integration of the development of skills into subsequent cycles has several advantages. First, children have the feeling of going along, and this makes the lesson more challenging, more motivating for them. Second, they are going along without loss of time. Third, skills are more efficiently developed in this way and become more ready for application, since they are developed in the course of their application rather than out of any context.

0.9.3   A third conspicuous feature of the pilot work in many reform projects is a delay in the verbalization, at least publicly, of what has been found – of rules, shortcuts and relationships. Again, this has several advantages. First, slower pupils have more opportunity to experience the discovery for themselves and do not just accept a formulation void of sense for them. Second, a certain delay before verbalization usually helps the idea to ripen. The act of verbalization in due course also has such an effect. Third, it may be a valuable – even though external – motivation to try to find a secret that some of the pupils know but do not share.

0.10   Individual differences

The growing consideration of the differences between pupils is another important trend. The basic idea is that every child should be given the opportunity to display his abilities as fully as possible, be he quick or slow, deep or superficial, thinking this way or that. This requirement is not specific to mathematics teaching, but here it is particularly important. In no other subject does a disregard of the differences influence so severely the efficiency of teaching.

Some ways of making allowances for such differences are the following:

(a) Children work individually or in small groups on more or less different tasks. The teacher certainly cannot decide which task will contribute most to the development of each child at a given time. Even if he could, it would be difficult to assign to each pupil the most suitable task every time. Evidently he has to allow pupils some choice and give them some autonomy in organizing their work. His main responsibility is to set going this 'self-regulating process', to control it, to correct its errors. Such organization of the work in the classroom is no stopgap arrangement. It has ingredients which are educationally valuable: pupils get used to independent, autonomous, self-reliant work; the possibility of choice adds to their morale; they are more likely to progress at their own pace than with the usual class organization.

Sometimes children of similar ability are grouped together. Sometimes groups are mixed and one child in each group is expected to act as a leader. Perhaps the best solution is to let children form groups so that friends are together; the quicker is rarely patient enough to help the slower unless they are friends.

(b) The class is divided by the teacher into two (or three) groups, according to ability or achievement. These groups are set apart and dealt with in turn. While there is discussion with one group the rest of the class may be involved in individual or group work. The groups are not inflexible divisions – there may be regrouping or minor adjustments from time to time.

(c) The 'streaming' of pupils in parallel classes of the same grade according to ability has a similar aim. In many countries the separation of pupils according to their interests rather than ability is preferred. Often there is a mathematical and scientific stream. The regrouping of the pupils within the class is nearer to 'interest streaming' than to streaming according to ability. The fact that it is related to one particular subject, mathematics for example, reduces such undesirable side-effects as the loss of self-esteem by those who are in a lower stream.

(d) In some countries, notably the USSR and Hungary, mathematical and mathematical–physical classes are being organized for the pupils gifted or interested in these subjects. Many other opportunities are given to such pupils: correspondence courses during their school years according to an additional programme, clubs, competitions, holiday activities, lectures, films, books, student journals.

The following points should also be noted:

(a) In considering individual differences, attention to the gifted or interested is only one aspect. The rest should also be given opportunities to make the most of their abilities. They have to avoid blind alleys and acquire knowledge which can be used and developed later. They, too, should have a positive attitude towards mathematics and certainly not one of fear or anxiety. The 'average' and the 'slow' learner can probably expect still more from the reform than the 'gifted'.

(b) In looking at differences the first step is for the teacher to be aware of the students, to see them, to pay attention, not only to their academic success, but also to their progress through the curriculum. In mathematics teaching failure to do this is the most common mistake, especially at higher levels.

(c) Recognizing these differences is not the same as removing them. It is a dangerous illusion to think that pupils in a class, even if they form a rather homogeneous group, can be 'kept together' in their mathematical development by 'bringing up the slower ones to the level of the rest of the class'. Efforts to level up often lead to levelling down.

(d) The harmful side-effects of the differences between pupils (such as the feeling of inferiority) are increased by the use of rewards and punishments.

(e) Emphasis on the differences between teachers and pupils usually entails emphasis on the differences between pupils themselves. If the teacher is not supercilious and is not afraid to go wrong, if he admits to an error or openly states that he does not know, if he is ready to give his ideas in an informal way and is willing to learn from his pupils, then he is likely to produce a similar attitude in his pupils towards others: the slower ones will not be so ashamed to go wrong, the brighter ones will be less likely to look down on the rest.

0.11   Discovery and exposition

0.11.0   'The best way to learn anything is to discover it by yourself,' writes Polya (1965, p. 103). This is more true in mathematics than in other subjects. The system of ideas exposed by Polya in his works about problem solving, plausible reasoning and mathematical discovery (1954, 1963 and 1965) has had considerable influence on several mathematics teaching reform projects. Among the ingredients of new school mathematics there is hardly one more important than that of leading the pupils to meet mathematics *in statu nascendi*, or to make them rediscover it.

0.11.1   This means first an approach to mathematics through problems. In the old-style teaching of mathematics sharp distinction is made between theoretical material and problems or exercises to which the theory is applied. In new approaches such a distinction becomes blurred. The law of sines, for instance, is not necessarily a theoretical item of knowledge to be deduced and then applied. It may be proposed as a problem, or rather as a link in a chain of problems. Books by Dynkin and Uspenskii (1963), and Yaglom and Yaglom (1964) are instances of this; they take topics from graphs, number theory, probability and geometry, and break them up into problems. Books of this kind may be of much help in the future.

0.11.2   The original discoverers of mathematics were not given ready-made problems. They were faced with 'problem situations' which they had first to realize and formulate. Sometimes they even solved the problem before having formulated it precisely.
   A similar approach is often instructive for the rediscoverers of mathematics. (See, for example, Polya, 1965, p. 107.) To begin with open problem situations has the advantage of developing an 'applicational attitude' in mathematics (cf. the study of Papy in *Mathematics Today*, OECD, 1964). Those who apply mathematics rarely deal with readily formulated mathematical problems. They are more often confronted with open problem situations which they have to mathematize, to translate into the language of mathematics, to find a fitting mathematical model (cf. section 0.4). While doing this they have no such cue as pupils often have: 'We are now on Chapter N, so this problem is likely to be solved by methods in Chapter N.'

0.11.3   Mathematics is not only a body of theorems and problems. To it belong also definitions and axioms, notation and terminology. In an up-to-date teaching of mathematics pupils learn not only names and symbols for mathematical entities, but also to name and to symbolize. Searching for a better name or symbol than that accepted by others is just as important as adapting themselves to standards and common usage. The same applies to forming concepts or to adopting axioms. Weighing the relative merits of various definitions or axioms, names or symbols is an important *mathematical* activity, even though it does not belong to formal mathematics.

0.11.4 The term 'discovery method' has different meanings according to the degree of originality involved.

One extreme is when the teacher determines that children should discover a certain fact or law, and leads them to it through sufficiently graded questions. If the teacher is skilful, success is guaranteed, but children may not see the wood for the trees.

At the other extreme the situation is so open that discoveries made by the children may be new to the teacher himself. Such moments are solemn for a teacher who understands what the children discover and the frequency of such solemn moments may be a measure of high-quality teaching. Yet it would be unrealistic to raise such a standard for mass education.

0.11.5 In learning mathematics, as in learning languages, the active aspects – expressing our own ideas, using mathematics and language as a tool – are of paramount importance, but they have to be supplemented by passive aspects – understanding the ideas of others, assimilating them, allowing them to bear fruit. Developing in students the habit of learning from books or from oral exposition is an important component of mathematical education. Those who have sufficient experience in the active aspects are more likely to behave actively during these passive periods. For example, they put the book aside before a proof starts and try to construct the proof themselves; or try to find examples from general statements, or to generalize from examples. On the other hand, they who have acquired competence in the technique of reading (or listening to) mathematics, gain a powerful means therein for widening the scope of their mathematical understanding; this widening is likely to help in their more active work, their rediscovering mathematics or discovering it anew.

0.11.6 Partisans of the discovery method may sometimes exaggerate its value, but they have good reasons to support it. First, they seek to counterbalance the prevalent use in schools of the expository method. Second, they trust that the time invested in it will be recovered later on by the higher degree of independent thought which it will produce in the children. Third, they find it indispensable to an early introduction of advanced mathematical ideas.

0.12 **Motivation**

Every child, by nature, likes learning just as he likes eating. Children reluctant to eat, and parents using promises and threats in order to make them eat, are not rare, yet they constitute perhaps rather an exception than a rule. In teaching, the situation is worse: to attach rewards and punishments to learning is more a rule than an exception. It is an institutionalized practice supported by social conditioning and by decrees. This practice exerts an unfavourable influence on the natural process of learning.

The reform movement contributes to the solution of this grave and intricate problem in many ways. It can provide children with mental 'food' necessary for their development, presented in an inviting form. Both the content and the form can induce children to regard the learning of mathematics as their own concern and not an activity forced upon them.

Success in the reform usually goes with the reconsideration of the motivational aspect of teaching. Davis (1964) writes about how this problem is dealt with by the Madison Project in the following terms:

We should admit at the outset that we use the ordinary rewards such as praise and affectionate warmth, etc. in securing reasonable *social* behaviour. *We try never, however, to use a teacher-imposed external reinforcement schedule to determine what a child thinks, how he answers a question, or how he attacks a problem.* (This last may be mild overstatement; perhaps the proper description would be : well, hardly ever.)

We try to use two forms of reinforcement only: first *intrinsic* rewards derived from solving a problem, from the reduction of cognitive strain which follows upon the discovery of an important concept or relationship, from the gratification of experimental verification of a prior theoretical prediction, etc., and, second, the reward that comes from being able to *tell* your classmates or your teacher about what you have just discovered or have just accomplished.

The limitation expressed in the remark made by Davis (in brackets) arises from the realization of the present situation. In a similar vein Polya (1965, p. 103) writes: 'The interest of the material to be learned should be the best stimulus to learning and the pleasure of intensive mental activity should be the best reward for such activity. Yet, where we cannot obtain the best we should try to get the second best, or the third best. . . .'

The interest may have its source both within and outside mathematics. Mathematics as an autonomous activity and mathematics as a tool, or a key to other activities, may both be challenging.

Without interest efficient learning of mathematics is hardly conceivable; nor is it without effort. These two are by no means opposed to each other. For an interesting and challenging activity we are more ready to make effort and even sacrifice.

0.13   Evaluation

Evaluation is a highly controversial issue. Paradoxically, that which can be evaluated with reasonable reliability (such as formal skills, problem-solving ability limited to specific kinds of problems, retention of factual knowledge) is much less worth evaluating than that which cannot (such as understanding or originality). Laying greater emphasis on evaluation, and on examinations in particular, entails the risk of a shift towards less valuable rather than more valuable aspects of teaching.

Yet one needs some reassurance, over and above the personal impressions of teachers and visitors, that the effort of reforming (or simply teaching) school mathematics is not wasted and that there is definite progress towards desirable goals. Some kind of objective evaluations are necessary to this end, without allowing them a central role in shaping classroom work.

The following points seem to be essential:

(a) Even if the evaluation of the more valuable aspects of mathematical learning is limited, the weight of these aspects in evaluations should be increased.

(b) Evaluations are to be considered as a feedback that helps to determine the subsequent course of the work. They serve first of all to help answer questions of this kind: 'Are children ripe (or, is this particular child ripe) for this kind of assignment, or for a more advanced, or rather a less advanced one?'

(c) Long-term evaluations (related to a period possibly of several years) are especially important, even with individual children and especially with populations large enough to make statistical inferences possible. These may serve to assess the relative merits of short-term evaluation procedures, for example, by checking how far predictions based on such procedures, related to further education and career, are verified later.

0.14 Towards a science of mathematical education

The contrast between *mathematics* as a prototype of exact science and *education* is so marked that one hesitates to speak about a science of mathematical education. No doubt, teaching is and remains an art and its laws (or secrets) can only partially be revealed by scientific analysis. But is this not true of every kind of human activity? The differences are of degree, depending on the variables involved. Even mathematics, the simplest of all sciences, had to go a long way before reaching the level of a science. A simple path is open to pedagogy, and in particular the pedagogy of mathematics, in spite of its many variables. Mathematical education, though still in a preliminary stage of reorganization, has become an increasingly important area of educational research. The results of this research form the theoretical counterpart of the practice of reforming school mathematics. Clearly, the empirical findings of the reform must lead towards certain generalizations as regards both the content and the form of teaching, and valid principles must have practical applications in actual classroom work.

Mathematical education as a field of research is gradually finding acceptance. Though its frontiers are not yet clearly defined, it is safe to say that the scientific approach of such researchers as Krygowska and Matthews is making a contribution to this specific field.

0.15 Programmed learning

In a book concerned with new trends in teaching mathematics, programmed learning cannot be ignored. It must be said, however, that opinions about this issue range wide, from those who proclaim its advent as a new era in education, to those who regard it as a plague on mathematical education. None of these views is acceptable.

One way of looking at programmed learning is to see in it the application of cybernetic ideas to education. The gains may be theoretical (the analysis of the learning process from a new angle) and practical (the introduction of automatic and semi-automatic devices into this process). The first is a real challenge furnishing and promising new insights, though there is also a danger of merely relabelling old phenomena. As to the second, it must be said that claims about the present and future merits of programmed learning of mathematics are too high in proportion either to evidence obtained from objective evaluations or to the material and mental investments.

As mentioned earlier, evaluating procedures are more sensitive to the formal elements of learning and less sensitive to such elements as understanding or original thinking. It may be thought that the merits of programmed learning lie in these latter fields. This is not so. The strongest claim for programmed materials is that they take over much of the routine drill, so freeing the teacher for more human aspects of the work.

In this respect it should be recalled that routine drill has a decreasing role in new mathematics teaching; practice in formal skills is preferably linked to some challenging hunt for new concepts and ideas. Even if drill remains, it is more efficient if it constantly changes its form and becomes individualized. Flexibility is, however, not the leading quality of present-day programmed materials.

The situation as described above may change. For example, the use of computers will, it is claimed, provide in the future for the mass introduction of flexible learning programmes. Computer-based instruction is perhaps the greatest promise of the programmed learning movement.

0.16 The growing role of the teacher

The shortage of qualified and competent mathematics teachers is a world-wide phenomenon. It is aggravated by the increasing demand on mathematics and mathematicians in so many fields of the modern world outside education. The quality of mathematics teaching should be increased at every level from primary to university. Yet there is an imminent menace of decrease because of teacher shortage due to the very reasons that demand the increase.

Most reformers probably agree that the proper way of breaking this vicious circle is not the partial or total replacement of some teachers by technical means and devices, but by measures tending to increase the social prestige of the teaching profession in general and of mathematics teachers in particular. The flight from this profession is evidently not an accident but a natural consequence of its still-insufficient prestige.

Computers have taught us to appreciate the mental power of man more than we did before. Education means, in a sense, the programming of human brains, those mighty instruments, to very complicated tasks, the most important of which is the continued programming of themselves and others. Is it possible that in the future teachers will be esteemed accordingly?

Progress towards this higher prestige goes hand in hand with the reform itself. It can be facilitated by administrative or financial measures, but substantial improvements cannot be achieved over night. Making the profession more attractive, improving the qualifications and competence of teachers and reforming mathematics teaching (its content and form) are mutually dependent.

Evidently, just as teaching should stem from the children's own interests and help them in realizing their intentions, the reform should realize the best intentions of the teachers; it should elicit and make use of their ideas. Imposing a reform on the teachers is just as bad as imposing mathematics on children. Bringing out the potentialities of teachers as well as of children is perhaps what matters most.

References

BRUNER, J. S. (1966), *Toward a Theory of Instruction*, Harvard University Press.
DAVIS, R. B. (1964), *Discovery in Mathematics*, Addison-Wesley.
DIENES, Z. P. (1960), *Building up Mathematics*, 2nd edn, Hutchinson.
DYNKIN, E. B., and USPENSKII, V. A. (1963), *Topics in Mathematics*, Heath; Harrap.
KRYGOWSKA, A. Z. (1962), 'L'enseignement de la geometrie dans la mathématique unitaire d'aujourd'hui', *Mathematica et Pedagogica*, no. 23.
OECD (1964), *Mathematics Today*, Organization for Economic Co-operation and Development.
POLYA, G. (1954), *Mathematics and Plausible Reasoning*, 2 vols., Princeton University Press.
POLYA, G. (1963), 'On learning, teaching, and learning teaching', *American Mathematical Monthly*, vol. 70, p. 605.

POLYA, G. (1965), *Mathematical Discovery on Understanding, Learning and Teaching Problem Solving*, vol. 2, Wiley.

PYSHKALO, A. M. (1965), *Geometriya v. I–IV Klassah (Geometry in Grades 1–4)*, Moscow: Prosveščenija.

SKEMP, R. R. (1962), 'The need for a schematic learning theory', *British Journal of Educational Psychology*, vol. 31, pp. 133–42.

VAN HIELE, P. M., and VAN HIELE-GELDOF, D. (1958/9), 'La signification des niveaux de pensée dans l'enseignement par la méthode deductive', *Mathematica et Pedagogica*, no. 16, pp. 25–34.

YAGLOM, A. M., and YAGLOM, I. M. (1964), *Challenging Mathematical Problems with Elementary Solutions*, Holden-Day.

Part One

New Ways of Teaching: Practice and Theory

1 Classroom Treatment of Some Essential Topics

To form an opinion on mathematics teaching, it is important to see what teaching methods and educational media are used. The best way to do this is in an actual lesson, that is, to observe classwork. Present trends need to be illustrated by concrete examples of the way certain subjects have been dealt with by pupils.

There are many ways of describing a lesson or series of lessons, and we have felt it best to vary our methods. In the case of the junior pupils, we have described what happens in the classroom, noting the children's attitude, their questions, their discoveries and their difficulties, as well as the teacher's explanations, his silences and his comments. When dealing with older pupils, we have progressively reduced the descriptive part, and given an outline of the material covered in a series of lessons.

No attempt has been made to reconstruct the life of the class – not even a film could do that – but we have tried to record with some accuracy what we have actually seen done. These lessons were actually given, and we have noted their merits, points on which there may have been omissions, and aspects of them which some people may perhaps consider open to question. They are not ideal or model lessons, but they have the advantage of being drawn from life. The pupils' lively interest and ready participation in these lessons show, as far as the observer can judge, that they have effectively grasped material which is sometimes considered to be too advanced or too abstract for their age.

From these few examples, the reader should gain a clearer understanding of what is meant by expressions such as an 'active lesson', 'the teacher's role as a guide', 'the use of educational situations', 'the use of examples drawn from the sciences', etc. In some cases, the account of the lesson is followed by comments on significant or noteworthy features. Our thanks are due to the teachers who have allowed us to observe their work or have reported on it: Mrs Papy, Mrs Oláh, Messrs Clersy, Delmotte, Dienes, Håstad, Matthews and Pescarini.

These lessons provide evidence of what can be done by schoolchildren from the outset and through secondary schooling in given circumstances. The question of knowing which topics are the most desirable or useful to treat at the various levels of a given curriculum is one open to experiment and discussion, but the experience of mathematics teachers and educationists has led to the definition of certain classroom conditions favourable for the learning of mathematics. In this connexion the following points were made at the International Symposium on School Mathematics Teaching in Budapest:

Teaching should rely on the natural intelligence of the student and not be limited to the acquisition of purely routine techniques which are quickly forgotten and are not very suitable for adaptation or transfer.

Personal activity of the student is indispensable for the development of his potential abilities.

The efficiency of learning is greater if the teacher presents pedagogical situations familiar to the student, who can put them into mathematical form himself, making his own discoveries and working at his own speed.

The conditions for learning such a systematic subject as mathematics should be organized in a manner which enables the student to acquire progressively a structured and active way of thinking.

There are various lines along which mathematics may be learned: practical and graphical work on a given topic, formal lessons given by the teacher, problem solving (individually or in groups), individual discovery work, discussion, reading of mathematical textbooks, films, study with the aid of teaching machines, television lessons. The respective pros and cons of these methods, for presenting various topics, should be studied with reference to levels of attainment and other circumstances.

1.1   **A lesson in logic**

Lesson given by Z. P. Dienes. Text prepared by T. Varga

1.1.1   This is a normal mathematics class in a French-speaking school in Sherbrooke, a city in Quebec, Canada. About thirty children, nine or ten years old, are distributed in groups of from three to five.

The groups are engaged in various activities. Some are drawing diagrams on blackboards, others are sitting at tables or on the floor working with sets of concrete materials. The teacher passes from group to group. Sometimes children come to consult her. The children are not silent, but it is a noise of industry not of idleness. They are absorbed in their work. There is no apparent compulsion or repression. If a child is tired or bored, he can change to another activity, such as building towers, or other play; but this rarely happens.

The multibase arithmetic blocks, associated with the name of Dienes, are among the materials used in the class. Here we are not concerned, however, with their use, but with various activities connected with the Dienes variant of Vygotsky's logic blocks. This is the material described in section 2.8 under the heading 'Logical materials'. Figure 4 is a semi-symbolic representation of one-third of a set, keeping the colour variable constant. (Shading on the right symbolizes thickness.)

Materials and assignments (through worksheets or orally) have been given out to each group by the teacher.

Dr Dienes, who pays regular visits in these classes, enters. The children smile at him; some exclaim, 'Monsieur Dienes!' He joins a group. The rest of the

Figure 4 Part of a set of Vygotsky's logic blocks

children continue their work. They know that Dr Dienes is very likely to join their group, too, during the period.

Dr Dienes, Hungarian by birth but equally at home in English, French, German and Italian language and environment, sits among the children enjoying the games himself like a child. He suggests that a set of logic blocks be sorted into four groups, according as they are yellow or not, squares or not. They sort the blocks in two boxes and their lids. It takes some minutes before they have this arrangement:

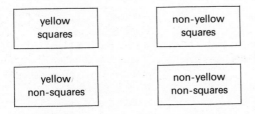

Dr Dienes now removes one of the boxes (or lids), the yellow non-squares, leaving this:

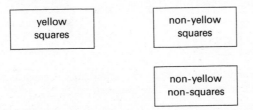

and asks, 'What could you say about each of the blocks remaining here? Something that sounds like "If ..., then ...." If it is yellow, then ...?'

They look at the yellow blocks remaining and are soon ready with the answer: 'If yellow, then square.'

'Right. Now see if you can say something about the squares. Or about those which are not square. Or which are not yellow.'

Some incorrect answers are rejected by the children themselves, or withdrawn by the proposers. Some answers are, though accepted, agreed upon as being not very interesting since they are always true. (For instance, that squares are yellow or not yellow.) Finally, 'If not yellow, then not square' is identified as another sentence which is true this time, but not always.

Putting back the first box, Dr Dienes asks the children to select another and find 'If . . . , then . . .' sentences again. Then he passes to another group leaving the children to struggle with the problem and to give him their conclusions in writing.

In the second group he invites children to pick out of the whole set three or four logic blocks. Here again he asks them about 'If . . . , then . . .' sentences which are true about *these* blocks (see Figure 5a). They may say some which are not true about all of them, even if they are true about some.

Figure 5a A selection of logic blocks for which the statement, 'If large, then blue' is true

Here are a few sentences of both kinds:

True	Not true
If red, then triangle	If red, then square
If triangle, then red	If triangle, then blue
If blue, then square	If square, then blue
	(not always; it can be yellow!)
If thick, then small	If small, then thick
If large, then blue	If blue, then large

They would like to go on but he changes the assignment. He writes the last true sentence on a slip of paper and invites them to add a fifth block which would make this sentence false (Figure 5b).

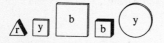

Figure 5b The addition of the large thin yellow circle negates 'If large, then blue'. Another true statement is 'If yellow, then thin'

' "If large, then blue" is no longer true. What else is true about this new set?'

There are a lot of such sentences. One of them is: 'If yellow, then thin.' 'Add a block to make it false.' (Figure 5c.)

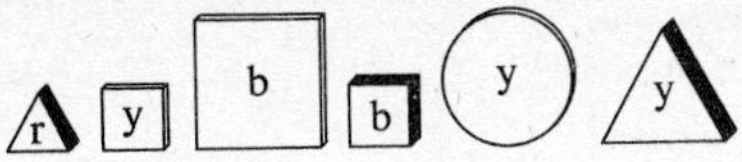

Figure 5c With the large thick yellow triangle, 'If yellow, then thin' is no longer true. A new statement is 'If triangle, then thick'

'What is still true? For instance, "If triangle, then thick." Make it false.'

This goes on for a while. With about ten blocks they cannot find a simple sentence that is true. They start again. The third time they can do it themselves, in pairs. One pair says and writes true sentences which the other pair turns to false by new blocks, and so on. Dr Dienes passes to other groups.

He starts new work with four groups almost simultaneously. To each he gives a large sheet of paper with a 'tree' on it. There are six different trees (Figure 6). He gives four to the children and reserves two for the quicker groups.

Each group has a set of logic blocks. They are told to use only the small blocks this time, and to put one at each branch end. This they do quickly without much attempt at systematizing.

'Now try to make it nicer,' Dr Dienes says to those children who are ready. He does not specify what he means by this. Only occasionally does he give hints such as these:

'On this branch almost every block is a square. Could you make them all squares, by changing some blocks? Now do something similar on the other branches.'

'All right, here are the squares, here the triangles, here the circles, here the long rectangles. But look, among the squares a yellow is in the middle, and with the triangles a red is. Try to make it still nicer!'

He passes quickly from group to group giving just a few hints here and there. They are mostly to their intuition – and perhaps their sense of beauty.

Those who arrive at a 'final' ordering can try their hands with other trees. Curiously enough, the second task is not always easier than the first. This is a good exercise to release children who tend to have fixed ideas of order.

With two groups who finished their trees he now starts a discussion.

'Suppose you arrange the blocks by placing the blocks you like best on the left and those which you like less on the right. What do you regard as more important: colour, shape or thickness?'

'Colour.'

'Which colour do you like best: red, yellow or blue?'

'Blue.'

'And which do you like less than blue but still almost as much?'

'Red.'

'Then we shall make every blue block precede every red block and every red block precede every yellow block. Thickness and shape are less important. They only count if blocks are of the same colour. Which of them would you

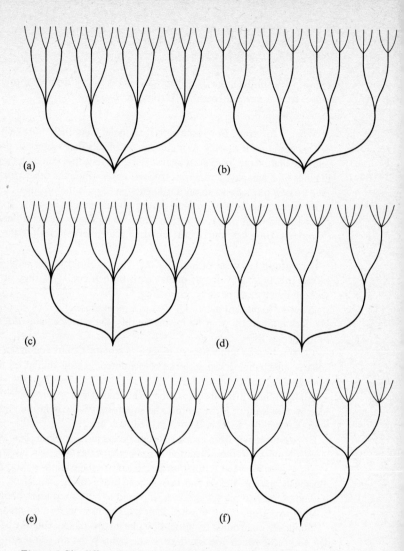

Figure 6 Six different 'trees' for ordering the logic blocks

say is more important, shape or thickness?'

Some say, 'Shape'; some say, 'Thickness'.

'All right, you choose one tree and the rest another tree. Remember that for you the order is colour, shape, thickness, and for you: colour, thickness, shape.'

After some guessing, they find the appropriate trees. They write on each branch the symbols expressing the attributes according to their order of preference. (See Figure 7, for example.)

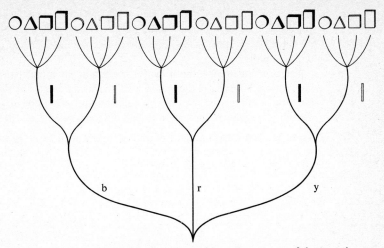

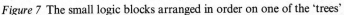

Figure 7 The small logic blocks arranged in order on one of the 'trees'

Then Dr Dienes shows them pairs of blocks and each time they decide which of the two is 'better' according to the rules for each tree.

Now the four 'tree' groups and some other children are around him, and he starts another discussion, based on pure imagery.

'It will soon be Christmas. Think of a very expensive gift you would like to receive.'

They agree on an electric train.

'And something less valuable?'

'A ball.'

'And something very cheap?'

'A pen.'

'Suppose that you can receive either no train or one train or two trains but you cannot receive more than two. In the same way, you can have no ball or one ball or two balls and no pen or one pen or two pens. Remember that balls are worth much less than trains, and pens much less than balls. Now tell me, what would be the most valuable set of presents you could receive?'

After some discussion they agree on two trains, two balls and two pens. He writes on the blackboard:

ttbbpp

'Now think of somebody who receives things which cost somewhat less. Still less! Something between!'

In this way they arrange the sets, as they did earlier with objects, according to superimposed criteria.

1.1.2 What was the subject matter of this unusual lesson? Much more than could have been related in the above report. One was the idea of implication (or conditional, in Quine's more coherent terminology), another the ordering of objects and sets. The first has more to do with speaking: that is how we use the words, 'If . . ., then . . .'; the second with doing: finding a way of arranging things in order.

The first situation, in both variants, contains far more than the idea of implication. To speak of the first variant, the layout created by removing one box can be interpreted not only by implications but also by disjunctions (in the sense of inclusive 'or'), both in two different ways* (see Table 2a).

Table 2a Two Interpretations of an Arrangement of Logic Blocks

	Yellow	Non-yellow
Squares	yellow squares	non-yellow squares
Non-squares		non-yellow non-squares

'If . . ., then . . .'   Inclusive 'or'
(implication, conditional)   (disjunction, alternative)
1. If yellow, then square   3. Non-yellow or square (may be both)
2. If non-square, then non-yellow   4. Square or non-yellow (may be both)

The lesson is again about language: that's how we use the word 'or' – to be sure, just one way of using it. To visualize another, remove two oppositive boxes (see Table 2b). This layout can then be read in several other ways, for example, by 'if and only if' (in short, 'iff') sentences.

Table 2b The 'Iff' and 'Exclusive "Or"' Interpretations of an Arrangement of Logic Blocks

	Yellow	Non-yellow
Squares	yellow squares	
Non-squares		non-yellow non-squares

'If and only if . . .'   Exclusive 'or'
(equivalence, biconditional)
1. Yellow if and only if square   3. Either yellow or non-square (but not both)
2. Non-yellow if and only if non-square   4. Either non-yellow or square (but not both)

*For a systematic treatment of these concepts see Appendix, section A.1.

In the first case (Table 2a) we have the union of two sets. In the second case we have a symmetric difference. The removal of three boxes leads to the intersection of two sets, the set-theoretical counterpart of the connective 'and'.*

The expert will see that the truth-table technique has been translated to the language of, say, seven to twelve year olds. Once the language is decided on the way is open to discovering a number of relationships: how an implication can be turned into another by interchanging the clauses and negating both; how a disjunction can be turned into an implication and vice versa by negating the first clause; and so on. The use of some symbolism then becomes more and more imperative. The increasing awareness of the relationships and the fluency in using symbols can grow into a powerful means of reasoning about our own reasoning, of being more conscious about the very stuff of mathematics.

The rest of the lesson is completely different from the first part. The use of the same set of concrete material is perhaps the only essential link between them. The technique presented here through directed discovery is basic in putting words in alphabetic order, using a dictionary or a directory, arranging numerals in increasing or decreasing order, and similar situations. In the cases listed there is a somewhat rigid pattern: the ordering goes according to the first letter or numeral, or if they are the same, according to the second, and so on. This is a convention – as is the use of ten for the base of the numeration – which, if stressed too much, tends to obscure the proper idea. The use of the logic blocks and of other situations is aimed at freeing the concept from convention and bringing out the main message, our double freedom in determining both the order of the attributes (colour, shape, thickness) and of their values (blue, red, yellow, etc.). Only if each of these is fixed, can a superimposed order situation be unambiguously determined in the order of any two elements – in this case, of two objects or of two sets.

There is a difference between these two cases, that of the objects and that of the sets, arising from the fact, that numbers are properties of sets, not of objects. The distinctly non-numerical character of the first activity changes in the second to something which has to do with numbers. One more step, making one train equal in value to three balls and one ball to three pens, gives us numbers expressed in base three, with their cardinal as well as ordinal aspect. But this step, intentionally, has not been taken. The accent is on the ordinal aspect and this it is hoped will become clearer if it is presented alone.

Words such as 'hope' are appropriate here, more than would be claims such as, 'it has been proved' or, 'this is the proper way'. In the strict educational sense nothing has yet been proved, but there is much to hope. One of the features of the Dienes approach is the scope for analysis of complex concepts into their

*If related to each single block and not to the set of blocks. The blocks 'each of which is yellow and square' are not the same as 'the yellow and the square blocks'. This second expression takes us back to the idea of union. It is like speaking of the blocks 'each of which is yellow *or* square'. It should be noted here that properly speaking the logical or linguistic equivalents of these arrangements would be, '*For every block*, if it is yellow, it is a square.' Technically, universal quantifiers are involved here.

elements (such as the ordinal and cardinal aspects of number) and presenting them separately. This is, of course, quite different from expecting children to analyse mathematical concepts at an age when they are not ready, a common and serious error. What is attempted here is a greater use of mathematical education to assist the natural growth of the thought processes in children. Yet the question remains, will the elements into which *we* analyse mathematical ideas, become integrated in *children's minds*? Some are sceptical about it. They are afraid that ideas presented in this way are swallowed by children in an 'insoluble capsule, unrelated to the wealth of experience that can make it come alive' (Hawkins, 1967, p. 8).* The main issue is perhaps the relative importance of the mathematical environment into which we put children (strongly advocated and in many ways created by Dienes) and of the natural environment implied in the words 'wealth of experience'. The benefits of the first are so evident that they could hardly be denied, and Dienes would be the last to deny the merits of the second. Their relation to each other will remain for some time to come.

1.2 The concept of a group

Lesson of about fifty minutes given by M. Delmotte to a class of twenty-six twelve-year-old boys. Text prepared by T. Varga.

1.2.1 The lesson begins with a short revision of the concepts of permutation (as a particular case of mapping, itself a particular case of relation) and the composition of two permutations. Three children changing places is used as an example.

Three children are having a game. [*He draws the sketch as in Figure 8.*] They leave their places and then return either to their original places or to another seat. In how many ways is this possible? The quickest, who therefore has first choice, is *a*.

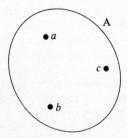

Figure 8 Three children, *a*, *b* and *c*, in their places

*His criticism is not explicitly directed against the Dienes approach, but it is a clear expression of one general point of view. References for chapter 1 will be found on p. 93.

Jean, show us how many moves it is possible for *a* to make.

Jean draws the three possible moves on the board:

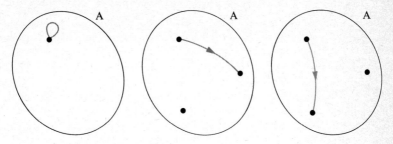

Figure 9 The three moves which *a* can make

The rest of the class draw the same in their exercise books.

Now it's *b*'s turn. How many choices does he have?

The class decides that two possibilities are open in each of the three cases. The following drawings take shape on the board and in the children's books:

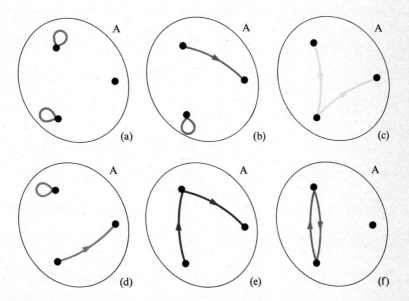

Figure 10 For each of *a*'s three possible moves, *b* has two

T   What about *c*? Does he have any choice?
P   No, he must take the only place left.

They complete the sketches, indicating *c*'s move in each case.

T   Do our drawings cover every possibility? Is there any repetition, any superfluous drawing? Tell me then, in how many ways can three children choose their places? How many possible permutations are there in a set of three elements?

    When all these questions have been answered, the teacher gives a colour to each of the six permutations, putting big coloured spots next to the six drawings. He combines the six cases into one drawing on another board, using the six colours for the lines. He begins to draw it; the children follow him until they have a diagram like Figure 11.

T   Have we got every possible game? Is each game represented only once? What kinds of relations are represented here?

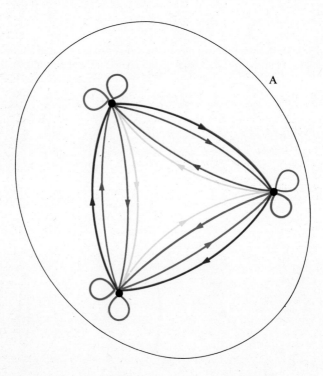

Figure 11 The six different moves that the three children can make, combined into one diagram

The teacher deliberately insists on such questions. When they have all been answered, the children declare that they have before them the set of the possible permutations in A.

T   We shall symbolize this set of permutations by $\mathscr{S}_A$. How many elements has $\mathscr{S}_A$? What is its cardinal? Let us enumerate these six elements using our colours.

While they answer these questions, they are all busy, their hands and minds are kept equally occupied. They draw:

$$\mathscr{S}_A = \left\{ \ \bullet \ , \ \bullet \ , \ \bullet \ , \ \bullet \ , \ \bullet \ , \ \bullet \ \right\}.$$

Now they begin to compose permutations. Here they make use of the introductory part of the lesson where they saw examples of such compositions. They still have in mind children changing places, but their way of speaking and thinking becomes more and more abstract.

T   Take a permutation, the green one for example. Form its composition with another, say the violet. [*He draws on the board.*] What is the composite of these two permuta-

$$\bullet \ \circ \ \bullet$$

tions? Try to find it, but don't tell the others your answer. Is it still a permutation of A?

They continue working, with one of the pupils at the board. As the big figure is too complicated, a little one is drawn for the two permutations to be composed (see Figure 12).
      The boy at the board finds the composition.

T   Have we got a permutation again? What happens if we take another two permutations? Michel, think of a permutation; you too, Pierre. I don't know which ones you have thought of, but I can guarantee that if we form the composition of them, it will still be a permutation. Let's write down what we have found.

He writes on the board:

1. For every $x, y \in \mathscr{S}_A$,

$y \circ x \in \mathscr{S}_A.$

T   This is usually expressed as: 'The operation of composition is internal and everywhere defined.' Are you sure that this is always true for any couple of permutations? (The word 'couple' is used in the sense of an 'ordered pair'.)
P   It must be true. Every permutation of A is a bijection of A onto A. And we have seen that the composition of two bijections is a bijection.
T   Thank you. That was an excellent explanation. Can you tell me something else about the composition of two bijections? or more generally, of two relations?

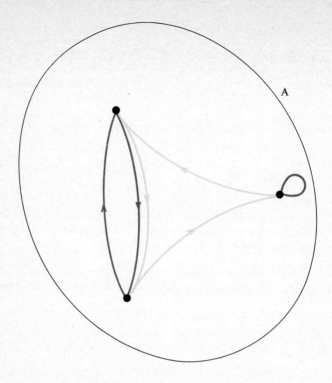

Figure 12 Two permutations to be composed into one

One of the pupils mentions associativity. The teacher asks for examples of it. They speak about the union and intersection of sets, and the composition of relations.

T   What does associativity mean in our case? Choose three permutations and try it. [*Everybody writes*:

one of the pupils writing it on the board.] Let us calculate the two members separately and see if they give the same result. [*He begins*:

and the children continue.]

Who knows what the result in the upper brackets is? [*Hands in the air.*] All right, continue. [*They finish the 'calculation' (most of them obtaining the same result).*] You see, if Alain thinks of a permutation, and Denis and Michel too, even though I don't know which ones they are thinking of, I am sure that if they form the composition of their three permutations in these two ways, the result in either case will be the same. This is another property of relations.

He writes under the first property:

2. For every $x, y, z \in \mathscr{S}_A$,

$z \circ (y \circ x) = (z \circ y) \circ x.$

The lesson continues with another problem. On the board, the teacher writes:

T   What can we write here [*pointing to the vacant place*] to make it true?
P   The empty set. [*Some laugh, the teacher does not.*]
T   What do colours symbolize here? They symbolize permutations. Which permutation should go there?

They go back to the diagram with the arrows (Figure 11). Having been given this opportunity to grasp the idea they fill in the empty place. Another example follows with another colour, and with the empty place on the right. They use the term 'identical permutation'.

T   Again this seems to be true of every permutation. We have now obtained a third property:

3. There exists an element $1_A \in \mathscr{S}_A$ such that, for every $x \in \mathscr{S}_A$,

$1_A \circ x = x = x \circ 1_A.$

He writes this, as he did earlier, with the help of the children, always waiting for their suggestions.

T   There is still one more property.

He draws:

$\circ$ ⬤   =   ⬤

on the board.

T   Can you think of a permutation which, when combined with this, gives us the identical permutation?

A pupil suggests a colour.

T   Let us see. Try it on the board.

51   The concept of a group

The boy comes out, explains his idea by means of arrows and then fills the empty place with the colour he had proposed.

T   And if we put them in the reverse order?

They try it and find the same result. The term 'reciprocal' or 'inverse' is introduced. They write:

Exercises follow concerning the reciprocal (inverse) of other permutations.

T   If we combine a permutation with its reciprocal (inverse), what do we get? Why?

He pretends to be dull-witted. The children explain the situation to him; they know it is a joke, but they enter into the spirit of it. Then they formulate the last property:

4. For every $x \in \mathscr{S}_A$, there exists an $x^{-1} \in \mathscr{S}_A$, such that

$$x \circ x^{-1} = 1_A = x^{-1} \circ x.$$

T   Every time we have a set with an operation in it having these four properties, we say that the set relative to that operation forms a group.

1.2.2   Some further comments:

(a) A concept has been introduced here to twelve-year-old boys, which traditionally appears only in the university curriculum. (This tradition is not very old, since in most universities it dates back less than half a century.)

(b) The introduction of this concept at this age-level is justified. It is a concept of basic importance which serves as a link between arithmetic, algebra and geometry. Moreover, it serves as a means to lessen this obsolete division of mathematics. The concept is not only important, it is also elementary, being within the grasp of twelve year olds.

(c) This was the first lesson where these pupils met this notion. Their acquaintance with it is bound to be superficial. Much further work is needed, until the concept ripens. The present lesson has achieved its aim. Children have made the first steps, through personal experience and work, towards assimilating the concept of a group.

(d) Most teachers would probably wait to introduce the word 'group' until pupils come across the idea in different contexts. They may argue that too close a connexion between the word 'group' and the concept of permutation is threatened. We share this view. (Integers with respect to addition, integers modulo a number, reflections of a square and many other examples will of course follow in subsequent lessons. Nobody would advocate an approach restricted to permutations. It is simply a question of when to introduce the word itself.)

(e) The use of colours and the most simple way of representation (namely the coloured spots) are, as can be seen, a major vehicle in promoting understanding and employing abstract concepts.

(f) 'Official' symbolism and 'adult' terminology have been used. There would be no point in avoiding them once children are willing to accept them.

1.3 Glide reflections

Lesson of ninety minutes given by Mme Papy to twenty-four girls aged from fourteen to fifteen years old. Text prepared by T. Varga

1.3.1 The teacher sketches two parallel lines on the board (Figure 13a), marking them 1 and 2, respectively. 'What would be the result of reflections relative to 1 and 2?'

One of the pupils volunteers: 'A translation.'

The teacher puts the same question concerning two coincident lines (Figure 13b) and two secant lines (Figure 13c). The pupils give the answers: 'Identical transformation', 'Rotation'.

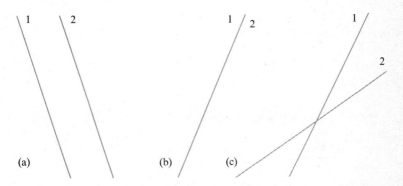

Figure 13 Pairs of (a) parallel lines, (b) coincident lines and (c) secant lines

In response to the teacher's questions, they re-form their answers (for example, 'Rotation around the point of intersection of the two lines').

The teacher now draws a red line parallel to the lines drawn first, puts a red '1' next to it, and asks: 'Could you trace a line, red 2, so that the reflections in respect to red 1 and red 2 result in the same translation as did white 1 and white 2?'

One of the girls goes to the board and accomplishes the task. She, like the teacher, draws free-hand diagrams, estimating the distances of the parallels by eye.

The same problem, this time related to a yellow line parallel to the others, is solved by another girl.

While they are working, the teacher writes on the board in a symbolic notation, using the respective colours:

$$t = s_2 \circ s_1 = s_2 \cdot s_1 = s_2 \circ s_1 = \ldots.$$

The pupils are apparently quite familiar with this symbolism.

'You see, we have now factorized the translation t.' (A short discussion follows about the number of ways to factorize t.)

'Now let us see this case.' The teacher points to the right-hand figure (Figure 13c). Some pupils come out to the board. The work is similar to that for the parallel lines. They get the factorization:

$$r = s_2 \circ s_1 = s_2 \cdot s_1 = s_2 \circ s_1 = \ldots.$$

In order to make a comparison and to sustain a possibly general idea of factorization, the teacher writes the number 12 on the board, asking: 'How could you factorize this number into two integers?' The class arrives at the conclusion that, in this case, only a finite number of factorizations is possible.

A discussion induced by the teacher's questions now follows about the possibilities of decomposing a product of more reflections. The girls distinguish the cases of an even and an odd number of reflections. The teacher asks the disputants to defend their views, evidently in the hope that the views themselves will become clearer during the discussion. A girl goes to the board and, with some help from the teacher, writes on it:

$$s_{2n-1} \circ s_{2n-2} \cdots \circ s_3 \circ s_2 \circ s_1$$

The girl would continue, but some of the others look perplexed. So the teacher stops the girl and asks her some questions concerning the possible values of n and the number of factors of the above product. Then the girl continues, inserting brackets: 'Here is an even number of reflections, their product is the product of two reflections:'

$$(s_{2n-1} \circ s_{2n-2} \circ \ldots \circ s_3 \circ s_2) \circ s_1 = s_3 \cdot s_2$$

Another girl volunteers: 'She has proved one of the statements, but she has not disproved the other. Perhaps we can substitute the product of three reflections by a single reflection?'

'Let's see! Could you sketch me some cases of three reflections?' suggests the teacher. Some girls go to the board and sketches like those in Figure 14 appear on it.

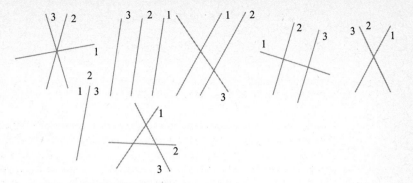

Figure 14 Various arrangements of three lines

After some trials, they establish that in some cases the product can be substituted by one single reflection, but not always. After a short discussion it becomes clear whose predictions were nearer to the point.

After this introductory part of the lesson, the class begins to study a new transformation: the product of a reflection and a translation parallel to the axis of reflection. To start with, the teacher draws a diagram (Figure 15) on the board.

Figure 15 Representation of a translation

Very few words are needed; the girls know what she means by such sketches. To make the point clearer for some of them, she puts questions like: 'What other couple of points would give the same translation?' 'Let us see still another, not on the axis.' 'Could you draw a different case, not represented by this picture?' The answers often consist merely of drawings appearing on the board, drawn by different girls. The last question proves to be too vague: some time elapses before they realize its meaning; they should not forget the translation of length 0. This case, too, is sketched on the board (Figure 16).

Figure 16 A translation of zero length

'Now let's look at this product:

$$\mathscr{P} = t \circ s_{\mathrm{A}}.$$

Your task is to construct the image produced by this transformation of . . .'; the girls suggest to her: '. . . of Joseph.' 'Let's call him Joseph,' she agrees. Joseph appears on the board (Figure 17).

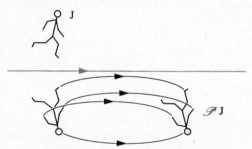

Figure 17 Joseph

The teacher invites one of the girls to come out, the rest work at their places. She walks around, encouraging some, discouraging others (who are on the wrong track), and giving them hints on how to continue. Remarks that may be instructive for others are made aloud. Part of the task accomplished, another girl goes to the board. She has some difficulty with the translation. To help her, the teacher breaks up the task into pieces, 'Show me a couple of point producing this translation – another couple – and another. Now the one whose origin is this point.' (Joseph's right hand after s_A.) The breaking-up works, the girl soon finds her feet. The drawing looks like Figure 18.

Figure 18 Joseph undergoes a glide reflection

'As you see,' the teacher summarizes, 'Joseph made a glide, apart from being reflected, so we will call this transformation a glide reflection. What do we mean by glide reflection?' The girls arrive at a correct wording.

'Does anybody see anything particular about this product, $t \circ s_A$?'

Some girls: 'It is commutative.'

'Do you think so? Let's see.'

One of the girls comes out and explains her idea by drawing. After all have agreed the teacher asks 'Who is willing to draw us $\mathscr{P}^2 J$ and $\mathscr{P}^3 J$?' While this is being done, she continues the conversation with the class about the transformation under discussion: 'What single transformation would produce the same effect as $\mathscr{P}^2 J$?; as $\mathscr{P}^3 J$? What transformation would bring this' (pointing at $\mathscr{P}^2 J$), 'to this one?' (pointing at $\mathscr{P}^3 J$).

Then they sum up their empirical findings by writing on the board:

$$t \circ s_A = s_A \circ t \qquad \mathscr{P} = t \circ s_A = s_A \circ t$$

$$\mathscr{P}^2 = t^2 \qquad \qquad \mathscr{P}^2 = (t \circ s_A) \circ (s_A \circ t)$$

$$\mathscr{P}^2 = t \circ (s_A \circ s_A) \circ t$$

$$\mathscr{P}^2 = t \circ I \circ t.$$

'Now I shall give you a problem. Try to prove this:' (pointing to the formula $\mathscr{P}^2 = t^2$) 'by means of this:' (the formula $t \circ s_A = s_A \circ t$).

During their individual work, she walks around the classroom as usual. After a while, a girl is requested to write on the board what she has found so far:

$$\mathscr{P}^2 = t \circ s_A \circ t \circ s_A$$

$$= t \circ s_A \circ s_A \circ t$$

$$= t \circ I \circ t$$

$$= t \circ t = t^2.$$

A little chat follows about brackets: they add and cancel some, but do not linger much on associativity.

The teacher continues, 'Kate, come here and factorize this translation.' She draws an arrow. 'Replace it by the product of two reflections, please.'

Kate draws a diagram like Figure 19.

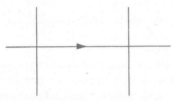

Figure 19 A translation as the product of two reflections. The pupil has not indicated the order in which the reflections take place

'I am not sure you are right. Show me the two axes,' the teacher asks. Kate points with her two forefingers to the two lines.

'I am still not sure you are right. Which is the first axis and which is the second?'

'Why didn't she ask this last question first?' one is tempted to ask, but it would have been a pedagogical mistake. To allow the students to grope, even to go wrong, is more instructive than to prevent them from making errors. It is through errors that we learn most.

Other factorizations are also found, then a problem is posed: 'As you see, $\mathscr{P}$ is the product of a reflection and a translation parallel to the axis of symmetry. Could you find another reflection and another translation parallel to its axis having as their product this same $\mathscr{P}$?'

Some girls are perplexed, some protest.

'Well, let's see. You say it is impossible. Try to establish your statement by calculation. Suppose that

$$\mathscr{P} = t_1 \circ s_1 = t_2 \circ s_2.$$

Are you sure then that t_1 must equal t_2 and so with the ss? Go on, try it.'

Seeing that very few of the girls find their way, she gives them a hint: 'You see, if they are equal, so are their squares.' This much is enough for the majority. Some need an explicit reference to the formula $\mathscr{P}^2 = t^2$ proved just now.

They arrive at $t_1^2 = t_2^2$ and establish that this implies $t_1 = t_2$.

'Now what about our problem?' asks the teacher, 'Have we solved it?' Some girls say they have; others point out, however, that the question of s_1 and s_2 is still pending.

'Are you sure that they are also equal? Well, I don't doubt you are, but you must show it to me *by calculation*. So far we have proved that $t_1 = t_2$ and this allows us to write

$$t_1 \circ s_1 = t_1 \circ s_2$$

instead of the original. But we must arrive from that at $s_1 = s_2$.' The girls work individually, as usual.

A girl then writes the following on the board:

$$t_1 \circ s_1 = t_1 \circ s_2 \Rightarrow t_1 \circ t_1^{-1} \circ s_1 = t_1 \circ t_1^{-1} \circ s_2.$$

'This is by no means false,' the teacher says after examining it carefully, 'still it is not quite logical. How did you arrive at it?'

They correct the proof and finish it.

They discuss what they have found. As an analogy, 7 is factorized in the set of natural integers. Time is running out, so the teacher sums up: 'Since there is a unique way of factorizing a glide reflection into a reflection and a translation parallel to its axis, we can speak of *the* axis of the glide reflection and *the* translation of the glide reflection.

At the end of the lesson she gives them some problems for homework:

1. Investigate the product of a reflection and a translation which is not necessarily parallel to the axis of reflection.
2. Try to show that the product of reflections in these three axes (Figure 20a) is a glide reflection.

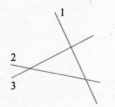

Figure 20(a) Three axes of reflection

About the latter, she gives a hint. 'Don't be puzzled if you arrive at a situation like this:' (Figure 20b). 'This seems to have nothing to do with glide reflection.

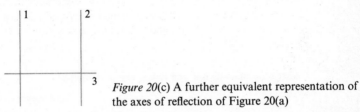

Figure 20(b) An equivalent representation of the three axes of reflection shown in Figure 20(a)

Still it has, because you may replace it by a situation like this:' (Figure 20c). 'Do you get the idea?'

Figure 20(c) A further equivalent representation of the axes of reflection of Figure 20(a)

1.3.2   The ease with which pupils use the symbolism is particularly characteristic here. After having introduced a new transformation and having marked it by a letter $\mathcal{P}$ they are able to see what $\mathcal{P}^2$, $\mathcal{P}^3$, etc. mean. Some still have difficulties, but they are encouraged by the comprehension of the others ('I must master it if they did; after all, it can't be witchcraft.') and by the constant assistance of the teacher. Pupils write products of not only two or three, but even n transformations, and they can use this symbolism in their reasonings.

There is a continuous interaction between this symbolic notation and the intuitive representation (in drawings and mental images). No demarcation line, like the one separating the traditional 'synthetic' and 'analytic' geometry, can be observed.

What do you think of Joseph? The girls are apparently delighted with him. He is certainly more attractive than, say, a triangle. He is also more versatile. He is visibly influenced by the transformations acting on him. Some are shown in Figure 21.

Notice the use of curved arrows (Figure 18). You may have found them unfamiliar. Aren't they being used to represent vectors? But can a vector be curved? Conditioned by the 'directed segment' approach, one may judge this representation inappropriate, but this is not so. Curved arrows suggest the important idea that between the origin and the endpoint 'anything can happen' and that the direction has 'nothing to do with it'.

Figure 21 Joseph is transformed

Still more important, arrows have a much wider meaning for these girls than just vectors or translations. They began the study of relations two years earlier. They often represented relations by arrows – curved arrows – between points of 'potatoes', which meant for them elements of sets. What they are doing here is just a particular case of what they did formerly. They consider transformations as special relations. They learn geometry in a much broader context than children usually do. Not only 'synthetic' and 'analytic' geometry are here integrated; the whole of geometry is merged into a unified mathematics course, based on sets and relations. These curved arrows point it out clearly.

1.4   Greatest common divisor and lowest common multiple

Prepared by W. Servais

1.4.1   Introduction

By the time pupils in the first class of secondary school (twelve years old) reach this lesson, they have grasped the basic theories of sets. The techniques of operations with sets (intersection, combination and difference) have become completely automatic. They understand the four arithmetical operations in the set of natural integers, as well as their properties, and they have studied raising to powers, including the power zero.

In previous lessons the following concepts have been made clear:

(a) *Divisors common to several numbers.* Common divisors of several numbers are introduced as the intersections of sets of divisors. As an example, consider the common divisor of 12, 18 and 27:

Set of divisors of 12 = div 12 = $\{1, 2, 3, 4, 6, 12\}$,

Set of divisors of 18 = div 18 = $\{1, 2, 3, 6, 9, 18\}$,

Set of divisors of 27 = div 27 = $\{1, 3, 9, 27\}$.

These sets of divisors and their intersections can be represented by a Venn diagram (Figure 22).

Set of common divisors of 18, 12 and 27 = div 18 $\cap$ div 12 $\cap$ div 27
$$= \{1, 3\}.$$

The greatest common divisor of 18, 12 and 27 is 3.

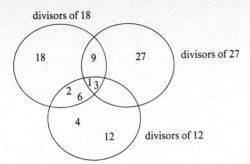

Figure 22 Venn diagram representing the sets of divisors of 18, 27 and 12, and the intersections of these sets

(b) *Prime numbers.* A prime number is one which is only divisible by exactly two divisors. The following examples illustrate the point:

3 is a prime number because 3 is divisible by 1 and 3.
1 is not a prime number because it is divisible only by 1.
6 is not a prime number because 6 is divisible by 1, 2, 3 and 6.

(c) *Primary numbers and primary divisors of natural numbers.* Let us call any power of a prime number a primary number. For example:

$81 = 3^4$ is a primary number,
$1 = 3^0$ is a primary number.

(d) *Primary factoring of a number.* As an example, let us find the set of primary divisors of 540.

540	2
270	2
135	3
45	3
15	3
5	5
1	

$540 = 2^2 . 3^3 . 5$

The set of primary divisors of $540 - p(540) -$ is $\{1, 2, 2^2, 3, 3^2, 3^3, 5\}$.

Any integer has one and only one set of primary divisors and, vice versa, any set of primary divisors yields one and only one whole number. For example:

$p(x) = \{1, 2, 2^2, 2^3, 3, 5, 5^2\} \Leftrightarrow x = 2^3 . 3 . 5^2 = 600$.

Any attempt to find the set of primary divisors of a number (and vice versa) affords an opportunity for many exercises in calculation.

1.4.2 *The lesson proper*

(a) *Exercise*. Find the lowest common multiple and the greatest common divisor of 54 and 90.

Pupils will draw up a list of divisors and multiples of 54 and 90.

Divisors of 54: 1, 2, 3, 6, 9, 18, 27, 54.
Divisors of 90: 1, 2, 3, 5, 6, 9, 10, 15, 18, 30, 45, 90.
Multiples of 90: 90, 180, 270, 360, 450, 540, and so on.
Multiples of 54: 54, 108, 162, 216, 270, 324, and so on.

The greatest common divisor of 90 and 54 is 18. Let us symbolize this fact by

$$90 \wedge 54 = 18.$$

The lowest common multiple of 90 and 54 is 270. This may be written

$$90 \vee 54 = 270.$$

Pupils are then asked whether this method would be practical in the case of very large numbers. They then realize the need for devising some other technique.

(b) *Use of primary divisors*. Pupils are asked to find and write down the set of primary divisors of 90, $p(90)$, and the set of primary divisors of 54 or $p(54)$:

$$p(90) = \{1, 2, 3, 3^2, 5\}, \qquad p(54) = \{1, 2, 3, 3^2, 3^3\}.$$

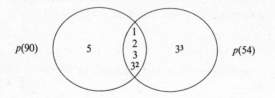

Figure 23 Venn diagram representing the sets of primary divisors of 90 and 54, and the intersection of these two sets

Pupils are invited to look for a relationship between 18 and 270 (i.e. $90 \wedge 54$ and $90 \vee 54$) and to work out this diagram (Figure 23). They may also look for $p(18)$ and $p(270)$.

The following results will be found:

1. The intersection of the sets of primary divisors of 90 and 54 gives the set of primary divisors of the greatest common divisor, 18:

$$p(18) = \{1, 2, 3, 3^2\} = p(90) \cap p(54).$$

2. The combination of the sets of primary divisors of 90 and 54 gives the set of primary divisors of the lowest common multiple, 270:

$$p(270) = (1, 2, 3, 3^2, 3^3, 5) = p(90) \cup p(54).$$

The first result indicates that the set of primary divisors of the greatest common divisor of two numbers is the same as the intersection of the sets of primary divisors of these numbers:

$$p(A \wedge B) = p(A) \cap p(B). \tag{1.1}$$

It will be seen that any divisor of a number is a product of primary divisors of this number. The greatest common divisor is therefore formed from the greatest primary divisors common to the two numbers: it is the number corresponding to the intersection of the sets of primary divisors.

The set of primary divisors of the lowest common multiple of two numbers is the same as the union of the sets of primary divisors of these numbers:

$$p(A \vee B) = p(A) \cup p(B). \tag{1.2}$$

Pupils then carry out exercises in which they look for the greatest common divisor and the lowest common multiple of numbers given.

The pupils are asked: 'What happens if one of the sets of primary divisors is included in the other?' Everyone studies this question by taking an example and it turns out that such a situation occurs if and only if one of the numbers is a multiple of the other.

For two sets A and B:

$$A \subset B \Rightarrow \begin{cases} A \cap B = A, \\ A \cup B = B. \end{cases} \tag{1.3}$$

When the two sets are sets of primary divisors, $p(A)$ and $p(B)$, implication 1.3 can be written

$$p(A) \subset p(B) \Rightarrow \begin{cases} p(A) \cap p(B) = p(A \wedge B) = p(A), \\ p(A) \cup p(B) = p(A \wedge B) = p(B). \end{cases} \tag{1.4}$$

Hence $\quad (A \text{ is a multiple of } B) \Rightarrow \begin{cases} A \wedge B = A, \\ A \vee B = B. \end{cases} \tag{1.5}$

(c) *Properties of the operations $\wedge$ and $\vee$.* Having defined two new operations $\wedge$ and $\vee$ concerning natural (nonzero) integers, the pupils will spontaneously look for the properties of these operations.

Q What is the property that we might examine first?
A Associativity.
Q What must be proved in order to show that operations $\wedge$ and $\vee$ are associative in $\mathbb{N}_0$?

A That $\quad \forall a, b, c \in \mathbb{N}_0 : \begin{cases} (a \wedge b) \wedge c = a \wedge (b \wedge c) = a \wedge b \wedge c, \\ (a \vee b) \vee c = a \vee (b \vee c) = a \vee b \vee c. \end{cases} \tag{1.6}$

Pupils may be at a loss to prove the derivations of this property.

Q What operations did we use to define the operations, $\wedge$ and $\vee$?
A Operations $\cap$ and $\cup$.

Q In the light of this, can we now prove that $\wedge$ and $\vee$ are associative?
A Yes, knowing that $\cap$ and $\cup$ are associative, we can conclude that $\wedge$ and $\vee$ are also.

Having demonstrated the associativity of $\wedge$ and $\vee$, we can now speak of the greatest common divisor and the lowest common multiple of more than two numbers.

The pupils will go on to study the commutativity of $\wedge$ and $\vee$. Since operations $\cap$ and $\cup$ are commutative, $\wedge$ and $\vee$ are also commutative and we have:

$$\forall a, b \in \mathbb{N}_0 : \begin{cases} a \wedge b = b \wedge a, \\ a \vee b = b \vee a. \end{cases} \qquad \textbf{1.7}$$

They will continue by investigating whether or not there is a neutral element for $\wedge$ and $\vee$.

Q What are the neutral elements of the operations with which you are already familiar?
A Zero is neutral for addition in the set $\mathbb{Z}$ of relative integers (as well as for all the sets of numbers with which we are familiar),

$$\forall a \in \mathbb{Z} : a + 0 = a = 0 + a. \qquad \textbf{1.8}$$

A neutral for multiplication in the set $\mathbb{Q}$ of rational numbers is 1 (as well as in all sets of numbers with which we are familiar),

$$\forall a \in \mathbb{Q} : a.1 = a = 1.a. \qquad \textbf{1.9}$$

The identical transformation I is neutral for the operation $\circ$ (product of composition) in the set T of translations, because

$$\forall t \in \mathrm{T} : t \circ \mathrm{I} = t = \mathrm{I} \circ t. \qquad \textbf{1.10}$$

Q In general when can it be said that an element n is neutral for an operation in a set $\mathscr{E}$?
A When $\forall a \in \mathscr{E} : n * a = a = a * n.$ **1.11**
Q What conditions must a number n fulfill in order to be neutral for $\wedge$ in $\mathbb{N}_0$?
A $\forall a \in \mathbb{N}_0 : a \wedge n = a = n \wedge a.$ **1.12**

Does this number exist? Pupils will look for it and will find that such a number does not exist.

On the other hand they will discover that

$$\forall a \in \mathbb{N}_0 : a \vee 1 = a = 1 \vee a \qquad \textbf{1.13}$$

and thus that 1 is neutral for $\vee$ in $\mathbb{N}_0$.

Similarly, pupils will discover that 1 is an absorbent element for $\wedge$ in $\mathbb{N}_0$ because

$$\forall a \in \mathbb{N}_0 : a \wedge 1 = 1 = 1 \wedge a. \qquad \textbf{1.14}$$

During these exercises, the pupils have discovered that every element of $\mathbb{N}_0$ is idempotent for operations $\wedge$ and $\vee$, as for example:

$4 \wedge 4 = 4$ and $14 \vee 14 = 14.$

When called upon to prove this property, pupils point out that every set is idempotent for $\cap$ and $\cup$,

i.e. $A \cap A = A$ and $A \cup A = A.$

Consequently $\forall a \in \mathbb{N}_0 : \begin{cases} a \wedge a = a, \\ a \vee a = a. \end{cases}$ **1.15**

Pupils then try to find out whether $\wedge$ is distributive relative to $\vee$. Since $\cap$ and $\cup$ are mutually distributive, the same holds for $\wedge$ and $\vee$.

$\forall a, b, c \in \mathbb{N}_0 : \begin{cases} a \wedge (b \vee c) = (a \wedge b) \vee (a \wedge c), \\ a \vee (b \wedge c) = (a \vee b) \wedge (a \vee c). \end{cases}$ **1.16**

Summary of properties

1. $\vee$ and $\wedge$ are associative (**1.6**).
2. $\vee$ and $\wedge$ are commutative (**1.7**).
3. $\vee$ and $\wedge$ are mutually distributive (**1.16**).
4. In $\mathbb{N}_0$, 1 is a neutral element for $\vee$ (**1.13**) and an absorbent element for $\wedge$ (**1.14**).
5. Every element of $\mathbb{N}_0$ is idempotent for $\wedge$ and $\vee$ (**1.15**).

1.4.3   *Remarks*

The whole of the material in section 1.4.2 has been covered in one period of about an hour. The pace was somewhat forced, in order to reach a certain completion. Under ordinary circumstances two periods are probably needed for the same topic. The reason for setting a pace quicker than the usual one was that it was a demonstration lesson, attended by about one hundred primary-school teachers. They had been taking a refresher course in mathematics, and they had to be shown in this lesson how certain concepts of modern mathematics could be linked with traditional topics such as the GCF and LCM. Some of the teachers present had taught these pupils before; knowing their ability and background, they were able to gauge the advance the pupils had made in less than one year.

Very often the consequence of a fast pace is that the teacher 'accomplishes' the task assigned for a given period, but the pupils do not. This was however not the case here. Pupils were not simply taught, they were given the opportunity to learn by personal experience.

The rules for finding the GCF and the LCM were not given to them: they themselves discovered these rules and why they work. This is the natural order of learning brought about by discovery. You cannot expect an average pupil to discover a rule and at the same time see why it works. If the topic is very simple, or the pupil is very bright, these two issues may coincide, at least apparently. In general, this is not the case. Pupils first discover a pattern, then they begin wondering why it works.

Note the simultaneous teaching of the GCF and the LCM. Usually these are taught separately – a logical set-up if the pattern is new for the children. For these boys it was not new; they were sufficiently familiar with the concepts of intersection and union of sets, and the transfer from this previous knowledge contributed strikingly to the assimilation of the new ideas.

The introduction of the 'primary divisor' concept may seem avoidable. The following diagram (Figure 24) and scheme might then serve as a substitute:

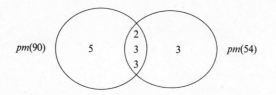

Figure 24 Diagram representing the prime divisors of 90 and 54

$$90 = 2 \times 3 \times 3 \times 5,$$
$$54 = 2 \times 3 \times 3 \times 3,$$

$$90 \wedge 54 = 2 \times 3 \times 3,$$
$$90 \vee 54 = 2 \times 3 \times 3 \times 3 \times 5.$$

Here *pm(a)* would mean, 'the set of the prime factors of *a*, taken with their multiplicities'. For instance, $pm(90) = (2, 3, 3, 5)$; $pm(54) = (2, 3, 3, 3)$. Yet there is a difficulty: set notation does not allow multiplicity; one and the same object cannot 'twice' be an element of a set. We may attribute a sense to $\{2, 3, 3, 5\}$, but then it must be equal to $\{2, 3, 5\}$. This may seem too severe a position, but it is unavoidable. If $\{2, 3, 3, 5\}$ were not equal to $\{2, 3, 5\}$ it would not be true that two sets are equal if and only if every element of either is an element of the other ('principle of extensionality'). A possible device to save the situation would be to distinguish the equal prime factors (here the 3s) by subscripts. Still, the use of primary divisors has the advantage that non-conventional new notation is avoided. The use of primary divisors has other advantages independent of the concept of set, viz. when the factors, their number and their sum have to be determined.

Taking the GCF and LCM of two numbers are traditionally not regarded as operations. They are looked upon as 'something else', what 'else' being conveniently unstated. This means depriving ourselves of interesting comparisons between these and other operations. Often it is easier to achieve more than less. We may spend hours of drudgery with commutative, associative, distributive laws applied to the 'four rules' with numbers, and they still will not be sufficiently clear. Applied under quite different circumstances, they receive the necessary background. The same holds for the existence of the neutral element (**1.13**) (note the counter-example with the operation ∧, **1.12**), for involution (raising to a power), which latter can be more fully appreciated after seeing examples of idempotence, and so on.

Note that the double distributivity between the GCF and the LCM (**1.16**) is certainly an awkward question if it is regarded independently of set concepts. The teachers present admitted that it was new to them and they found it difficult. Nevertheless, the children who were familiar with the mutual distributivity between the intersection and the union of sets, had only to grasp the idea that here again, as so often formerly, they were dealing with these same two fundamental operations.

1.5 The use of environmental interests in developing a project

Prepared by A. Pescarini, secondary-school mathematics teacher at Ravenna, Italy

1.5.1 *The idea of using naval charts*

The teaching experiment described here was carried out during three months (February, March, April) of the 1955/56 academic year with second and third grade boys and girls (from twelve to fourteen years of age) in the Pietro Damiano Secondary School, Ravenna.

The teacher, an ex-naval officer, recalled his enthusiasm and that of his comrades when, at the same age as his present pupils, he was first given the opportunity to do practical work with charts in a naval school.

The vividness of his memories suggested to him the idea of introducing similar practical work to his class in order (a) to exploit this rich source of motivation for an interesting introduction of mathematical ideas, and (b) to develop in pupils the heuristic attitude needed for solving open problems raised by projects of navigation.

It was important to reconcile this approach with the official mathematical curriculum which is emphasized at this stage by the approach of a final examination at the end of grade 3. The Hydrographical Institute of the Italian Navy readily provided charts.

1.5.2 *Preliminary knowledge*

The pupils had a common background of practical arithmetic: some proficiency in calculations with decimal numbers; in measuring angles in degrees and time in days, hours, minutes and seconds; in simple geometric ideas and the use of instruments; and in the use of signed numbers. They had an informal knowledge of the concepts of longitude and latitude.

1.5.3 *The lesson*

The presentation of the charts so excited the pupils that the teacher wondered how he could focus their diffused interest and energies towards the objectives of the project in the limited time available. They spontaneously raised a multitude of problems and it was not easy to restrict them to a selection without either damping their enthusiasm or dealing with problems which were too difficult. The teacher found it convenient to lead the discussion through problems which, though not directly mathematical, arose naturally in the given context. These related to reading a chart, to the use of a compass and its role in navigation etc. The following excerpt from a taperecorded lesson (in the second grade) may give some idea of the course of the work:

T	What have you got in front of you?
P	A map.
T	Do you think that this map has some pecularity?
P	It represents the Adriatic Sea.
T	Can you tell the land from the sea?
P1	The colour of the sea is lighter.
P2	Please, teacher, inside the land towns are not indicated ...
P3	... neither are mountains – nor roads. ...
T	What do you think this map is for?
P	?
T	As you said, roads are not indicated, towns only at the coast. ...
P1	They are used by shipmasters.
P2	I know – by pilots.
T	That's right. So from now on you are all pilots.
P	Shall we start steering at once?
T	But do you know what the harbours are for?
P1	For the ships to rest. ...
P2	For loading and unloading goods and passengers.
P3	Also for repairing ships.
T	And then?
P	?
T	What else happens with a ship in a harbour?
P1	I know! It is refuelled.
P2	Refuelled with what?
P3	With coal.
	[*Pupils laugh*]
P4	With oil! Today all ships are driven by oil.
T	Let us say, almost all. At any case, how many miles do you think a ship can travel without being refuelled?
P1	It depends on how large its tank is ...
P2	... also on the speed. ...
P3	On the consumption of its motors. My car does ten kilometres on a litre of petrol. ...
P4	On the conditions of the wind, of the sea. ...
T	Let us simplify the situation. Supposing average weather conditions, and a certain speed in knots, what other data do you think essential?
P1	I have said: the capacity of the tank.
P2	The consumption per kilometre.
T	Rather per nautical mile [*1852 metres*]. At sea this unit of measure is used. I think that's all. Let us formulate our problem: supposing that a ship consumes a certain

	quantity q of oil per mile at a speed of say 20 knots, and that its tanks can hold T metric tons of oil, how many miles can the ship travel without refuelling?
P	What do q and T mean?
T	Why, q means the quantity of oil consumed per mile, and T means the capacity of the tank in metric tons.
P	Why don't you give us the numbers? We could make a word problem.
T	Why not solve it without the numbers?
P	I could solve it if I had the numbers.
T	Tell me, how.
P	I would divide the number of tonnes in the tank by the consumption per mile.
T	Why can't you indicate the division?
P	I could, but I don't know what to divide by what.
T	But you do, you have all you need. Try to tackle it. Use the letters: T for the number of tonnes, q for the quantity of oil consumed per mile. What would you write for the unknown?
P	Let's call it A.
T	All right then, what will A be equal to?
P	A is equal to T divided by q.
T	How would you write it if you had numbers? Come to the blackboard.
P	Oh yes, this way:

$$\frac{T}{q} = A.$$

T	I agree. This is the right formula if q is expressed in tonnes per mile. And what if it is expressed in kilogrammes per mile?
P	I would convert the kilogrammes into tonnes.
T	Would you try it?

P	q in kilogrammes $= \dfrac{q \text{ in tonnes}}{1000}.$

T	This means, if we use this new q, q in kilogrammes, we shall have

$$\frac{T}{\dfrac{q}{1000}} = A$$

or, recalling how we divide by a fraction,

$$\frac{1000T}{q} = A.$$

Now you can formulate as many particular problems as you will. But you should use reliable data. I didn't want to improvise numerical data but, as you see, we have solved the problem all the same. Moreover we have a solution formula that you can use in every case of concrete numbers.

P	Yes, teacher, but where should we look for data?
T	Isn't there a harbour in Ravenna? Go on board a ship and ask for it.

1.5.4 Remarks

The approach used by the teacher is apparent from this text. The problem was open, indeterminate. Because of the motivation boys soon became involved. One can distinguish the usual phases of problem solving. The teacher first helped the boys to problematize a situation and then to formulate a definite problem.

In the next phase the problem was easily solved using literal notation which was new to the pupils. Doing so they made definite progress towards more abstract and generalized problem solving than they were accustomed to.

After a number of problems solved in this way the teacher found it possible to discuss with the pupils the merits of this general way of solving problems.

1.6 A lesson on linear programming

Ninety-minute lessons given by Mrs Oláh to a class of six girls and ten boys, aged from fifteen to sixteen years. Text prepared by T. Varga

1.6.1 Background and aims

During the earlier lessons the pupils learnt of linear inequalities. They represented the solution sets by open or closed half-planes. They 'played' with the intersections, unions and differences of such sets, and with their complementary sets in respect to the plane. This offered a good opportunity for introducing the symbols $\cap$, $\cup$, etc. The concept of the slope of a line was already well known to them. For example, they had some awareness of the fact that the slopes of lines with equations of the form

$$ax + by = c$$

only depended on a and b, not on c.

The object of this lesson was to present a practical application of linear inequalities, so far little more than a mathematical curiosity to the pupils.

1.6.2 The lesson

At first sight the problem has little to do with half-planes:

One division of a factory produces two articles that we shall call X and Y. It would be desirable to produce as many as possible, with a value as high as possible and to make as much profit as possible.

A discussion follows on these ideas. Pupils raise questions. Partly as answers to these questions, partly on the teacher's initiative, the data in Table 3 appear on the blackboard. Other divisions also need the same workshops and machines, hence the restrictions expressed in the last column.

Table 3 Production of Articles X and Y

	X	Y	Machine–hours available daily, as a maximum
Cost of production per piece/$	1·28	4·65	—
Price per piece/$	2	5	—
Profit per piece/$	0·72	0·35	—
Time needed for milling/hours	2	0	90
Time needed for compressing/hours	0	2	80
Time needed for grinding/hours	2	1	100
Time needed for painting/hours	5	5	300

The problem begins to take shape. The students examine it and look for a mathematical model. They decide to use x and y to represent respectively the number of pieces of X and Y manufactured daily. The teacher allows them to work independently. When it is time she asks a student to write on the board what he has found:

$$2x \leqslant 90, \qquad 2x + y \leqslant 100,$$
$$2y \leqslant 80, \qquad 5x + 5y \leqslant 300.$$

She asks those who seem to be uncertain, 'What does this inequality express?' 'Couldn't we write the same information in a more simple form?'

Here and there some silly remarks are made. The atmosphere of the lesson allows them to be made; ideas are clarified, misunderstandings need not survive.

Now they use the techniques developed earlier. They make sketches of the intersection of four half-planes (Figure 25).

The teacher asks questions about different points of the coordinate plane: 'What does this point represent?' 'What do we know about that point?' This serves to make students realize two tacit conditions: if either x or y were negative, it would mean that articles were being destroyed in the factory, instead of being produced.

The conditions reach their simplest forms:

$$x \leqslant 45, \qquad y \leqslant 100 - 2x, \qquad x \geqslant 0,$$
$$y \leqslant 40, \qquad y \leqslant 60 - x, \qquad y \geqslant 0.$$

Even a sketchy representation shows that the points satisfying them simultaneously lie within a closed hexagon OABCDE.

What is the problem? They agree to subdivide it as follows: How many items X and Y should be manufactured daily to maximize (for the two articles

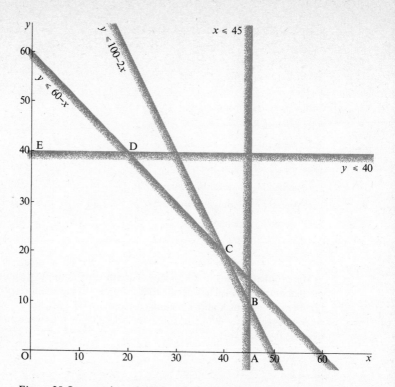

Figure 25 Intersection of the four half-planes, $x \leqslant 45$, $y \leqslant 40$, $y \leqslant 100 - 2x$, $y \leqslant 60 - x$. These half-planes, together with the two half-planes representing non-negative x and y, intersect in the hexagon OABCDE

together) the number of items n, the value produced v and the profit p?

The number of items is seen to reach a maximum of sixty when the painting shop is maximally utilized. This condition is satisfied at points on segment CD. This gives for x and y the non-independent conditions:

$20 \leqslant x \leqslant 40,$
$40 \geqslant y \geqslant 20.$

A student points out that, according to the condition of maximum v, y should be equal to 40 and x should be equal to 20. One Y item is of more value than one X, and this makes it clear that the production of Y should be favoured for making v a maximum.

But the profit on X is higher and so the same argument holds for producing 40 X items and only 20 Y, if our primary goal is the higher profit, not the higher value produced.

'Have we finished? Is this the final answer to our questions?' asks the teacher.

The students are startled by this question. One of them remarks, 'We treated the number of pieces as most important. The answers 20 and 40 are valid if we make the combined number of X and Y items a maximum. But what happens if it is not?'

'Indeed, what does happen if it is not? Could we then obtain a greater profit? Or a higher total value? Let us see. The profit if x items of X and y items of Y are produced is

$$p = 0{\cdot}72x + 0{\cdot}35y.$$

What lines do these equations represent if p varies? What about their slopes? Would you plot one of them, Kate? What if p is higher? Where can p be the highest? Watch the restrictions! Yes, it will be at point B.

'Now the value of the production. Leslie, you have it already. You say, at the point D. That is, p and v cannot be maximized together. It is a pity. But what if we were to modify the conditions? We might demand more time for the painting and polishing, in order to reach a higher production value and a higher profit at the same time.'

Here the lesson had to stop. Students will plot the diagrams at home on graph paper, and work out suggestions for reorganizing the production conditions in the factory.

1.6.3   Discussion

Should we approach mathematical topics from theory or from practice? Should we first take a mathematical model and apply it to solving problems, or should we rather raise problems that lead us to formulate mathematical models?

These are controversial questions. The second approach is known to have at least two advantages.

Firstly, among pupils – as among people in general – theoreticians are less numerous than those who are practically minded. Therefore a practical approach can be expected to have a higher motivational value than a merely theoretical one.

Secondly – and this is the main point – those who apply mathematics to solving a real problem very rarely have a ready-made mathematical model to hand. They themselves have to find and sometimes to create the necessary means. Starting with the practical problem helps to develop a useful way of thinking.

All that is true; yet the following points are also true. (a) The acquisition of a new mathematical idea can be motivated by considerations within mathematics itself: getting rid of an exception to a principle, rounding off a treatment, etc. The more we can reveal to the students the inherent laws and beauties of mathematics, the more this kind of motivation increases. (b) Practical problems that can be made interesting are rarely available. There is also a danger that unnecessary details will distract attention from the essential ideas. (c) Finding (not to speak of creating) a mathematical model for a practical problem needs considerable time, especially if the components of the model are not all at our disposal.

The teacher has to ponder these different points before he decides between a purely mathematical approach and one based on the outside world environment.

Further consideration shows that the two points of view are not as far apart as they seem. Motives can be taken partly from mathematics itself, partly from the environment in a wide sense. Part of the mathematical equipment may be prepared beforehand, the discovery of another part may be expected to arise from the problem.

Let us consider the lesson from these viewpoints. There may be arguments against pre-arranging the mathematical equipment. Some teachers (including this writer) might have tried to motivate the introduction of half-planes by some environmental problem at an earlier stage. Still they have little right to blame the teacher for having chosen a different way. There are too many factors involved in such decisions: the pupils' and the teacher's preferences, the syllabus to be covered, etc. In this particular case, deeper interest could be expected for intrinsic mathematical problems than in an average class; this is apparent from the discussion.

Is the topic and its presentation appropriate to this age level? Since linear programming itself is new, it is not surprising that it found its way into secondary schools only recently (and so far only in the simple intuitive presentation as seen above, restricted to two dimensions). After the pioneering work of Mansfield and Thompson, whose textbook (*Mathematics: A New Approach*) adapts the topic for as young an age group as from twelve to thirteen years, and the work of other pioneers, there remains little doubt that linear programming will have a permanent place in secondary-school syllabuses at some age level or another, in some form or another. The first introduction of the topic to mathematical classes, as in Hungary, can only be regarded as a preliminary to its wider spread.

Consider the strictly pedagogical aspects of the lesson. The same topic was taught some days later for the other half of the class by another teacher. The problem itself was the same, and this rendered the pedagogical differences especially conspicuous.

The first teacher planned a lesson, and followed her plan; the second teacher also planned a lesson, but deliberately ceded half of the initiative to the class. This involved a risk of not being able to finish in time, and indeed this was what happened. Yet her compliance paid fair dividends in the creative activity and independent work of the class.

The first teacher posed the problem in a mathematically impeccable form; the second gave the students only a rough outline of the situation and let them develop it with a mathematical problem.

This treatment, of course, takes more time, and it is up to the teacher to decide again and again about the usefulness of his time investment. This may not always be worth enough, it may tend to degenerate into formal ceremonies even under the label 'heuristic'. In the reported lesson this was not the case. It is true that most of the forty-five minutes were over before it became clear to the students what the problem really was. But this groping about the problem *was* a worthwhile activity, through which the problem became *their* problem. The crop grew ripe while time was seemingly wasted; it had just to be gathered in.

There is another aspect of this 'wasting time'. Recall the moment when the teacher let them err about the maximization of *n*, *v* and *p*, snatching them back at the last minute from the mistake of considering *v* and *p* only after *n* had been maximized. Without stumbling upon this error, few of them could reach a clear idea of the problem. This is a typical example of what might be called learning by mistakes.

1.7 Probability and statistics

Prepared by M. Håstad, Secretary of the Nordic Committee for the Modernization of School Mathematics

1.7.1 Finite outcome spaces

The empirical background of probability theory must first be studied: that is, the empirical phenomenon called the stability of relative frequencies. The students should themselves perform experiments such as tossing drawing-pins or coins. These experiments and the following simple properties of relative frequencies are used to motivate the model of probabilities in finite sample spaces.

If $f(u)$ is the relative frequency of the u,

then $f(u) \geqslant 0$ and $\sum f(u) = 1,$ **1.17**

where the summation is made over the set of all possible outcomes. If A is an event then

$$f(A) = \sum_{u \in A} f(u),$$ **1.18**

that is, the relative frequency of A is equal to the sum of relative frequencies belonging to outcomes in A.

The concept of outcome space is then introduced as the set of all possible outcomes of an experiment. Some examples of outcome spaces are given in Table 4.

Table 4 Some Simple Experiments and their Outcome Spaces

Experiment	Outcome space
Tossing a die	$\{u_1, u_2, u_3, u_4, u_5, u_6\}$
Tossing a thumbtack	$\{$up, down$\}$
Tossing two thumbtacks	$\{$up, down$\} \times \{$up, down$\}$
Tossing three coins	$\{$head, tail$\} \times \{$head, tail$\} \times \{$head, tail$\}$

Subsets of the outcome space are called events. If we throw a die and get an even number, this corresponds to the event $\{a_2, a_4, a_6\}$. If we take a natural number between 1 and 100 the outcome space is $\{u \in \mathbb{N} : 0 < u \leqslant 100\}$ and the event that the number is between 0 and 50 is $\{u \in \mathbb{N} : 0 < u \leqslant 50\}$.

With every outcome u in the outcome space Ω we now associate a number $P(u)$ such that

$$P(u) \geqslant 0 \quad \text{and} \quad \sum_{u \in \Omega} P(u) = 1. \qquad \textbf{1.19}$$

These numbers are called elementary probabilities. Table 5 describes some examples of simple outcome spaces with their elementary probabilities.

Table 5 Some Simple Outcome Spaces and their Elementary Probabilities

	Outcome u	Elementary probability $P(u)$
Tossing a drawing-pin	$\perp$	0·6
	λ	0·4
Sex of newborn baby	boy	0·52
	girl	0·48
Tossing a coin	head	0·5
	tail	0·5
Tossing a die	1	$\frac{1}{6}$
	2	$\frac{1}{6}$
	3	$\frac{1}{6}$
	4	$\frac{1}{6}$
	5	$\frac{1}{6}$
	6	$\frac{1}{6}$

The probability $P(A)$ of an event A is defined as the sum of elementary probabilities belonging to outcomes in A,

i.e. $\quad P(A) = \sum_{u \in A} P(u). \qquad \textbf{1.20}$

It is then easy to show that

$$P(\varnothing) = 0 \leqslant P(A) \leqslant 1 = P(\Omega), \qquad \textbf{1.21}$$

$$P(A) + P(\mathscr{C}_A) = 1, \qquad \textbf{1.22}$$

$$P(A \cup B) = P(A) + P(B) - P(A \cap B), \qquad \textbf{1.23}$$

$$A \cap B = \varnothing \Rightarrow P(A \cup B) = P(A) + P(B) \quad \text{(A and B are disjoint).} \qquad \textbf{1.24}$$

One important special case is when the elementary probabilities are chosen equal to each other. One can often use some symmetry of the experiment to justify this choice. If there are n outcomes in Ω, we have $P(u) = 1/n$, and if we use definition **1.20** of $P(A)$, we will get

$$P(A) = \frac{\text{number of outcomes in A}}{\text{total number of outcomes}}. \qquad \textbf{1.25}$$

If $P(A \cap B) = P(A)\,P(B)$ the events A and B are called independent.

1.7.2 *Sample problems*

1. The number of accidents in a certain city on Sundays gave the following elementary probabilities.

Outcome accidents	Elementary probability
0	0·819
1	0·164
2	0·016
more than 2	0·001

Calculate the probability that there is (a) at most one accident, (b) at least two accidents, (c) at least one accident, (d) one or two accidents.

2. The probability that a unit produced in an automatic industry will be defective is equal to p. In the experiment of selecting four units and counting the number of defectives amongst them, the following elementary probabilities may reasonably be assumed.

Outcome defections	Elementary probability
0	$(1-p)^4$
1	$4(1-p)^3 p$
2	$6(1-p)^2 p^2$
3	$4(1-p)p^3$
4	p^4

Suppose that $p = 0\cdot2$. (a) Check that the sum of the elementary probabilities is equal to one. (b) Calculate the probability that at least one of the four units is defective. (c) Suppose that the units are packed in cartons with four units on each carton. In how many, out of one thousand cartons, can one expect to find exactly two defective units?

3. Show that $p(A \cap B) \leqslant p(A) \leqslant p(A \cup B) \leqslant p(A) + p(B)$.

4. In a farming experiment a square field is divided into sixteen equal squares, arranged in four rows and four columns. Four squares are chosen at random. Calculate the probability that these squares (a) lie in the same row, (b) lie in the same column, (c) lie in the same diagonal, (d) lie such that there is one in each row and one in each column.

5. In a newly built business centre there are eight shops on two levels: four stores on each level. On each level the shops are arranged in a row. The different shops are assigned at random to eight shopkeepers. Two of these people, A and B, are thinking of opening shoe stores. Calculate the probability that (a) A and B receive shops on the same level, (b) A and B receive shops next to each other on the same level.

1.7.3 *A statistical investigation*

The following investigation about the children's habits with their mathematics homework may be performed by a group of students.

The purpose of the investigation is to select a random sample of pupils, give the group a questionnaire, sort out the replies by diagrams and tables, and eventually to try to draw conclusions about the whole population by means of statistical inference. The work is composed of six parts.

(a) Discussion of the aims of the investigation.

(b) Drawing up the questionnaire. The questions must be formulated so that it is possible to give unique answers.

(c) The selection of the random sample of students which is to answer the questions. Here the notion of random sample, and possibly stratification of the sample, is discussed. The use of random numbers for selecting the sample is introduced.

(d) The questionnaires are distributed and answered.

(e) The material is treated and presented in tables and diagrams. Means, medians, quartiles and standard deviations are calculated.

(f) By using tables of the binomial or normal distribution some confidence intervals are calculated. For instance, if seventeen out of eighty students in the sample have said they listen to music when doing their mathematics exercises, what can be said about the percentage of the 900 children in the whole school who combine music and mathematics in this way? The answer should be given as a confidence interval.

The results of points (e) and (f) could be published as a theme or as a lecture for the whole class. Other topics may be treated in a similar way.

1.7.4 *A problem about statistical inference*

'A metallurgist has performed four determinations of a melting point: 1263, 1259, 1270 and 1268°C. Estimate the real melting point and tell how accurate this estimate is.'

The students should understand the concepts of the mean and standard deviation of statistical data, expectation and standard deviation of a stochastic variable, and the normal distribution.

The measurement of the melting point is a stochastic variable X which may be supposed to be approximately normally distributed. The mean μ of X is the melting point if the measuring process is unbiased. As an estimate of μ we use the mean $\bar{X}$ of the four observations 1263, 1259, 1270 and 1268. Calculations give $\bar{X} = 1265$. We wish to give a confidence interval round $\bar{X}$ in which μ lies with 95 per cent likelihood.

We suppose that X has the standard deviation $\sigma = 5$. (Calculation of the standard deviation of the four observations gives the value 4·97 and does not contradict this assumption.) At this point we must make use of the theorems which say that the distribution of the mean $\bar{X}$ of four observations on X is approximately normal with the same mean and a standard deviation

$$\bar{\sigma} = \frac{5}{\sqrt{4}} = \frac{5}{2}.$$

A table of the normal distribution shows that the value of X with a probability of 0·95 lies within 1·96$\bar{\sigma}$ from the mean. This can be written

$$P(\mu - 1{\cdot}96\bar{\sigma} \leqslant \bar{x} \leqslant \mu + 1{\cdot}96\bar{\sigma}) = 0{\cdot}95.$$

In this case $\bar{\sigma} = \frac{5}{2}$ and the observed value of $\bar{x}$ is 1265. The inequalities can thus be written

$$\mu - 1{\cdot}96 \times 2{\cdot}5 \leqslant 1265 \leqslant \mu + 1{\cdot}96 \times 2{\cdot}5,$$
$$1265 - 4{\cdot}9 \leqslant \mu \leqslant 1265 + 4{\cdot}9.$$

The melting point can thus be estimated with a 95 per cent confidence interval of $1265 \pm 4{\cdot}9$.

1.8 Matrices

Prepared by G. Matthews, Project organizer for the Nuffield Foundation Mathematics Teaching Project

Matrices may be introduced to children at the age of thirteen or fourteen, when the 'product' is defined naturally in terms of successive geometrical transformations. However, psychologically there is much to be said for a preview. Matrices can be introduced to eleven or twelve year olds with the help of a contrived motivation. They are then 'old friends' when they crop up later. Further, the important idea of a non-commutative algebra has been introduced satisfactorily early. Encounters with different structures do not confuse children of twelve, or even a little younger; on the contrary, they learn to take greater care with familiar situations. (Is 63 421 × 59 186 the 'same' as 59 186 × 63 421?)

Introduction to matrices can be made via codes. For example:

A	B	C	D	E	F	G	H	I	J	K	L	M
9	2	20	7	19	14	17	13	5	10	1	12	8

N	O	P	Q	R	S	T	U	V	W	X	Y	Z
6	11	21	4	18	25	16	15	26	24	23	3	22

BUDA can be encoded by writing the corresponding numbers $\begin{bmatrix} 2 & 15 \\ 7 & 9 \end{bmatrix}$ and premultiplying by an 'encoder', say $\begin{bmatrix} 2 & 1 \\ -1 & 0 \end{bmatrix}$:

$$\begin{bmatrix} 2 & 1 \\ -1 & 0 \end{bmatrix}\begin{bmatrix} 2 & 15 \\ 7 & 9 \end{bmatrix} = \begin{bmatrix} 2\times 2+1\times 7 & 2\times 15+1\times 9 \\ -1\times 2+0\times 7 & -1\times 15+0\times 9 \end{bmatrix}$$

$$= \begin{bmatrix} 11 & 39 \\ -2 & -15 \end{bmatrix}.$$

The rule for multiplying matrices is stated without explanation. The notion of a row 'diving' onto a column has been found useful.

The message is then sent as 11 39 −2 −15. At the other end, decoding is effected through multiplication by a 'decoder', in this case $\begin{bmatrix} 0 & -1 \\ 1 & 2 \end{bmatrix}$, obtaining

$$\begin{bmatrix} 0 & -1 \\ 1 & 2 \end{bmatrix}\begin{bmatrix} 11 & 39 \\ -2 & -15 \end{bmatrix} = \begin{bmatrix} 2 & 15 \\ 7 & 9 \end{bmatrix} \quad \text{as above.}$$

After this artificial start, there is plenty of scope for discoveries; for example, the children can discover: (a) the rule for finding the correct decoder for a given encoder, (b) the unit and zero matrices, (c) that they are working with an arithmetic modulo 26, (d) that the determinant of the encoder should be unity to avoid fractions. They then investigate what happens if the encoding clerk makes a mistake and reverses the order of multiplication:

$$\begin{bmatrix} 2 & 15 \\ 7 & 9 \end{bmatrix}\begin{bmatrix} 2 & 1 \\ -1 & 0 \end{bmatrix} = \begin{bmatrix} -11 & 2 \\ 5 & 7 \end{bmatrix}.$$

At the other end, the message is decoded according to the correct procedure:

$$\begin{bmatrix} 0 & -1 \\ 1 & 2 \end{bmatrix}\begin{bmatrix} -11 & 2 \\ 5 & 7 \end{bmatrix} = \begin{bmatrix} -5 & -7 \\ -1 & 16 \end{bmatrix},$$

i.e. −5 −7 −1 16
or 21 19 25 16 (adding 26 where appropriate)
giving, instead of BUDA, PEST.

Matrices of other orders can now be introduced, and a procedure can quickly be evolved for solving simultaneous equations. The relevant rules (associative law etc.) are emphasized as they crop up.

$$x+2y = 5$$
$$3x+4y = 11$$

$$\Leftrightarrow \quad \begin{bmatrix} 1 & 2 \\ 3 & 4 \end{bmatrix}\begin{bmatrix} x \\ y \end{bmatrix} = \begin{bmatrix} 5 \\ 11 \end{bmatrix}$$

$$\Leftrightarrow \quad \begin{bmatrix} 4 & -2 \\ -3 & 1 \end{bmatrix}\begin{bmatrix} 1 & 2 \\ 3 & 4 \end{bmatrix}\begin{bmatrix} x \\ y \end{bmatrix} = \begin{bmatrix} 4 & -2 \\ -3 & 1 \end{bmatrix}\begin{bmatrix} 5 \\ 11 \end{bmatrix}$$

$$\Leftrightarrow \quad \begin{bmatrix} -2 & 0 \\ 0 & -2 \end{bmatrix}\begin{bmatrix} x \\ y \end{bmatrix} = \begin{bmatrix} -2 \\ -4 \end{bmatrix}$$

$$\Leftrightarrow \quad \begin{bmatrix} -2x \\ -2y \end{bmatrix} = \begin{bmatrix} -2 \\ -4 \end{bmatrix} \Leftrightarrow x = 1, \quad y = 2.$$

The matrix $\begin{bmatrix} 4 & -2 \\ -3 & 1 \end{bmatrix}$ introduced into the second matrix equation is obtained from $\begin{bmatrix} 1 & 2 \\ 3 & 4 \end{bmatrix}$ by changing over the 1 and 4 and reversing the sign

of the remaining elements. Several examples like this, made up by the children themselves, are worked through.

The pernicious use of the symbol $\therefore$ ('therefore') can be brought out by the following demonstration:

$$x + 2y = 5$$
$$3x + 6y = 11$$

$$\therefore \quad \begin{bmatrix} 1 & 2 \\ 3 & 6 \end{bmatrix}\begin{bmatrix} x \\ y \end{bmatrix} = \begin{bmatrix} 5 \\ 11 \end{bmatrix}$$

$$\therefore \quad \begin{bmatrix} 6 & -2 \\ -3 & 1 \end{bmatrix}\begin{bmatrix} 1 & 2 \\ 3 & 6 \end{bmatrix}\begin{bmatrix} x \\ y \end{bmatrix} = \begin{bmatrix} 6 & -2 \\ -3 & 1 \end{bmatrix}\begin{bmatrix} 5 \\ 11 \end{bmatrix}$$

$$\therefore \quad \begin{bmatrix} 0 & 0 \\ 0 & 0 \end{bmatrix}\begin{bmatrix} x \\ y \end{bmatrix} = \begin{bmatrix} 8 \\ -4 \end{bmatrix}$$

$$\therefore \quad \begin{bmatrix} 0 \\ 0 \end{bmatrix} = \begin{bmatrix} 8 \\ -4 \end{bmatrix}$$

$$\therefore \quad 0 = 8 = -4$$

The horrible snowstorm of dots has produced an absurdity. If '$\therefore$' is replaced by the implication sign, $\Rightarrow$ (and not by '$\Leftrightarrow$' unless every step is clearly reversible), then the last example reads quite logically, according to the English adage, 'Ask a silly question and you'll get a silly answer'.

After this, the way is open to link matrices with geometry. Even at the age of nine or so, children can appreciate, for example, reflections in mirrors.

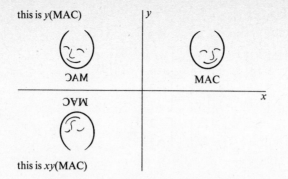

this is y(MAC)

y

ƆAM

MAC

x

MAƆ

this is xy(MAC)

Figure 26 Reflections in a pair of perpendicular axes

In Figure 26, y(MAC) is the reflection of MAC in the y-axis and xy(MAC) is the reflection of y(MAC) in the x-axis; xy(MAC) = yx(MAC), but not if the mirrors are not at right angles to each other. At thirteen or fourteen, this can be taken up again in terms of matrices. The transformation of the column

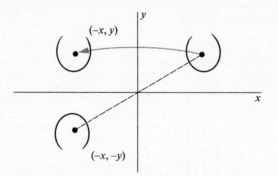

y

$(-x, y)$

x

$(-x, -y)$

Figure 27 Coordinates of a point and of its reflections in a pair of perpendicular axes

vector $\begin{bmatrix} x \\ y \end{bmatrix}$ into $\begin{bmatrix} -x \\ y \end{bmatrix}$ or MAC into y(MAC), is given by A $= \begin{bmatrix} -1 & 0 \\ 0 & 1 \end{bmatrix}$, since

$$\begin{bmatrix} -1 & 0 \\ 0 & 1 \end{bmatrix}\begin{bmatrix} x \\ y \end{bmatrix} = \begin{bmatrix} -x \\ y \end{bmatrix}.$$

Similarly the matrix representing reflection in the x-axis is B $= \begin{bmatrix} 1 & 0 \\ 0 & -1 \end{bmatrix}$ and the product of these is

$$\begin{bmatrix} -1 & 0 \\ 0 & 1 \end{bmatrix} \begin{bmatrix} 1 & 0 \\ 0 & -1 \end{bmatrix} = \begin{bmatrix} -1 & 0 \\ 0 & -1 \end{bmatrix} = C$$

say; that is, successive reflection in the axes is equivalent to the half-turn

$$\begin{bmatrix} x \\ y \end{bmatrix} \rightarrow \begin{bmatrix} -x \\ -y \end{bmatrix}.$$

A group table can now be constructed:

	I	A	B	C
I	I	A	B	C
A	A	I	C	B
B	B	C	I	A
C	C	B	A	I

and this can be compared with other situations (addition modulo 4 etc.) so that the two distinct groups of order 4 are discovered.

The affine transformations represented by

$$\begin{bmatrix} a & b \\ c & d \end{bmatrix} \quad (ad \neq bc)$$

can next be investigated, and eventually there is hardly a branch of mathematics which cannot be illuminated in some way by matrices. That they are truly 'polyvalent' is indeed the justification for their early introduction.

1.9 Calculus

Prepared by G. Matthews, project organizer for the Nuffield Foundation Mathematics Teaching Project.

Teaching calculus at school involves compromise: the mathematician demands rigour, the pupil demands motivation. Concepts must therefore be introduced intuitively and the need for refinement of ideas then gradually make itself felt. A start can be made at the age of about fourteen in terms of travel graphs.

Example. A particle moves in a straight line so that the distance s metres it has travelled after t seconds is given by $s = \frac{1}{2}t^2$. Plot accurately the graph of s against t for values of t from 0 to 4.

(a) Read off from the graph the total distance covered (i) between $t = 0$ and $t = 3$; (ii) $t = 0$ and $t = 2$.

(b) What is the distance travelled in the third second (i.e. between $t = 2$ and $t = 3$)?

(c) What is the average velocity between $t = 2$ and $t = 3$?

(d) Find the average velocity (i) between $t = 2$ and $t = 2.5$; (ii) between $t = 2$ and $t = 2.1$; (iii) between $t = 1.7$ and $t = 2.3$.

(e) Estimate the velocity when $t = 2$.

(f) Draw by eye, as accurately as possible, the straight line touching the graph at the point for which $t = 2$, and calculate its gradient (the tangent of the angle it makes with the t-axis).

(g) What do you infer by comparing the answers to (e) and (f)?

The *gradient* of a curve is first introduced graphically, by observing the behaviour of the gradient of a chord PQ as Q approaches P.

By this time, it is possible to make three fair guesses about motion in a straight line:

(a) The gradient of any $s(t)$ curve at any point gives the velocity at that instant.

(b) The gradient of any $v(t)$ graph gives the acceleration.

(c) The area under any section of a $v(t)$ graph gives the distance travelled in the corresponding time.

Even at this stage problems like the following can be set.

(a) Give a rough sketch of the $s(t)$ and (t) graphs of a schoolboy who starts slowly for school, panics because he thinks he is late and then dawdles again as he approaches the school gate.

(b) Treat similarly a more complicated journey (e.g. he could set out and have to return for a forgotten book, jump on a bus, etc.).

(c) If a few bacteria are put into a closed vessel, they will first breed slowly (as there are few of them), then more rapidly (as more become available to breed) and finally more slowly again (as they become cramped in the full vessel).

Reword this statement in terms of the gradient of the graph of number of bacteria present plotted against time, and give a rough sketch of this graph (cf. Steinhaus, 1964, p. 249).

Our idea of 'gradient' is then shown to be inadequate for, say, x and a second look is necessary. At this stage it is pointed out that mathematicians cannot be bothered to deal in turn with x^2, $3x+1$, $1/x$ and so on, but would rather deal in more general terms, and so the idea of *function* is introduced, as a many-to-one mapping. Eventually, again with the help of diagrams, the final definitive formula is evolved.

There is still a danger that

$$\lim_{h \to 0} \frac{f(x+h)-f(x)}{h}$$

will become a meaningless slogan, to be brought out whenever the word 'gradient' is mentioned. We now therefore digress briefly to re-examine some of the underlying ideas.

This will scarcely give a preview of the rigorous treatment given in more advanced courses, but at least perhaps show the need for it.* First, the idea '$h \to 0$' here implies that, as h changes from one value to a numerically smaller one, it takes up 'all' values in between. Just what do we mean by 'all'? This leads to a discussion (probably in the nature of revision) of the different sets of numbers.

We next look a little more closely at the meaning of 'limit'.

Example. Find $\lim_{x \to 2} (x^2 + 3)$.

The answer is 'clearly' 7, since if x is given values closer and closer to 2, then $x^2 + 3$ gets nearer and nearer to 7. This, however, is careless talk. (How close is 'closer and closer'? Do we mean for *all* values of x close enough to 2? How near to 7 is near enough?)

If A writes, '$\lim_{x \to 2} (x^2 + 3) = 7$', this implies that if x is *any* number within a close enough range of 2, then $x^2 + 3$ is as near to 7 as any challenger B pleases. The 'close enough' range for x centred on 2 *does not necessarily apply to 2 itself*, as 'tending to 2' does not involve actually reaching it. The argument might go as follows:

B You reckon $\lim_{x \to 2} (x^2 + 3) = 7$. Very well, I name 7 ± 0.01 as the boundaries for $x^2 + 3$.
You find an interval centred on 2 such that, for all x in that interval (except possibly 2 itself), $x^2 + 3$ lies between $7 + 0.01$ and $7 - 0.01$.

A Certainly If x is between 2 ± 0.002, your condition is satisfied.

B All right. Now I name 7 ± 0.0001 as the boundaries for $x^2 + 3$ ... (and so on).

If A is sure he can answer *any* such challenge, and come up with a corresponding interval for x, only then can he correctly assert that '$\lim_{x \to 2} (x^2 + 3) = 7$'.

Example. Examine $\lim_{x \to 2} \dfrac{x^2 - 4}{x - 2}$.

This is not quite so 'obvious' as the last example, for $(x^2 - 4)/(x - 2)$ is meaningless when $x = 2$. All the same, if $x \neq 2$, $(x^2 - 4)/(x - 2) = x + 2$, and, as x tends to 2, this expression tends to 4.

A could stand up to any challenge by B, the conversation running similarly to that of the previous example. The reader should verify this, remembering, that as x is *tending* to 2, what happens, or fails to happen, if $x = 2$ does not affect the argument.

Thus $\lim_{x \to 2} \dfrac{x^2 - 4}{x - 2} = 4$.

*Learning to speak, small children first pick up a number of words, and only later stop to analyse their precise meaning. Similarly here it is time to stop and at least reflect a little on what we are really talking about.

The graph of $y = (x^2-4)/(x-2)$ is a straight line 'with a hole in it', that is, the line whose equation is $y = x+2$ with a point missing at $x = 2$.

(If we had started instead with the equation $y(x-2) = x^2-4$, this would have been equivalent to 'either $x = 2$ or $y = x+2$', and the graph would then have consisted of the whole of the two straight lines $x = 2$ and $y = x+2$.)

Example. Investigate $\displaystyle\lim_{h\to 0}\frac{|h|}{h}$.

This limit does not exist, for if $h>0$, $|h|/h = 1$, while if $h<0$, $|h|/h = -1$. It would therefore be impossible to find an interval for h centred on 0 such that $|h|/h$ was 'as near as you please' to any given number.

This last example shows that $|x|$ does not have a gradient when $x = 0$, for the following problems are equivalent.

(a) Investigate the gradient of $|x|$ at $x = 0$.

(b) Investigate $\displaystyle\lim_{h\to 0}\frac{f(x+h)-f(x)}{h}$ if $f(x) \equiv |x|$, when $x = 0$.

(c) Investigate $\displaystyle\lim_{h\to 0}\frac{f(h)-f(0)}{h}$ if $f(x) \equiv |x|$.

(d) Investigate $\displaystyle\lim_{h\to 0}\frac{|h|}{h}$.

We have just seen that the last limit does not exist.

We can now return with more conviction to our definition of the gradient of a function $f(x)$ for a particular value of x, say $x = a$. To avoid having to write $y = f(x)$ and referring to dy/dx (or to write clumsily '$d\{f(x)\}/dx$'), we introduce the notation $f'(x)$ for the gradient of $f(x)$, and we have

$$f'(a) = \lim_{h\to 0}\frac{f(a+h)-f(a)}{h}$$

provided the limit on the right-hand side exists. (If it does not, then $f(x)$ has no gradient when $x = a$.)

The existence of the right-hand side implies that x can take all values within a certain range centred on a, and further that $f(a+h)-f(a) \to 0$ as $h \to 0$. This last condition means that the function is *continuous* at $x = a$;* that is, $f(a)$ exists, and by taking h small enough, $f(x)-f(a)$ is as small as you please for *all* x between $a+h$. But if a function is continuous at a point, this does not ensure that it has a gradient there (cf. $|x|$ at $x = 0$); it is, in fact, a necessary condition, but not a sufficient one.

The way is now open for differentiation of polynomials and applications

---

*This is roughly equivalent to saying that the graph of $y = f(x)$ could be drawn in the neighbourhood of $x = a$ without taking the pencil off the paper.

(tangent and normal, maxima and minima, kinematics, approximations).

Integration can be introduced by returning to the three 'fair guesses' (p. 84). The first two of these will by now have been justified and can be re-stated, mathematically, as

(a) $\dfrac{ds}{dt} = v,$ (b) $\dfrac{dv}{dt} = f.$

Guesses (a) and (c) form a pair:

Gradient of $s(t)$ graph is v.   Area under $v(t)$ graph is s.

This suggests a connexion between gradients and areas as, roughly speaking, opposite processes.

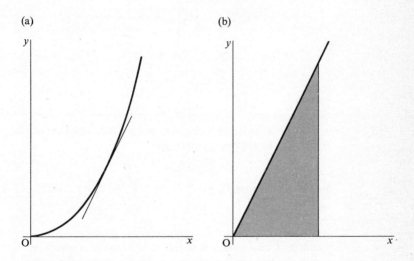

(a)   (b)

Figure 28 (a) Gradient of $y = x^2$ is $2x$; (b) area 'under' $y = 2x$ is x^2

Integration is then defined in three distinct ways, 'opposite of differentiation', 'area under graph' and 'limit of sum', the latter by means of an example.

Example. Find the area 'under' the graph of $y = x^2$, between $x = 0$ and $x = a$.

The area required is that bounded by the curve, the x-axis and the line $x = a$. We first divide the interval between O and a on the x-axis into n parts, each

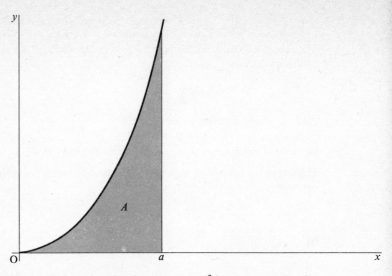

Figure 29 Area A under the curve $y = x^2$ between $x = 0$ and $x = a$

of length δx, so that $n\,\delta x = a$. Labelling the points along the x-axis $A_1, A_2, \ldots$; $A_{n-1}, A_n (x = a)$ (Figure 30), we have

$$OA_1 = A_1 A_2 = \ldots = A_{n-1} A_n = \delta x.$$

Since $OA_1 = \delta x$, $A_1 P_1 = (\delta x)^2$; $OA_2 = 2\delta x$, $A_2 P_2 = (2\delta x)^2$; $\ldots$;

$$OA_{n-1} = (n-1)\delta x, A_{n-1}P_{n-1} = \{(n-1)\delta x\}^2; OA_n = n\,\delta x, A_n P_n = (n\,\delta x)^2.$$

We next construct two 'staircases' consisting of rectangles, as in Figure 30. The area A which we seek is greater than the area under the 'staircase' in Figure 30a, and less than the area under the 'staircase' in Figure 30b.

The area under the first staircase is

$$A_1 P_1 \times \delta x + A_2 P_2 \times \delta x + A_3 P_3 \times \delta x + \ldots + A_{n-1}P_{n-1} \times \delta x$$
$$= \delta x [(\delta x)^2 + (2\,\delta x)^2 + (3\,\delta x)^2 + \ldots + \{(n-1)\delta x\}^2]$$
$$= (\delta x)^3 \{1^2 + 2^2 + 3^2 + \ldots + (n-1)^2\}.$$

Similarly, the area under the second 'staircase' is

$$(\delta x)^3 \{1^2 + 2^2 + 3^2 + \ldots + (n-1)^2 + n^2\}.$$

We thus have

$$(\delta x)^3 \{1^2 + 2^2 + \ldots + (n-1)^2\} < A < (\delta x)^3 \{1^2 + 2^2 + \ldots + n^2\}.$$

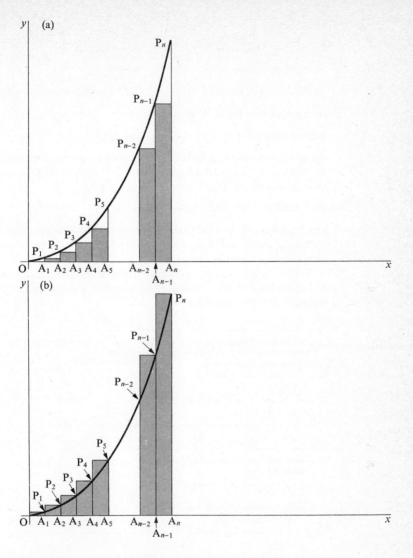

Figure 30 (a) 'Staircase' with area less than A; (b) 'staircase' with area greater than A

It can be shown that

$$1^2 + 2^2 + \ldots + n^2 = \tfrac{1}{6}n(n+1)(2n+1)$$

and that $1^2 + 2^2 + \ldots + (n-1)^2 = \tfrac{1}{6}(n-1)n(2n-1).$

Thus we have

$$(\delta x)^3 \times \tfrac{1}{6}(n-1)n(2n-1) < A < (\delta x)^3 \times \tfrac{1}{6}n(n+1)(2n+1).$$

This can be written

$$\tfrac{1}{6}(n\,\delta x - \delta x)(n\,\delta x)(2n\,\delta x - \delta x) < A < \tfrac{1}{6}(n\,\delta x)(n\,\delta x + \delta x)(2n\,\delta x + \delta x)$$

or, remembering that $n\,\delta x = a$,

$$\tfrac{1}{6}(a - \delta x)a(2a - \delta x) < A < \tfrac{1}{6}a(a + \delta x)(2a + \delta x).$$

We now let $\delta x \to 0$ and n become large in such a way that $n\,\delta x$ remains equal to a, that is, we increase the number of small subdivisions of OA_n, correspondingly decreasing the length of each. Now, as $\delta x \to 0$,

$$\tfrac{1}{6}(a - \delta x)a(2a - \delta x) \quad \text{and} \quad \tfrac{1}{6}a(a + \delta x)(2a + \delta x)$$

both tend to $\tfrac{1}{6} \times 2a^3 = \tfrac{1}{3}a^3$. As A lies between these amounts, however small we take δx to be, it follows that $A = \tfrac{1}{3}a^3$. (This is consistent with the first definition of integration, by which $\int x^2\,dx = \tfrac{1}{3}x^3 + c$.)

This can be followed by an informal treatment of the fundamental theorem and application to areas, volumes, mass-centres, kinematics, and a possible sequence after this as follows:

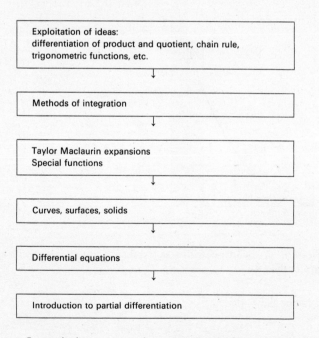

Exploitation of ideas:
differentiation of product and quotient, chain rule,
trigonometric functions, etc.

Methods of integration

Taylor Maclaurin expansions
Special functions

Curves, surfaces, solids

Differential equations

Introduction to partial differentiation

In particular, we now give a note on the introduction of the exponential function and its inverse, the logarithm, to the future scientist.

The subject matter is, of course, quite traditional, but the presentation suggested is not the usual one of starting with

$$\log t = \int_1^t \frac{1}{x}\,dx$$

and developing the theory with as much rigour as possible from the start. Interest tends to wane with this approach, as the student can't 'see the point'.

The following, then, is a suggested sequence:

1. Start with a number of examples, such as:
(a) Formulate mathematically the law, 'If bacteria breed without restraint, the rate of increase is proportional to the number of organisms.'
(b) Translate into mathematics the law of cooling: 'If a hot body is placed in a cool room, the rate at which its temperature changes is proportional to the difference between the temperature of the body and that of the surrounding medium.'
(c) Formulate the law of radioactive decay.

In each case, an equation of the form

$$\frac{d}{dx}\{f(x)\} = k f(x) \qquad\qquad \textbf{1.26}$$

is found, so there is now a strong motivation for finding a solution of this.

2. Start with the case $k = 1, f(0) = 1$ and use Maclaurin's series,

$$f(x) = f(0) + x f'(0) + \frac{x^2}{2!} f'(0) + \dots ,$$

quite recklessly to obtain

$$f(x) = 1 + x + \frac{x^2}{2!} + \dots .$$

Differentiate term by term, obtaining $f'(x) = f(x)$ and so a solution of equation **1.26**.

Also, multiplying two series together,

$$f(x)f(y) = \left(1 + x + \frac{x^2}{2!} + \dots\right)\left(1 + y + \frac{y^2}{2!} + \dots\right)$$

$$= 1 + (x+y) + \frac{1}{2!}(x+y)^2 + \dots$$

$$= f(x+y).$$

This suggests the index law and we let $f(x) = \exp x = e^x$, defining e as

$$1 + 1 + \frac{1}{2!} + \frac{1}{3!} + \dots .$$

3. This is the key move in the lesson. Many students (alas) may have accepted the above all too readily. Questions such as the following are now discussed by the class:

(a) The series

$$\sin x + \frac{1}{2}\sin 2x + \frac{1}{2^2}\sin 2^2 x + \frac{1}{2^3}\sin 2^3 x + \ldots$$

converges. What happens on differentiating term by term and then setting $x = 0$?

(b) Have we *proved* that $\exp x \times \exp y = \exp(x+y)$?

(c) The series $1 - \frac{1}{\sqrt{2}} + \frac{1}{\sqrt{3}} - \frac{1}{\sqrt{4}} + \ldots$ converges.

What about the Cauchy product of this series with itself, i.e.

$$\sum \frac{1}{\sqrt{1}\sqrt{n}} + \frac{1}{\sqrt{2}\sqrt{(n-1)}} + \ldots + \frac{1}{\sqrt{n}\sqrt{1}}?$$

The class can soon discover that the nth term of the last series does not tend to zero as n tends to infinity, and so the series is divergent.

After such a series of shocks, the class will now accept the traditional approach with interest, being now aware of (i) the importance of the topic, and (ii) the dangers of a reckless approach.

The introduction of simple differential equations to pupils of sixteen or seventeen can be justified not only in terms of intrinsic interest but also since so many physical problems can then be tackled, for example:

(a) Solve the equation

$$\frac{d^2 y}{dt^2} + n^2 y \equiv A \cos pt.$$

What phenomenon is illustrated when $p \simeq n$? Show that a particular integral of

$$\frac{d^2 y}{dt^2} + n^2 y = k \cos nt \quad \text{is} \quad y = \frac{k}{n} t \sin nt.$$

(b) A particle of mass m and charge e moves in the plane xOy under the action of constant electric and magnetic fields of strengths E and H respectively. The fields exert forces eE in the direction of Ox and eHv along the normal to the path of the particle, v being the velocity of the particle at any instant. Write down the equation of motion of the particle.

Show that the equations are satisfied by

$$x = A + B \cos \alpha t, \qquad y = Ct + B \sin \alpha t,$$

where the constants C and α are given by the formulae

$$C = \frac{E}{H}, \qquad \alpha = \frac{eH}{m}.$$

Evaluate the constants A and B if the particle is initially at rest at O; and prove that in these circumstances the particle comes momentarily to rest when $t = 2\pi n/\alpha$, where n is any positive integer.

(c) A particle of unit mass is projected vertically upwards in a medium whose resistance is λv^2, where v is the velocity at any instant. Find the greatest height attained when the initial velocity is v. Show that, when λ is small compared with v the greatest height is approximately

$$\frac{v^2}{2g}\left(1 - \frac{v^2}{2g}\right).$$

As already indicated, emphasis should be placed throughout on motivation and understanding rather than mechanical learning. Thus, for example, the idea of gradient is first shown to be useful, and later the underlying concept of limit is discussed in more than customary detail. Again, the exponential function and Taylor's theorem are introduced most informally, more rigorous treatment being deferred until after their importance has been justified.

References

HAWKINS, D. (1967), 'Mathematics – practical and impractical', *Mathematics Teaching*, no. 41, pp. 4–8.
MANSFIELD, D. E., and THOMPSON, D. (1963–66), *Mathematics: A New Approach*, 5 vols., with teachers' guides, Chatto & Windus.
STEINHAUS, H. G. (1964), *One Hundred Problems in Elementary Mathematics*, Basic Books.

2 The Use of Teaching Aids

Prepared by W. Servais

2.0 Introduction

It is appropriate to begin this review of the equipment and aids used in teaching mathematics by emphasizing the part they play in the development of mathematical thinking. Some teachers are opposed to the use of concrete illustrations as a basis of support for abstractions. They demand strict logic and strict logic alone, with no compromising admixture of imprecise empiricism. At the other extreme are those who want the concrete illustration for its own sake and who replace proof by demonstration, in the belief that the concrete is immediate, that it exerts some magic power and that mathematics is subsumed by the concrete. In fact, it is by working with concrete examples that we come by our first notions of mathematics. We gradually build up from our perceptions and actions relating to the concrete a mental picture which we can then call up by itself. The relations between perceptions and actions which have thus been given an abstract form constitute the first subject of mathematical study.

In an experiment with physical objects our attention is focused on the results, satisfactory or otherwise, ensuing from our actions. With mathematics in the abstract, objects are stylized and free from imperfections. For this reason, when we use sketches and tangible models to reinforce these abstract mental operations, we pay no attention to the imperfections in their representation of mathematical concepts. The mathematical experiment and the subjects with which it works are at a second stage and are not to be confused with the physical experiment and subjects, which are at an earlier stage. No doubt it is impossible for us to attain the second stage without having carried out the operations of the first. Most people, if not all, need to give a concrete form to their mental activity; this is where the vehicular language of diagrams and mathematical symbols comes in. These symbols and diagrams are physical models governed by precise rules of manipulation and thus, ultimately, they convey the rigour of the abstract original.

All types of material equipment are, in their conception, isomorphic (Servais, 1958),* fulfilling the same role from the mathematical point of view, although from the psychological point of view some of them may be better adapted than others to our idea of things by their colour, their manageableness

*References for chapter 2 will be found on pp. 120–23.

or their appeal to the intuition. Once their isomorphism has been acknow-ledged, we can delegate to them the task of giving support to a mathematical activity to which they automatically run parallel. This is the function of mathe-matical machines which work the other way round to make the abstract concrete.

The term 'model' is thus employed in two complementary senses, corres-ponding to the two ways in which the physical and the mathematical interact: the physical material is a concrete model of the mathematical relation which it illustrates, the mathematical structure is an abstract model of the physical situation which it explains.

Educationally, the greatest value of concrete material is that it allows the pupil to acquire mental experience at his own pace, outside the authority of the teacher. There are conscientious teachers who think they can teach any-thing by saying it and repeating it, not realizing that their efforts are wasted unless the intellectual activity of the pupils is deeply engaged. There are teachers who do not fully realize that their business is to see that children learn. Well-designed material aids can, to a certain extent, protect the pupil against the teacher, protect his unspoiled creativity from adult knowledge which has become a little stale by constant repetition. For mathematical teaching aids to fulfil their purpose, they must be manipulated by the pupils themselves, thus helping them to clarify, co-ordinate and organize their ideas. There would, therefore, be very little point in a complicated ready-made model. The best that teaching-aid firms can do is to supply the teaching profession with geometrical, mechanical, electrical, algebraic and logical construction games to encourage pupil activity and save teaching time.

2.1 Drawings and diagrams

2.1.1 Drawing with instruments is an integral part of the teaching of geometry. Not only does it enable pupils to draw figures correctly; its essential purpose is to create, by this exercise, a whole field of ideas and notions without which the pupil cannot form geometrical concepts.

At the same time, the commentary which accompanies these operations brings into active play a vocabulary which will later become familiar through its use in definitions and proofs.

The exact drawing of figures gives the pupils an inkling of the perfection of pure geometrical concepts. Observations made experimentally upon physical figures provide, in suitable cases, a means of checking theoretical results in practice and of discerning new abstract properties. These exchanges and relationships between drawing operations, mental images and abstract notions are very useful for nourishing geometrical thought.

However, the transitions between the plans of action, comprehension and conceptualization occur so readily and so often in this way that, unless care is taken, they set up and perpetuate a confusion between the experimental and the theoretical, and elementary geometry takes on too much the appearance of physics with ruler and compass.

It is true that metric geometry has its roots in the properties of solid physical bodies, but this is no reason why an attempt should not be made at a fairly early stage to rid geometrical thinking of its early connexions so that its relational content may be more easily grasped.

In this way, abstract geometrical shapes may be used as mathematical models suitable for dealing with the most varied questions. For instance, a simple cube can be used as a model for the solution of a problem involving the counting of numbers from zero to seven in the binary system (Pollak, 1965), or to represent the inter-character relations in a three-factor characterology (Servais, 1955/6).

2.1.2   Drawing of rough diagrams is much more common than accurate drawing with instruments. An important original contribution of modern teaching has been to introduce the use of graphs systematically and at a very early stage. This makes it possible for pupils to realize at the conceptual level properties which are normally observed only at the perceptual level.

Thus, in order to grasp the full significance of the axiom of the determination of a straight line by two points belonging to it, it is a useful exercise to map a straight line A and a straight line B on a Venn diagram and to ask which will be the empty parts if it is known that separate points p and q both belong to both A and B.

In this way, the figurative representation involved, while it is still perceptual, is of a more advanced nature and is being used to give a sharp, abstract form to a geometrical fact which is too closely tied to the visual evidence of a straight line drawn through two points. In a similar way, Venn diagrams can be used to show two disjoint parallel lines or two intersecting lines (Papy, 1963).

Schoolchildren of about the age of twelve who already have some grounding in sets and Venn diagrams show astonishing ease in dealing with such problems. They therefore have the necessary background for understanding that all the notions involved apply equally to sets which are determined by any two of their elements and by pairs of objects in particular (Servais, 1965).

2.1.3   Because of its perceptual realism, traditional geometrical drawing is unsuitable for illustrating certain ideas. It is easy enough to draw a segment, but how is it possible to indicate on the figure that the interval formed by the points within this segment is regarded as open? Some conventional representation is required. The elements to be excluded from consideration might, for instance, be coloured red whilst the elements to be taken into consideration might be coloured green (Papy, 1963). The two ends of the segment would thus be coloured red and the interior would be drawn in green. The same convention makes it possible to represent the interior of a circle and, more generally speaking, the interior of a region by adding to it certain elements of the border.

2.1.4   Geometrical drawing is usually something static. It does not, of itself, provoke transformations, relationships, in short, dynamism. Later on we shall look at some methods of achieving this dynamism by means of moving models or films.

Arrow graphs are used to represent binary relations by sets of arrows (cf. chapter 1 and the Appendix). The finished graph, being formed of arrows, preserves the memory of the dynamic operation involved in drawing it. This is one reason why such graphs are an effective means of representing reciprocal relations by reversing the direction of the arrows or by the composition of successive relations. They thereby give particularly evocative images of the reflexivity, symmetry or transitivity of relations (Papy, 1963). They are really perceptual drawings fulfilling an abstract purpose. Coloured graphs have made a powerful contribution to the elementary understanding of relational notions by representing these notions, which were supposed to be on a higher level of abstraction, in perceptual form.

It is a simple matter to add arrows to figures illustrating geometrical transformations to produce a striking result. For example, on a classical figure illustrating axial symmetry, it is only necessary to join points to their respective images by arrows and to indicate a few fixed points by a loop in order to obtain a really clear representation.

2.2   **Geo-boards**

Drawing requires a certain dexterity, particularly drawing with instruments. This does not mean that we must abandon the idea that young children, even the unskilful, can be taught to construct correct polygonal figures. A simple and ingenious procedure has been devised by Gattegno (1958a, 1963a) to overcome this problem. Nails are fixed into a board at regular intervals along the edges of a sheet of squared paper, for instance, and a variety of polygons can be obtained simply by stretching elastic bands between these nails. The ease with which figures can be made, changed and erased gives wide scope for investigation, even to pupils who are not gifted with much imagination.

The variety of shapes thus obtainable develops the pupil's skill in handling concepts. For example, the concept of area will be easier to grasp after a number of exercises to find the area of a polygon by reference to that of the unit square. Nails evenly spaced around a circle make it very easy to construct and study regular polygons and other inscribed figures.

Some large geo-boards have been built for use by teachers in front of classes, but it is important initially for each pupil to use an individual geo-board twenty-five to thirty centimetres square which will give him an opportunity to discover the essential geometrical concepts in his own time.

This method has already been introduced at primary-school level with good results.

2.3   Three-dimensional models

The normal representation of solid figures on paper or on a blackboard frequently fails to give the beginner a clear idea of the geometrical relations which they are meant to suggest, especially when the conventions governing the drawing of such figures are not made plain.

For this reason, teachers have long used models of the solids – prisms, pyramids, cones, cylinders, spheres and regular polyhedra – which could be drawn on if necessary as a teaching aid for elementary geometry. In the same way, models of surfaces of the second degree, surfaces of a higher degree and ruled surfaces are used in higher education (Gattegno, 1958b).

Here again a distinction must be made between the lesson delivered by the teacher with the help of a model which the pupils may examine, and the construction of models by the pupils themselves, which helps them develop their own skills.

The construction of polyhedra in cardboard raises elementary problems and demonstrates the usefulness of many simple geometrical constructions. These operations can be made more alive by careful choice of colours for the faces of the solids. In addition to the aesthetic effect obtained, there are interesting considerations of symmetry between faces of the same colour (Cundy and Rollett, 1961). Pupils find construction techniques employing new materials or procedures particularly attractive. An exciting example is the construction of solids with transparent materials such as acetophane, perspex and polythene. With such models diagonals and axes of symmetry can be shown inside the solids by means of differently coloured pieces of elastic. The construction of wire models using an electric soldering iron or a soldering kit with small transformer also has its strong supporters (Ministère de l'Instruction publique, Belgium, 1956).

The construction of models by the pupils obviously requires time and should ideally be restricted to manual work periods separate from the mathematics lessons proper. If the time for this extra work is not available, simpler procedures will be needed. A few knitting needles, balsa-wood rods, coloured drinking straws or sheets of Bristol board or plastic are sufficient for demonstrating lines and planes. They can be fastened together with plasticine, glue, adhesive tape or elastic bands. These last have the advantage that, when tight they hold the model solidly together and, when loosened a little, allow enough play for one rod to pivot or slide over another. A combination of colours brings out certain elements more clearly and makes it possible to point them out (Ministère de l'Instruction publique, Belgium, 1956). Operations such as these are very helpful to the pupil and help him to become more easily acquainted with spatial relations.

Another useful point is to show, by examples drawn from ancient and modern architecture, engineering and everyday life, the use made of geometrical properties by builders and designers. The natural forms of plants and animals are another rich field of investigation (Weyl, 1952).

2.4 Space frames

This is the name given to apparatus which makes it possible to construct three-dimensional figures supported by a frame. The frame suggested by Adam (1958) is made of wooden strips forming a rectangular parallelepiped. The figures are supported by parallel slats on the faces.

In the Geospazio system of Pescarini (Pescarini and Serra, n.d.), the frame is a large cube of plexiglass with regularly spaced holes in its faces. Some of the faces are hinged to provide access to the inside of the cube.

The 'universal stereograph' of Delugas (Walusinski, 1965) is made of three square panels arranged in a trihedron and mounted on hinges. Each panel consists of a wooden frame to either side of which is fixed a very fine metal grid. Knitting needles inserted in the two parallel grids remain fixed. The inner surfaces of the trihedron are covered with paper so that drawings and in particular projections can be made. The paper is then folded to obtain the required design.

2.5 Moving models

Models are a useful way of developing concepts of figures. They are even more useful for conceptualizing distortions, transformations and movements.

Even at an elementary level, distortions of figures lead to a better understanding of the properties of those figures. For example, four Meccano strips of equal length bolted together at their ends form a rhombus. Elastic can be used to give a physical representation of the diagonals. Distortion of the rhombus displays the classic properties very clearly. It may be seen in passing under what conditions the rhombus is a square. In the same way, it is possible to construct a parallelogram and its diagonals and to note at what point it produces a rectangle. It is also an interesting exercise to construct these quadrilaterals by taking two Meccano strips bolted together in the middle as the diagonals and stretching elastic between them to form the sides. If no Meccano strips are available, strong cardboard strips may be used and these may be fastened together with split-pin type paperclips.

A quadrilateral formed with two pairs of knitting needles, each pair fastened together with elastic bands, can be distorted to give a square, a rhombus, a rectangle, a parallelogram, a trapezium, any quadrilateral and a complete quadrilateral with its six points of intersection.

A distortable prism can easily be obtained by stretching elastic between the corresponding apexes of two cardboard bases held parallel. By moving the bases, one can obtain prisms of different heights and vary the direction of the lateral edges at will. When one of the bases is rotated through 180° in its own plane, all the lateral edges cross, thus forming two pyramids, having a common apex, and which can be distorted at will.

By replacing the polygonal bases by two discs of the same radius we obtain a variable cylinder. If one of the discs is turned slowly in its own plane, we can obtain a hyperboloid of one sheet and then a cone.

Two Meccano strips of equal length with parallel strips of elastic stretched between them produce a ruled surface of the second degree (paraboloid or hyperboloid) when the two strips are placed in different planes. If they are placed in the same plane, with one at right angles to the other, the elastic bands will form tangents to a curve of the second degree.

A number of models demonstrating the affine or metric projective properties of curves, particularly conics, can be constructed by using sliding and pivoting knitting needles (Servais, 1956a).

The simplest way of obtaining conic sections is to project the light beam of an electric torch on a plane surface. A section of a wire or transparent plastic model may be obtained by passing light through a rectilinear slit and placing the model between the slit and a plane surface in a darkened room. Even a rough and ready apparatus in which a box takes the place of the dark room gives satisfactory results. Pupils can vary the illuminated section of the model at will by simply moving the model.

An ingenious device for obtaining simultaneous horizontal, frontal and profile projections of a wire model consists of two mirrors inclined at 45° to each other and illuminated from above, with a box acting as screen. Movement of the model produces mobile figures, curves in particular, on the planes of projection (Tombs, 1961).

Jointed models made from Meccano can be used for a number of elementary geometrical transformations such as translation (Kempe's translator), dilatation (pantograph), similarity (Sylvester's pantograph) and inversion (Hart's and Peaucelier's inverters).

These pieces of apparatus can be used to trace the transforms of certain figures, lines in particular. It is also possible to compose transformations (Gattegno, 1958b; Ministère de l'Instruction publique, Belgium, 1956).

The simplest way to show axial symmetry is by reflection in a mirror. If a sheet of dark glass held perpendicular to the drawing board is used, both sides of the figure can be seen at once, one through the mirror and the other by reflection (Adam, 1958a).

Many everyday objects and mechanical devices may be used as ready-made jointed models. Adam (1958a) has made very ingenious use of french-window bolts, umbrellas and folding music stands.

2.6   **Films**

At first sight, films would seem to be ideal means of showing transformations, variations and motion, being pre-eminently suited to representing movement. While the number of mathematical films is increasing, many are lacking scientific and educational quality.

The United States National Council of Teachers of Mathematics has subjected a sample of more than 250 films to examination by several committees. The report of three of these committees analyses 158 films and draws the following general conclusions:

Several committee members have commented that the mathematical quality of many of the films is poor even in cases where a mathematics consultant is listed in the production. This is an unfortunate situation which might be remedied by more effective use of these consultants in the actual production of the film. Moreover, there seem to be relatively few films designed to illustrate a particular topic in less than ten minutes, say, and a great many films thirty minutes long, each covering a great many topics. Animation seems to be used less extensively and effectively than one might expect in view of the number of topics in mathematics which involve motion of some sort. Many members felt that short films on the history of mathematics would be of particular value to the mathematics teacher. In short, the consensus of the reviewers seems to be that more mathematics films should be designed to do tasks that the ordinary classroom teacher cannot do effectively, and fewer films designed to 'teach' an entire course. (Reviews of films, *Mathematics Teacher*, December 1963, p. 578.)

These criticisms go to show that it is not easy to make a successful mathematical film. This makes it all the more interesting to take another look at the work of one of the pioneers of mathematical films who made more than twenty films meeting all the requirements expressed or implied above and not included in the list under consideration.

Each of Nicolet's films deals accurately with a single mathematical subject and each lasts approximately three minutes. They have no soundtrack and illustrate no points which the teacher and pupils could perfectly well work out for themselves. In addition, the purely technical quality of the most recent films is outstanding. Anyone who has used Nicolet's films knows how effective they are (Gattegno, 1958c).

Here is a summary of the action of the best known of these films as Nicolet himself described it in 1942:

Three fixed points appear on the plane surface.

A circle revolves freely. This circle enjoys three degrees of freedom: its centre can move in two dimensions and its radius can vary independently of the position of the centre.

Apparently by chance the circumference of the circle comes into contact with one of the points. It is now less free than before.

The circle swings, its radius increases until one of the other points coincides with a point on the circumference. The circle has now lost another degree of freedom and retains only one.

Its radius can still increase. Its centre moves along a straight line as the radius varies. The circle ends by passing through the third point. A second circle, moving freely like the first, goes through the same adventures as the first.

It passes through one of the three points then through a second and finally merges with the first circle.

A third, fourth and more circles appear, inside the existing fixed circle or cutting it or completely surrounding it. They go through a number of variations, always ending up by passing through the three fixed points and merging into a single circle (Nicolet, 1942).

As we can see, the author's mathematical thinking is very clear as is also his educational aim, which he expresses as follows:

The film lasts one to two minutes. The facts are presented and speak for themselves. The pupils recognize them after passing through the natural stages of discovery. Now they have to be proved. We see how far removed this film is from the film used to supply the proof, how intuition is aroused, how impressions and views are allowed to meet, collide, merge, come together and form ideas of greater or less stability which must then be examined, criticized, analysed and finally expressed in as simple and clear a form as possible.

Nothing else can inculcate so well what Henri Poincaré calls 'the healthy habit of analysing one's sensations'. Not a word has been read or heard; there is only the viewing of moving, living figures and this viewing has encouraged the pupils to think about what they have seen and awakens in them the hope of discovering a truth. Intuition has done its part: logic can now be brought in and used to good effect on material worthy of it (Nicolet, 1942).

We have quoted Nicolet because he expresses so well the part played by the intuitive exploration of a situation: the creation of a world of mental images and problems upon which logic can build. One educational factor of which the author emphasizes the importance consists in varying at will the elements in the situation under consideration.

This should be the case in every question at any level. Since in mathematics one is always dealing with a set of objects, a sufficiently broad idea must be given of the extent of the class to which these objects belong. Dienes (1960) refers to what he calls the 'mathematical variability principle', which states 'that all features inessential to the structure of the concept must be varied, so as to spotlight what is really constant'. The dynamic way in which Nicolet handles the question of making a circle pass through three non-aligned points, so different from the way in which it is usually handled, is a striking illustration of this principle.

In the example quoted, the final aim of the author is determined in advance, but although the film proceeds inflexibly towards its conclusion and the activity of the spectator is to this extent limited, the film is developed in such a way as to raise a variety of problems in passing: location of the centre of a circle with constant radius passing through a fixed point, location of the centre of a variable circle passing through two fixed points, relative positions of two or more circles, etc. This abundance of matter for thought explains why over-long films which contain a substantial amount of information have to be chopped up into shorter sections, except in the case of films giving a summary of a subject.

Films thus face the same problem as any other teaching aid: the problems of how they are to be used and how they are to be integrated in teaching. Not having thought out the special methods and techniques required for educational films, the producers of some of these films have reproduced on the screen the various stages of a classic proof; in so doing, they are simply lifting the logical exposition out of a textbook and on to the screen instead of using the film for what it can do better than any textbook – throwing wide open the windows of visual imagination.

Films have a variety of recognized uses. Figures in movement can be shown several times over if necessary and then questions can be put on what the pupils have seen. It is often surprising to find how many facts they have been able to observe and retain after seeing a film once. The problems raised by the film will also be considered. Drawings must be made, data must be put in their proper place and the class must examine what is actually happening (Gattegno, 1958c). The film is thus a method of initiating pupils into new subject matter and encouraging in them a wide variety of motivated activity.

At some point, the film may be shown again so that a new point for research may be taken up, for every showing of the same film is, from the psychological and intellectual points of view, new.

When a particular subject has been studied, a film is a very valuable way of summing up clearly the material which has been dealt with and retained.

Other applications of films have been discovered, for example by Fletcher (1958), the author of a series of masterly films full of interest, ranging from *The Simson Line to Four-Line Conics*.

When setting out to make a motion film on some fairly complicated but well-known subject, Fletcher has often discovered geometrical properties new to him as a mathematician as he has gone along. Analysing the language of films, he has emphasized that it makes it possible to produce methods of proof outside the verbal, literal context. Noting that nearly all mathematical films consist of drawings repeated in cycles and that the number of drawings required becomes smaller as the symmetry of the figures becomes greater, Fletcher studies the mathematical structure of these figures, which is 'one of the most important lessons the film can give, particularly as it is difficult to translate it into words'.

As seen by Fletcher, one of the most important roles of the mathematical film is to serve as an introduction to the magic and beauty of mathematics. 'People watching a mathematical film can forget that it is the expression of a logical sequence and can contemplate its beauty regardless of the discursive form.' Pupils and teachers who have had the privilege of seeing the colour film *Four-Line Conics* recognize it as a thing of beauty.

Although we have made a point of stressing the characteristics of the mathematical film as such, this does not mean that the documentary value of films for the teaching of mathematics should be neglected. A film may be used as a technique of instructing pupils in the use of the slide-rule, for example, since this is a very good way of drawing attention to points of detail. However, in view of the cost and difficulty of production, it is not a good idea to present on film the sort of demonstration given in a book or by a teacher in class, unless there is a shortage of qualified classroom staff for this purpose. The use of films to take the place of the teacher in the classroom requires the lessons to be of very high educational quality. The same applies to television lessons.

Documentary films can be used to show the applications of mathematics in the arts, in industry, in science and in economics. An amusing example is Disney's *Donald in Mathemagic Land*, which is interesting even for the very young.

A third use to which the documentary film may be put is to present actual lessons so as to show teachers educational methods and techniques being put into practice. For films of this sort to fulfil their purposes, it is important that they should be shot live, using several cameras like a television film as, for example, in the experiment carried out by the Canadian National Film Office. Films made in this way provide objective documentation suitable for being shown, studied and discussed at leisure by teachers and trainee teachers.

Mathematical films are not as widely used as they might be, but this is no doubt due to temporary factors. At present not enough of the films being produced are good enough from a mathematical and educational point of view. The effectiveness of certain films does not justify their price. The theory of educational film production has not been sufficiently developed. Too many teachers expect the new method to teach the same things more quickly than the traditional procedures; they do not ask themselves what new lessons they, as well as their pupils, can learn from the film.

What is needed is for mathematics teachers to take an active part and increased responsibility in production. This is the way in which many valuable films are made. Costs both for production and for use of the film are fairly high for 16 mm, but the 8 mm and super 8 mm formats are less expensive. Television size projectors with built-in screens allow films to be shown in subdued light without blacking the room out completely. Five-minute film loops can now be obtained in cassettes which need only to be inserted into the projector. The film can be projected several times over without being handled.

Film strips are easy to use. They make it possible to stock much documentation – figures, diagrams, pictures, formulae, photographic illustrations – without taking up much space. They can often be made at minimal cost: all that is needed is a 36 mm camera with an extra lens and a tripod for taking several shots in succession. Colour films can be used just as they are as coloured film strips. By making their own films teachers have material that is adapted to their own teaching requirements.

Although the mathematical film strip lacks the movement of film, it does make it possible to present separate illustrations of the successive stages of a proof, a considerable improvement on the traditional representation, where several constructions are superimposed on the same drawing. The sequence of operations in a geometrical proof thus develops without words like that of an algebraic computation. The books of Papy (1963) show how this strip cartoon technique can be exploited.

Diascopes and episcopes are well known. A newer device, the overhead projector, also under other names, uses an objective lens and a mirror to project onto a screen any figure drawn on a transparent horizontal panel through which the light passes. The teacher can thus face his audience and at the same time show on a screen figures and formulae which he draws and writes out as he goes along on a strip of cellulose acetate; this strip can be rolled up after use. Ready-made colour drawings on transparent sheets can also be projected. These can be superimposed on each other, so that one can be moved in relation to another (see e.g. Osborne, 1962; Unkrich, 1962).

2.7 Algebraic aids

2.7.1 The teaching aids we have considered so far all have a mathematical structure, often a complicated one, bound up with perception and visual images. In this sense they are geometrical. We now turn to teaching aids which, in addition to their geometrical aspect, illustrate certain structures when they are used to carry out certain operations. Handling of this equipment helps pupils to gain an insight into these structures and their properties. For this reason they may be called algebraic aids.

2.7.2 The idea of using rods, tiles and blocks in the teaching of arithmetic is more than a century old (Smith, 1965). The Montessori system with its rulers, squares and cubes illustrating regular divisions has been in use since 1914. There are many other similar sets of apparatus of varying complexity and varying ingenuity all of which aim to provide a sensorimotor basis for the learning of arithmetic.

2.7.3 The apparatus most widely used at present is Cuisenaire's 'Numbers in Colour', which has been popularized by the research and demonstrations of Gattegno (1962). Although it is the simplest possible form of apparatus, it enables the pupil to learn, through his own activity, about such topics as natural numbers, fractions, negative numbers, arithmetical and geometrical progressions, permutations and combinations, length, area, volume, the metric system, orthogonal projections, etc.

Other apparatus can fulfil certain of the functions of Cuisenaire rods and can be used by the teacher to demonstrate certain relations. Is there any other apparatus which allows the pupil to discover so many things? There is a whole range of literature on this subject (Gattegno, 1963b; Goutard, 1963; Trivett, 1963; Lenger and Servais, 1956).

Without trying to sum up the value of this apparatus as a whole, we shall point out those structures which it illustrates and which the pupils discover for themselves as they handle the rods.

The first thing that strikes anyone seeing these rods is their colours: vermilion, light green, carmine, yellow, dark green, black, brown, blue, orange and the small cube which is white. Identity of colour signifies equivalence; the rods can be divided into classes according to their colour. A variety of games is possible with the set of rods. By playing construction games with them the children learn that rods of the same colour can be superimposed on each other; they are of the same length.

Separation by colours is identical with separation by length. The set of rods is made up in such a way that they can all be arranged in order of increasing length. The order is strict as long as rods of different colours are used. An order exists between the lengths (or colours) so that any rod can be substituted for any other rod of the same length.

The order of lengths and colours is:

1 white	6 dark green
2 vermilion	7 black
3 light green	8 brown
4 carmine	9 blue
5 yellow	10 orange

One simple form of activity is to build 'trains' by putting the rods end to end, thus adding the lengths. Pupils learn that addition is associative and commutative without necessarily knowing the numerical value of the rods. This value depends on the unit length: if this is the length of the smallest rod, the measures of lengths go from one to ten; if the length of the light green rod is the unit, the lengths are fractions with denominator three, etc. This shows that the addition of natural numbers and fractions is associative and commutative. Multiplication of natural numbers is discovered from the iteration of the addition of rods of the same length.

'Tiling' a flat surface with the same set of rods produces equivalent areas. By means of tiling, the rods produce surfaces. The multiplication of integers and fractions is thus connected with the areas of rectangles. This demonstrates that multiplication is distributive in relation to addition. To demonstrate blocks of the same volume, blocks composed of the same set of rods have to be found. The differences between two rods, taken in either order, serve as a lead-in to positive and negative numbers.

From the foregoing, it should be clear that by using the rods in different ways – comparison, placing end to end, tiling, block-building, differences, iteration of addition or multiplication, etc. – various structures may be introduced and the pupil may gradually become acquainted with them through his contact with the apparatus.

When the pupil has realized that the addition of two rods is commutative, regardless of the choice of rods, and that this property is not changed by substituting rods, he has grasped the psychological significance of the idea of variables. This example demonstrates that the commutative law exists independently of the numerical value of the terms of the addition: it precedes any measurement.

One of the reasons why Cuisenaire rods are so multivalent is that there are no subdivisions to restrict their use. Colour was the clearest way of making equivalent rods individually recognizable. One reason why Cuisenaire's simple invention is so effective (see Wheeler, 1963) is that it arranges the rods in the easily recognizable colour scale described above.

2.7.4   The intuitive learning of place value can obviously be helped by using coloured rods, but Dienes's Multibase Arithmetic Blocks (MAB) (Dienes, 1964a, 1964b) are, by their structure, more directly suitable for making the rules of arithmetical operations to any base understandable.

The MAB originally consisted of boxes representing base values 3, 4, 5, 6 and 10. Subsequently the base 2, now so important, was added. Each box contains a series of blocks representing various powers of the base which we write in ascending order from right to left as in the notation of numbers using place value. For example, the box for the base 4 contains:

a block of	a flat of	a long of	a unit of
4^3 cm^3	4^2 cm^2	4 cm	1 cm^3

Signs inscribed on the blocks show their position in relation to the unit. Using this material, pupils learn: (a) to reduce any set of blocks to its equivalent decomposition in terms of powers of the base; (b) to add the numbers expressed in this form; (c) to subtract numbers, making natural use of the borrowing method; (d) to multiply given numbers in one of the bases.

The most interesting thing about this material is that it makes children realize that the underlying principle is the same whatever base is being used, so that the base ten is not given the special status which is allotted to it in traditional teaching.

The use of five or six different bases illustrates the mathematical variability principle stressed by Dienes, but research by Leith and Clark has shown that there is an optimum: it is better to study *two* bases than four or one (see section 4.4).

Dienes has developed apparatus for introducing children to the concepts of algebra constructively. A traditional apparatus for carrying out equations is the balance. Dienes replaces this with a simple balance beam with hooks at equal intervals from the fulcrum. Identical rings may be hung on different hooks. The children discover the law of moments experimentally (Dienes, 1964a, p. 78) and hence it becomes possible to prove that multiplication is distributive over addition and to set problems of the first degree. To introduce the second degree, an interesting elementary adaptation is made of the geometrical method of proving the identity

$$(a+b)^2 = a^2 + 2ab + b^2$$

by means of squares and rectangles. The law is, however, arrived at inductively, by asking the pupil to construct from juxtaposed identical small squares a larger square and then to examine how the second square can be made larger so that a succession of squares is obtained.

To vary the practical work, the problem of forming large equilateral triangles from juxtaposed identical small equilateral triangles may be set.

By forming rectangles beginning with a square and using rulers and small squares, pupils learn factorizations such as

$$k^2 + 5k + 6 = (k+2)(k+3).$$

Pegs and pegboards may be used to present problems of this kind from a different angle. Pupils can be trained in this way to solve simple problems of the second degree.

By means of the system of blocks representing successive powers of a base, pupils learn that to multiply two powers of the same base, the indices are added. They can later learn how to divide powers. In this way, they are making their first contact with logarithms.

2.8 Logical materials

Under this heading, we include structured materials for teaching Boolean algebra and introducing children to logic.

2.8.1 Intersection, union and complementation between the elements of a set are operations in Boolean algebra. Venn diagrams (see section A.2) provide a very intuitive method of presenting Boolean algebra (section A.2.4), particularly if the outlines are drawn in colour.

To enable young children, even at nursery-school age, to play with these diagrams, Dienes has put forward a logical game involving blocks with four attributes which can take the following values:

(a) Colour: yellow, blue, red.

(b) Shape: round, square, triangular, rectangular.

(c) Thickness: thick, thin.

(d) Size: big, small.

If all the conjunctions of these attributes are each to be represented in a set by one piece only, the set will need to comprise $3 \times 4 \times 2 \times 2$, = 48 pieces. By playing with these blocks, the children learn to recognize their attributes and to identify each block by its characteristic attributes (Dienes, 1964b). A similar game is to make up a set of dominoes in such a way that each one is different from the previous one in either one or two of its attributes.

Games involving the negation of simple or composite attributes are introduced, followed by games which introduce the children to conjunctions, disjunctions and implications of attributes (see sections A.1.8–10). A hoop of soft plastic wire with, for example, a red tab is placed on a table or on the ground and inside it are placed red blocks and red blocks only. Rectangular pieces only are placed inside a second hoop bearing the rectangular tab. The two hoops must overlap in such a way that the red rectangles can be placed in the area of overlap. In this way the children are making Venn diagrams with two or three attributes. They realize that complements of sets correspond to 'not', intersections to 'and' and unions to 'or', and they observe that some sets can be described in two different, but logically equivalent, ways (see section A.2.2).

2.8.2   Logical symbols are introduced for the names of sets (Dienes, 1964b). The simple attributes are designated by the following abbreviations:

(a) Colour: *y* (yellow), *b* (blue), *r* (red).

(b) Shape: *ro* (round), *sq* (square), *tr* (triangular), *re* (rectangular).

(c) Thickness: *tk* (thick), *tn* (thin).

(d) Size: *bg* (big), *sm* (small).

Reference will be made to the yellow set, the set of squares, etc. The negation of an attribute is denoted by placing the letter *N* in front of the abbreviation which stands for that attribute; thus *Ny* stands for not yellow and can be applied to the set of blocks which are not that colour. In the same way *NNb* means not not-blue – that is, blue.

To signify the conjunction of two attributes, the letter *K* is placed to the left of the two symbols indicating the attributes:

K y ro indicates 'both yellow *and* round'.
K y Nro indicates 'both yellow *and* not-round'.
K Ny ro indicates 'both not-yellow *and* round'.
K b K re tn indicates 'both blue *and* thin rectangle'.

These symbols also stand for the sets which are extensions of the attributes.

Disjunction of two attributes is indicated by placing the letter *A* to the left of the two symbols, for example, *A b sq* (blue *or* square), *A b Nsq* (blue *or* not-square), *A Nb sq* (not-blue *or* square), *A tn K y sm* thin *or* (yellow *and* small). *A K b tr Ny* (blue *and* triangular) *or* not-yellow.

One game consists of getting children to imagine names of sets and getting other children to form them.

When every yellow block in a set is square, we have: 'If yellow, then square.' This implication (see section A.1.10) is designated by writing the symbol of implication *C* to the left: *C y sq*. The equivalence of two attributes, *b* and *tr* for example, is shown as *E b tr*, the letter *E* being the symbol for equivalence. *E b tr* indicates that if a block is blue then it is triangular and that if a block is triangular then it is blue, that is, that there is a conjunction of implication (section A.1.8):

K C b tr C tr b.

The notation used in the above examples was devised by the Polish logician Lukasiewicz and has the advantage of not using brackets.

2.8.3 Games familiarizing children with the handling of symbols and giving them practice in abstract thinking, and which help in teaching mathematical logic, have been introduced by the Accelerated Learning of Logic (ALL) project team working at Yale University under Allen (1963). The original series consisted of twenty-four games; this has been replaced by a new series of twenty-one games, played with thirty-six dice and a set of cards. The two basic ideas of the games are a definition of well-formed formulae and a definition of proof; hence the name of WFF 'N' PROOF games (well-formed formula and proof). The WFFs, written with the Lukasiewicz notation, are defined as follows:

An expression is a WFF if and only if:

(a) it is a p, q, r or s; or

(b) it is formed of N followed immediately by exactly one WFF; or

(c) it is the expression formed by C, A, K or E followed immediately by exactly two WFFs.

Altogether thirteen ideas are introduced and used in the WFF 'N' PROOF games; the definition of a WFF as given above, the definition of a proof and eleven rules of inference covering the calculus of propositions. The twenty-one WFF 'N' PROOF games vary greatly in their complexity; the first have been mastered by children of six whilst the last are interesting for professors of logic.

2.8.4 A set of punched cards provides a concrete method of practising Boolean algebra. All the cards are the same size. Along one edge of each card, a sequence of n holes or slits, as the case may be, are punched. In the first position a hole or slit relates to property A; a hole in a card corresponds to 'belongs to the set having the property A', whilst the open slit corresponds to the negation, 'does not belong to the set having the property A'. When the cards are all together in a pack, the holes and slits representing property A are superimposed. When a knitting needle is inserted through the holes and slits of A, the set of cards with holes representing the property A can be lifted out, leaving behind the set of cards with slits representing not-A and complementary to the former set. A second property B and its negation not-B can be indicated respectively by a second hole and a second slit, and so on. To cover all possible combinations of properties and their negation, 2 cards are needed for one property, 2×2 for two properties and 2^n cards for n properties.

Given a pack of punched cards, how does one remove the sets of cards (section A.2.2)

$$X \cup Y, \quad X \cap Y, \quad X \backslash Y, \quad X \triangle Y,$$

where X and Y are parts of the pack corresponding to two given holes?

If in one each of the cards of the pack a slit (or hole) is made along the lower edge to correspond with each hole (or slit) in position X along the upper edge, it is possible to remove one part of the pack or its complement at will. Thus, the complement of the union of two sets represented by two holes on one edge of the cards is the intersection of the complements represented by the two corresponding holes at the other edge. This illustrates De Morgan's laws.

An article by Fletcher (1963) gives examples of amusing logical puzzles to be solved with a pack of punched cards.

2.8.5 Switches in electric circuits obey a Boolean algebra: the current passes or does not pass in accordance with whether a switch is closed or open. A switch A' which is open when switch A is closed and vice versa is the negation of A. If two switches are wired in series they give an 'and' circuit; if they are arranged in parallel they give an 'inclusive or' circuit. In the same way, various logical operations can be illustrated by simple electrical circuits which the pupils can discover and set up for themselves (Servais, 1956b; Giles, 1962).

Adam has devised a circuit board which makes allowance for the duality of the operations, thus making it possible to represent logical operations on propositions and to compose them at will. Tagged flexible wire is used for the leads. The construction of a circuit board connecting a battery, sockets and lights is described in Fletcher (1964, pp. 155–6). Several examples of lessons given with this apparatus to pupils at different levels are also given.

Simple, cheap electronic systems can be built to handle logical problems. Apparatus described by Flanagan and Molyneux (1965), uses 'NOR units' which can be connected to each other to express a problem. The NOR unit with its two inputs A and B functions like the negation of the inclusive or (sections A.1.6 and A.1.8): it gives a true output only when A and B are false, hence its name. Any logical operation can be carried out by combining these NOR units, and they are suitable for the construction of calculators (Birtwistle, 1962).

2.9 Calculating machines

Calculating machines are becoming ever more numerous and powerful. There are thus good reasons for developing pupils' calculating abilities by helping them to a better understanding of the logic of such operations and by acquainting them with the means of extending their possibilities. In this way an incentive is provided for the study and practice of calculation and the subject will be given more attention.

2.9.1 The realization that one can add two numbers together simply by sliding one ordinary graduated ruler along the top of another comes as a revelation to young children. Going on from there the teacher can explain to them how small desk adding and multiplying machines work (Birtwistle, 1962, 1965). Primary schoolchildren enjoy working on office calculators (French, 1962, 1964).

In the conclusions to his report on the introduction of desk calculators in primary and secondary schools, Kerr (1963) remarks that, at the very least, use of the machines was interesting and stimulating. It resulted in a clearer idea of numbers and of place value.

Mathematics Teaching, 1965, no. 31, carried a supplement devoted to calculating machines, containing two reports of significant experiments. The report by Denniss refers to 'Calculators with seven and eight year olds'.

Pupils working with these machines improved their results by an average of 30 per cent in an arithmetic test whilst the control group showed a progress of 15 per cent. Hopkins used two calculating machines in a remedial class. She analysed the different attitudes of girls and boys. The general attitude towards arithmetic changed: fear was replaced by pleasure and confidence. The same issue contained an appraisal of desk calculators suitable for use in schools and a list of special prices to schools.

2.9.2 *The slide rule*

The slide rule has a long history, but sufficient use is still not made of it in secondary education. When it is used, it is generally used too late, after theoretical study of logarithms; this leaves the pupil little time to acquire sufficient practice in calculating with the rule. There are sound reasons for starting to use the slide rule as soon as possible; as soon as pupils know the rule that whole-number powers of a number are multiplied by adding the indices.

Fandreyer (1961) ingeniously suggests that the question be studied by beginning from the fact that where $d(a)$ and $d(b)$ are distances on the scale corresponding to two numbers a and b, the sum of the distances $d(a)+d(b)$ has to be made to correspond to their product ab. The scale is then calibrated step by step on the basis of this functional relation. Cundy and Rollett (1961) also give a method of calibration.

Circular slide rules have the advantage over straight ones that multiplications can be carried out by moving the rule in one direction only. Calculators of this sort printed on card are marketed commercially (Birtwistle, 1962), but they can be made by sticking two logarithmic scales opposite each other, one on the side of a circular box and the other on its lid (Adam, 1958b).

2.9.3 Construction of even a rudimentary calculating machine is an interesting activity. The binary system is the system best suited to such a machine.

A childishly simple binary adder using scales was described in *Mathematics Teaching*, 1963, no. 24. Several other mechanical models were described in *Mathematics Teaching*, 1964, no. 26: 'A pegboard computer', Mastrantone; 'A simple mechanical model', Haines; 'A hydraulic model', Reinstein.

A booklet by Lemaître (n.d.) describes a method of notation and computation which enables operations to be carried out 'mechanically'. This clever invention is worth trying out to lighten the effort of memory required even by written computation.

To improve the elementary arithmetical knowledge of his pupils, which was in some cases very poor, Clark (1964) built a very simple calculating device, the movable part of which consisted of a disc with twenty holes arranged as on a telephone dial. Addition and subtraction can be carried out by turning the disc with the finger clockwise or anticlockwise by the number of holes required; the answer appears in a little window. The results can be seen during the movement of the disc, while the operations are being carried out. Multiplications are obtained by repeated addition, divisions by repeated subtraction. This apparatus can be used by very young children. Here, the function of an elementary calculating machine is to establish a relationship between a practical activity, numbers and numerical symbols.

Building an electric binary adder raises problems of logical organization which it is useful for pupils to understand. The justification for building such an apparatus, which performs operations that could quite easily be carried out without it, is that it exercises logical thinking.

An article by Giles (1964) suggests a way of constructing a similar machine using eight identical elements corresponding to each of the figures and connected to each other. The rapid growth in the use of electronic computers makes it necessary to introduce pupils to this subject. A good method is to build with them a simple electronic computer. How to do this is suggested in an article by Meredith (1962). The author explains how the machine adds and how the component elements of a computer – input, logic, storage, control, output – are built. His article includes a diagram of the elementary circuit and a view of the apparatus indicating the component parts. All the pupils worked together to build the separate elements of the computer; each element was put into limited service as it was built. The teacher obtained material assistance and technical advice from several firms to whom he had outlined his project.

Using NOR units, Wilkinson (1965a) built a BEATLE (Binary Electronic Adder with Transistorized Logical Elements) apparatus with his pupils. This apparatus is capable of:

(a) counting in the binary system;

(b) converting small numbers to binary;

(c) storing a number, retrieving it and adding it to any number present in one unit;

(d) producing a number at random;

(e) calculating a person's reaction time;

(f) producing musical notes of certain frequencies and showing their value.

The author provides a number of diagrams, a view of the BEATLE and a bibliography. In conclusion, he emphasizes that the experience gained by his pupils in the construction of the apparatus gave them a clear idea of the uses of a transistor as an interrupter switch. Several pupils are now building their own circuits for other uses.

2.9.4 *Flow charts*

From the mathematical point of view, it is important to understand the logical sequence of operations performed by a calculating machine. For this purpose, it is useful to introduce pupils to flow charts, which make it possible to represent the whole sequence of operations to be carried out in order to solve a problem step by step. Children can learn to construct these diagrams on the basis of familiar situations such as the series of acts which a pupil performs in proceeding from home to school (Fletcher, 1964, p. 108; NCTM, 1963a).

By analysing planned action, pupils realize that their plans have to include in whole or in part:

(a) Putting down things that have to be done.

(b) Noting initial data (input) and final results (output).

(c) Questions involving decisions to be taken for subsequent operations.

These data are noted in three separate types of box:

(a) Rectangular operations boxes.

> Add two to three

(b) Rectangular data boxes with the top right-hand corner cut off.

> 729

(c) Decision boxes with straight horizontal sides and curved vertical sides.

> Is number A positive?

These boxes mostly contain questions requiring the answer 'yes' or 'no'. The choice of the next operation depends on the answer, which is indicated by the two arrows 'yes' and 'no' emerging from the box.

A flow chart consists of a diagram in which the commands and decisions are linked by arrows indicating their order. The diagram may also include loops. As an example, Flow Chart 1 illustrates factorization of an integer.

As will be readily understood, such charts are of great educational value in analysing operations involving many steps. The uses to which it might profitably be put in education include analysis of methods of calculation, solutions of equations, geometrical constructions, etc. (Fletcher, 1964; McDonald, 1965; Forsythe, 1964; Watson, 1965; Varsavsky, 1964). By getting pupils to draw charts of familiar operations it is possible to find out which of them have a thorough knowledge of the operations.

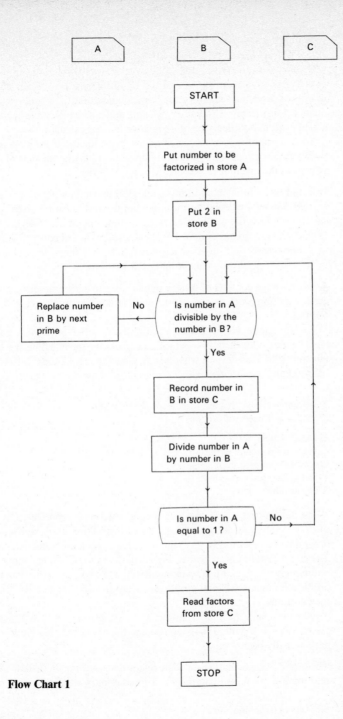

Flow Chart 1

The chief stages in the use of a calculating machine are shown by McDonald (1965) in Flow Chart 2.

Examination of this diagram shows the extent to which the application of flow charts to calculations carried out by ordinary methods can train pupils to approach such calculations in a critical and attentive attitude, which is so often lacking. Pupils with whom checking and assessment have become reflex actions will undoubtedly be more reliable in their calculations.

To carry out the instructions of a flow chart, the calculating operation has simply to be divided among several pupils, each playing the part of one component in the machine (Fletcher, 1964, pp. 117–18).

2.9.5 It would be useful if, in addition to a logical understanding of the operations carried out by a calculating machine, pupils could also be given an understanding of how the machine carries out these operations. For this purpose, Wilkinson (1965b) has designed a demonstration board consisting of ten NOR units and one OR unit. In his article he explains how these elements may be set up to solve logical problems or make calculations.

2.9.6 A further stage consists of getting pupils to write a program for a machine in code. Knitting patterns are a form of code familiar to girls (Fletcher, 1964, pp. 115, 117).

To familiarize young children with the essential parts of a calculating machine and with the way in which a program for the machine can be coded, Horton (1961) has devised what he christened the Hobladic (Horton's Blackboard Digital Computer). He describes it as follows:

The Computer in its simplest form is merely a blackboard, in one instance 3 by 4 feet, divided into five general sections:

1. The accumulator
2. The read-in section of memory
3. The read-out section of memory
4. The remainder of memory
5. The arithmetic unit.

The author uses a code in which each instruction is represented by a group of three letters and he gives examples of instruction cards and calculation programs. His method is very simple and is capable of being extended (Van Tassel, 1961). It has been devised in such a way as to encourage pupils to carry out numerical calculations by manipulating the code, since they can choose a problem for themselves and program it. They thus acquire an orderly approach to operations.

Other teachers use real computer codes (Pierson, 1963; Whitacre, 1963; Sweet, 1963; Forsythe, 1964) and some of the programs drawn up in this way have actually been used.

2.9.7 The training of calculating-machine operators is not the immediate aim of the information given on these machines in secondary education. One aim is to

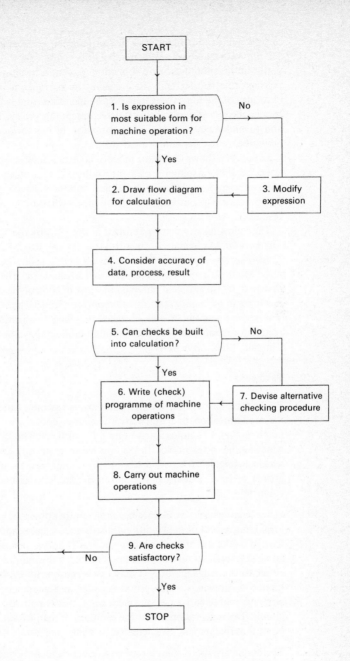

Flow Chart 2

provide a motivational basis for the learning of mathematics. Using machines, the pupils are doing applied mathematics within the framework of mathematics itself. Moreover, this applied mathematics is closely linked with the physics of electrical circuits. Before using the machines, it is essential to have a clear idea of the logical organization of operations and hence to analyse step by step the procedures to be used, to represent this process by means of charts and to understand the logical formulation of the various stages. All these activities are of clear educational value.

Experience shows that these modern questions interest pupils and that they are capable of grasping the elements of them. The problem is to find teachers with sufficient knowledge of the subject and the means of putting these ideas into practice. The outline given above shows what can be done with available resources.

The following two texts, published in the USA by the National Council of Teachers of Mathematics, are of particular use to teachers: *Report of the Conference on Computer-Oriented Mathematics and the Secondary School* (NCTM, 1963b) and *Computer-Oriented Mathematics* (NCTM, 1963a). The first analyses the problem raised by the introduction of the study of calculating machines in secondary schools and reports on some achievements in this field. The second sets out the basic ideas and their application to problems at secondary-school level. It also contains a bibliography. (See also Thomas and Thomas, 1962; Lovis, 1964.)

2.10 Textbooks

Books form part, the most important part, of teaching material. As a result of the modernization of mathematics teaching, books are appearing in such numbers that it is impossible to give a list of them. The Bibliography gives a wide sample of textbooks. Below, we try to point out some of the features which distinguish the new textbooks from older works and which are to a greater or lesser extent to be found in the modern textbooks of the various countries.

2.10.1 School mathematics books are becoming more attractive, in contrast with the forbidding aspect of the traditional textbooks. Figures and diagrams are enlivened by the use of two or more colours. The style, instead of being general and impersonal, adopts a more familiar and individualized tone, bringing it closer to the language of everyday conversation. Illustrations often include humorous drawings which put the reader in a good mood and show that, although mathematics is a serious science, this is no reason for presenting it glumly. Documentation about the pioneers of mathematics brings home the point that mathematics was created by men.

2.10.2 Textbooks are more stimulating and richer in ideas. Dynamic relations are indicated by numerous graphs and diagrams. Definitions and proofs can be presented clearly and concisely thanks to comprehensive modern symbolism.

Photographs illustrate the part played by mathematics in the arts, sciences and industry.

2.10.3　Textbooks are written with greater rigour than they used to be. Even those written for beginners endeavour to bring out the rules of the mathematical game: axioms. Definitions have become more precise with the acquisition of the basic notions of sets. Proofs are stricter and reduced more nearly to essentials. Stripped of inessentials, they often have a more widespread validity than formerly. The elementary symbolism now used can convey clearer ideas.

2.10.4　The structure of textbooks has been improved. They aim at presenting mathematics as an entity based on the idea of set structures. Research into effective methods of presentation made in connexion with programmed instruction is producing a better understanding of the psychological elements to be taken into account in gradually introducing and consolidating the ideas to be learnt and in firmly fixing them in pupils' minds.

2.10.5　Something still remains to be done to increase awareness of these resources and to exploit them to the full in presenting mathematics with a logical appearance, agreeable and open to the world of its actual and potential uses. With this aim in view, a new type of textbook is now being published: books and booklets written to be read by the pupils themselves. Pupils should be encouraged to read this sort of material, whether it is complementary to the course of study or not, since it trains them to understand a text for themselves and leads them on to further reading material of a broader nature.

From this point of view, the example of the United States, the Soviet Union and Britain is worthy of emulation. In the United States, bibliographies of books specially intended for pupils' reading have been published by the National Council of Teachers of Mathematics (Hardgrove, 1962; Schaaf, 1962). Bibliographies can also be found in NCTM (1963c, 1963d). In Russia, collections such as *Popular Lectures in Mathematics* and *The Mathematics Club Bookshelf* are meant to be read by, among others, students in the upper classes of secondary schools. Several of the volumes already published have been translated into English. In England, two series of books for school-children have been published under the general title *Contemporary School Mathematics*. The first series can be read in the lower secondary school. Another collection by Johnson and Glenn can also be used to stimulate interest in mathematics (see Bibliography, 'Series').

2.11　**The mathematics laboratory**

Abstract subjects can be taught dogmatically in a bare room furnished only with desks and seats and containing no other teaching aid but a blackboard. Live mathematics teaching flourishes best in a classroom specially designed to encourage the use of the material now available. Obviously everything depends on the resources at the school's disposal. It is possible to give a new look to teaching, even in unfavourable conditions, if the teacher possesses the necessary conviction and ingenuity. Conversely, the best equipment is useless unless it is properly used. In planning schools today, thought should be given to organizing laboratories for mathematics in the same way as they are organized for physics and the other natural sciences. Useful works have been published for classroom designers and suppliers of equipment (Bartnick, 1960; Jones, 1963). These references will give them ideas on classroom sizes, heating, ventilation, lighting and flooring, and advice on the composition and arrangement of blackboards, placards, book cupboards and shelves, display cabinets, storage cupboards, desks, work tables and chairs. The texts are accompanied by plans and photographs of models.

In addition to the books and booklets already mentioned in this chapter, there are useful reference works on mathematical aids and equipment proper (Berger and Johnson, 1959; NCTM, 1945).

The pupils' mathematics library will include several types of work: representative textbooks, reference books, supplementary reading matter, booklets and periodicals written for the young.

Countries where the difficulty of recruiting good teachers at all levels adds to the burden of those concerned with the promotion of education should look hopefully towards teaching aids and equipment. The ideal set of teaching aids would be that which helps most to turn pupils into students, that is, into young people who, for the most part, find their way to knowledge.

References

ADAM, P. P. (1958a), 'El material didáctico matemático actual', *Enseñanza media*.
ADAM, P. P. (1958b), 'Modèles prêts et modèles faits', in C. Gattegno (ed.), *Le matériel pour l'enseignement des mathématiques*, Neuchâtel: Delachaux & Niestlé.
ALLEN, L. E. (1963), 'Toward autotelic learning of mathematical logic', *Mathematics Teacher*, vol. 56, January.
BARTNICK, L. P. (1960), *Designing the Mathematics Classroom*, National Council of Teachers of Mathematics.
BERGER, E. J., and JOHNSON, D. A. (1959), *A Guide to the Use and Procurement of Teaching Aids for Mathematics*, National Council of Teachers of Mathematics.
BIRTWISTLE, C. (1962), 'Calculating aids in the secondary school: 1', *Mathematics Teaching*, no. 19.
BIRTWISTLE, C. (1965), 'The number tutor', *Mathematics Teaching*, no. 30.
CLARK, J. (1964), 'A calculating device for teaching elementary arithmetic', *Mathematics Teaching*, no. 26.
CUNDY, H. M., and ROLLETT, A. P. (1961), *Mathematical Models*, 2nd edn, Clarendon Press.
DIENES, Z. P. (1960), *Building up Mathematics*, 2nd edn, Hutchinson.
DIENES, Z. P. (1964a), *The Power of Mathematics*, Hutchinson.

DIENES, Z. P. (1964b), *Le mathématique moderne dans l'enseignement primaire*, OCDL.

FANDREYER, E. E. (1961), 'Introducing the slide rule early', *Mathematics Teacher*, vol. 54, March.

FLANAGAN, G. J., and MOLYNEUX, L. (1965), 'A system of logic to aid in teaching mathematics', *Mathematics Teaching*, no. 30.

FLETCHER, T. J. (1958), 'Les problèmes du film mathématique', in C. Gattegno (ed.), *Le matériel pour l'enseignement des mathématiques*, Neuchâtel: Delachaux & Niestlé.

FLETCHER, T. J. (1963), 'Teaching aids and logic', *Mathematics Teacher*, vol. 56.

FLETCHER, T. J. (ed.) (1964), *Some Lessons in Mathematics*, Cambridge University Press.

FORSYTHE, A. (1964), 'Mathematics and computing in high school: a betrothal', *Mathematics Teacher*, vol. 57, January.

FRENCH, P. (1962), 'Calculating machines in a primary school', *Mathematics Teaching*, no. 15.

FRENCH, P. (1964), *An Introduction to Calculating Machines for Schools*, Macmillan.

GATTEGNO, C. (1958a), *From Actions to Operations*, Reading: Cuisenaire.

GATTEGNO, C. (ed.) (1958b), *Le matériel pour l'enseignement des mathématiques*, Neuchâtel: Delachaux & Niestlé.

GATTEGNO, C. (1958c), 'L'enseignement par le film mathématique' in C. Gattegno (ed.), *Le matériel pour l'enseignement des mathématiques*, Neuchâtel: Delachaux & Niestlé.

GATTEGNO, C. (1962), *Eléments de mathématiques modernes par le nombres en couleur*, Neuchâtel: Delachaux & Niestlé.

GATTEGNO, C. (1963a), *Algèbre et géometrie pour les écoles primaires*, Neuchâtel: Delachaux & Niestlé.

GATTEGNO, C. (1963b), *Mathématiques avec les nombres en couleur*, manuals A, B. 5–9, Neuchâtel: Delachaux & Niestlé.

GILES, G. (1964), 'Electrical circuits for binary adders', *Mathematics Teaching*, no. 28.

GILES, R. P. (1962), 'Building an electrical device for use in teaching logic', *Mathematics Teacher*, vol. 55, March.

GOUTARD, M. (1963), *Les mathématiques et les enfants*, Neuchâtel: Delachaux & Niestlé.

HARDGROVE, E. (1962), *The Elementary and Junior High School Library*, National Council of Teachers of Mathematics.

HORTON, G. W. (1961), 'Hobladic', *Mathematics Teacher*, vol. 54, April.

JONES, B. W. (1963), 'The mathematics room', *Mathematics Teaching*, no. 24.

KERR, E. (1963), 'Experiments in the use of desk calculators in schools', *Mathematics Teaching*, no. 22.

LEMAÎTRE, G. (n.d.), *Calculons sans fatigue*, Louvain: E. Nouwelaerts.

LENGER, F., and SERVAIS, W. (1956), 'Les reglettes en couleur', in Ministère de l'Instruction publique, Belgium, *Les modèles dans l'enseignement mathématique*, Documentation no. 5, p. 27.

LOVIS, F. B. (1964), *Computers*, 2 vols., Arnold.

MCDONALD, E. (1965), 'Computing by calculating machines', *Mathematics Teaching*, no. 31.

MEREDITH, M. D. (1962), 'A digital computer demonstration', *Mathematics Teaching*, no. 22.

Ministère de l'Instruction publique, Belgium (1956), *Les modèles dans l'enseignement mathématique*, Documentation no. 5.

NCTM (1945), *Multi-Sensory Aids in the Teaching of Mathematics*, 18th Yearbook, National Council of Teachers of Mathematics.

NCTM (1963a), *Computer-oriented mathematics*, National Council of Teachers of Mathematics.

NCTM (1963b), *Report on the Conference on Computer-Oriented Mathematics and the Secondary School*, National Council of Teachers of Mathematics.

NCTM (1963c), *Enrichment Mathematics for the Grades*, 27th Yearbook, National Council of Teachers of Mathematics.

NCTM (1963d), *Enrichment Mathematics for High School*, 28th Yearbook, National Council of Teachers of Mathematics.

NICOLET, J. L. (1942), *Intuition mathématique et dessins animés*, Lausanne: Payot.

OSBORNE, A. R. (1962), 'Using the overhead projector in an algebra class', *Mathematics Teacher*, vol. 55, February.

PAPY, G. (1963), *Mathématique moderne*, 6 vols., Paris and Brussels: Didier.

PESCARINI, A., and SERRA, N. (n.d.), *Il Geospazio*, Bologna: Ed. Fem.

PIERSON, E. (1963), 'Junior high mathematics and the computer', *Mathematics Teacher*, vol. 56, May.

POLLACK, H. O. (1965), 'Applications of modern mathematics for use in teaching secondary school mathematics', *Mathematics Today*, OECD.

SCHAAF, W. L. (1962), *The High School Mathematics Library*, National Council of Teachers of Mathematics.

SERVAIS, W. (1955/6), 'Présentation de la caractérologie', *Mathematica et Pedagogica*, no. 7.

SERVAIS, W. (1956a), 'Modèles relatifs aux coniques', in Ministère de l'Instruction publique, Belgium, *Les modèles dans l'enseignement mathématique*, p. 73.

SERVAIS, W. (1956b), 'Modèles logiques', in Ministère de l'Instruction publique, Belgium, *Les modèles dans l'enseignement mathématique*, p. 92.

SERVAIS, W. (1958), 'Concret-abstrait', in C. Gattegno (ed.), *Le matériel pour l'enseignement des mathématiques*, Neuchâtel: Delachaux & Niestlé.

SERVAIS, W. (1965), 'Axiomatisation et mathématique élémentaires', *Records of the ICMI Symposium in Echternach, 1965*.

SMITH, I. M. (1965), 'The psychological case for using structural apparatus', *Mathematics Teaching*, no. 30.

SWEET, R. (1963), 'High school computer programming in the junior high school', *Mathematics Teacher*, vol. 56, November.

THOMAS, L., and THOMAS, A. (1962), *Mathematics by Calculating Machine*, Cassell.

TOMBS, P. M. (1961), 'Visualization of functions of the complex variable wire models' in B. Thwaites (ed.), *On Teaching Mathematics*, Pergamon.

TRIVETT, J. V. (1963), 'Coloured rods in mathematics teaching', *Mathematics Teaching*, no. 24.

UNKRICH, H. (1962), 'Using the overhead projector in teaching geometry', *Mathematics Teacher*, vol. 55, October.

VAN TASSEL, L. T. (1961), 'Digital computer programming in high school classes', *Mathematics Teacher*, vol. 54, April.

VARSAVSKY, O. (1964), *Algebra para escuelas secundarias*, Editorial Universitaria de Buenos Aires.

WALUSINSKI, G. (1965), L'espace affine à portée de la main', *Bulletin de l'Association des professeurs de mathématiques de l'enseignement publique*, no. 247.

WATSON, R. (1965), 'Solution by computer', *Mathematics Teaching*, no. 33.

WEYL, H. (1952), *Symmetry*, Princeton University Press.

WHEELER, D. (1963), 'Structural materials in the primary school', *Mathematics Teaching*, no. 22.

WHITACRE, L. (1963), 'Computer programming for high school sophomores', *Mathematics Teacher*, vol. 56, May.

WILKINSON, A. (1965a), 'A small computer demonstration model', *Mathematics Teaching*, no. 31.

WILKINSON, A. (1965b), 'A computer logic demonstration board', *Mathematics Teaching*, no. 32.

3 Treatment of the Axiomatic Method in Class

Prepared by A. Z. Krygowska, Professor of Mathematics and Mathematical Education, Higher Teacher Training College, Cracow

Opinions regarding the pupil's introduction to the axiomatic method and its place in school mathematics as a whole are very conflicting. Some see it as the essential element in mathematical education at every level, and therefore consider initiation into the axiomatic method as an essential condition for modernizing mathematical education. But the teaching aspect of this proposition is not clear and its feasibility has not yet been adequately verified. Others consider that the secondary-school pupil is not capable of comprehending the axiomatic concept and does not need it. This negative opinion is often justified by reference to observations made during traditional teaching of deductive geometry. But this cannot be conclusive, since modern concepts of axioms and axiomatization are not the same as traditional concepts. That is also why the question of how to teach the axiomatic method must be treated from a modern standpoint; the results of experiments based on this new concept may differ from those of the traditional school. The question is therefore entirely open and requires objective research.

When undertaking such research, we must distinguish two aspects of the axiomatic method:

(a) The axiomatic method in action, as an instrument of mathematical thinking in the three phases of its activity: *axiomatization* (search for an adequate definition of a structure, which is also quite easy to handle), *deduction* (logical development of the theory of the structure thus defined), *interpretation* (application of this theory in fields containing the given structure).

(b) The axiomatic method as the subject of metamathematical research (conditions of coherence and independence, scope of method, etc.).

This distinction between the operative instrument of thinking and the subject of methodological analysis is necessary in order to avoid possible confusion.

In educational research on the axiomatic method, we shall be solely concerned with the first aspect. The essential problem is to work out educational approaches to (a) the initiation of the pupil into the processes of active axiomatic thinking (axiomatization, deduction, interpretation) adapted to the level of his intelligence and the content of the curriculum; (b) the formation in the pupil's mind of a concept which, although not yet formalized, would nevertheless correspond in its essentials to the *modern* axiomatic concept.

The preparation of an 'axiomatic teaching method', thus conceived, calls for experimental research on a large scale. In order to mark the direction of work in this field, we must:

(a) Reveal the natural basis of the axiomatic method, that is, the underlying intuitions in which the educational approach always seeks its starting point.

(b) Compare with the results of this analysis the traditional manner of presenting the 'deductive method' (in geometry) to the pupil, so that on the one hand we can obtain a better grasp of the postulates of the new teaching in this field, combined with a better understanding of the concepts involved, and so that on the other hand we can avoid from the outset teaching errors resulting from a misinterpretation of such concepts.

(c) Prepare teaching projects which might be used as starting points for educational experiments in class.

Some points of this programme are outlined below. We shall concentrate on general methodology, and omit the detailed discussion of the various axioms already available for use in teaching.

3.1   Intuitive meaning of axioms

We shall take as our starting point the axiom conceived as the *definition* of a structure. The first question concerns the object thus defined.

Contemporary mathematics defines the object of its research as the structure underlying elementary set relations in all fields of the mathematician's activity.

The foremost problem today for mathematics teaching is the following. Is it possible for secondary-school pupils to understand the axiomatic concept in this sense? Is it necessary? These questions are new and important, because the emphasis in teaching is frequently placed on the deductive phase and on the rigour of reasoning. Rigour is only one aspect of the axiomatic method, the natural aspect for someone who understands the object of mathematical research. We insist on this point, for the formalism of mathematical statements, while impressive, conceals the mechanism of mathematical thinking itself, and this is undesirable in the classroom.

If the teacher considers the deductive links paramount and not the underlying ideas, then what is natural for the mathematician becomes artificial for the pupil. Rigour becomes for him a strait-jacket imposed by the teacher.

There are psychological reasons to suggest that this situation can be avoided by introducing into teaching the axiomatic concept as the definition of a structure. Such an introduction is clear and free of the incomplete arguments which weaken the pupil's mathematical thinking.

This may be regarded as over-ambitious or even illusory, in view of the degree of abstraction of the concepts in question.

Of course, if it were not possible for us to teach pupils the axiomatic method by starting from their intuitions, their personal experiences, their natural flow of thought, and the concepts already familiar to them, we should have to eliminate our programme from our educational considerations from the outset. Happily the intuitive aspects of the concept of structure are immediately apparent. Moreover, the axiomatic process, devoid of formalism, is revealed in its essence and its psychological genealogy as a natural process of human thinking which, even in its naïve form, could not orient itself into reality nor transform that reality without an awareness of relations, without the two fundamental operations of schematization and extrapolation of real data, by means of which reality in its different aspects is reflected in thought, in the form of different structures.

It is true that the path leading from this primitive, though universal, concept of structure to the formalized concepts of modern mathematics is very long and very complicated, and that these concepts were defined formally only after many centuries of scientific history, but it is also true that contemporary mathematics has brought into prominence an underlying concept of creative mathematical thinking. Mathematics has always been relational, whether we like it or not. The modern approach consists in realizing this and expressing it clearly and precisely from the methodological standpoint.

This realization of the structural character of mathematics and its formal expression make it easier for the naïve thinker to understand abstract concepts, which may appear paradoxical. Let us consider the attitude of naïve thought to axioms: the axioms of group theory and of Peano's natural integers, for instance. For the naïve thinker there is an essential difference between these two situations, the first axiom being a true 'definition' determining the meaning of the term 'group', that is, expressing the *necessary* and *sufficient* conditions for a system of a set and an operation to be a group, while the second axiom is understood as an expression of the conditions *necessarily* satisfied by the intuitive concept of the natural integers, but *by no means sufficient*. The isomorphic models of Peano's axiom are treated by the naïve thinker as concretely different, and he is, therefore, disinclined to accept the axiom in question as a 'definition' of this natural number, which has been familiar to him since childhood. The discussions of philosophers and even mathematicians prove that these difficulties are not confined to naïve thought. Still considered from the standpoint of intuition the situation becomes quite different if Peano's axiom is interpreted as the definition of the structure called 'natural order', this structure being understood as the essential structure of the set of these 'natural numbers' which have been known since childhood and used in practice. Peano's axiom in this sense is for the naïve thinker a 'true definition' of the natural order, being nevertheless not a 'true definition' of the natural number. And despite the fact that, from the formal standpoint, a distinction is made between the natural numbers used in metamathematics and those encountered in Peano's axiomatic theory, it would not be possible to make this distinction in teaching. Happily this is not necessary in the light of the concept of structure. The same is true for geometry.

It is a very important educational discovery of our time that it is often easier to find ways of transplanting 'scientific concepts' in school education by starting with the analysis of these concepts in their pure, logically perfect form than in this apparently more intuitive, but vague, form. The educational interest taken in their analysis derives from this impressive lesson of research on the foundations of mathematics; work on the precise and formal organization of a field of abstract ideas often reveals the primitive, natural germ of these ideas. This also applies to the modern concept of the axiomatic method which enables us to perceive its unsuspected sources in naïve thinking itself. To demonstrate this, it is only necessary to have the courage to bring out the intuitive aspects of formalism. We say 'courage' because, from the standpoint of precise mathematical thinking, our considerations may be regarded as a misuse of scientific concepts, as an inadmissible pandering to the popular level. Traditional didactic thinking, on the other hand, may regard them as playing with abstractions in a somewhat irresponsible manner from the point of view of education. We have that courage and, in order to give a concrete illustration of our remarks regarding the natural sources of the axiomatic method, we shall now analyse an example of the reasoning of a child, chosen from among others collected as illustrations of 'teaching the axiomatic method'.

Paul (aged $6\frac{1}{2}$) wants to persuade his parents that he can go by himself from the station to his grandparents' house without crossing the main street (forbidden because of its heavy traffic). To prove his point Paul draws on a sheet of paper the network of lines and points representing the streets and places relevant to his argument (station, grandparents' house, intersections of roads). In this way Paul constructs a graphic model of a certain topological structure: a model of the particular linear complex, without realizing its polyvalence and without extrapolating real data. During this construction Paul is concerned only with two relations acting in the finite set of points and roads: (a) 'You can go from point x to point y by road m.' (b) 'Point x is the intersection of road m and road n.' He visibly neglects the other relations (distances, magnitudes, geometrical figures) of which he has acquired a practical knowledge during his daily personal experience. The diagram thus obtained concerns the system of these two relations which are not isolated, but represented in their mutual relationships. We observe the agreement between Paul and his father with regard to the initial data thus fixed in the chosen symbolism.

Paul tries to prove his argument using the same code. He tries this time to prove an argument regarding a particular topological structure. This demonstration does not succeed. In admitting that the diagram does not have the property in question, Paul does not seek any further arguments. He is sure that his premise was false and observes that it is impossible to go from the station to his grandparent's house without crossing the main street. In this way he decodes the result of his search, made in a representation of reality, by projecting it into the reality represented.

Paul does not know scientific concepts and terms. He is not aware of having isolated a particular structure from many others embedded in reality, nor of having defined that structure correctly by using the topological structure of his graphic diagram.

Three extremely important phases in this process must be emphasized. The first is the fabrication of the diagram and the decision that the diagram is complete and that it expresses everything one wished to bring out. In this way one has finished *presenting premises*; from this point on the structure question has acquired a certain independence of the initial situation. The second phase is *deduction – sui generis –* which relates only to the structure thus defined, and therefore uses only the premises and the 'rules of procedure' corresponding to concrete operations in reality (movement of pencil – crossing the street). This phase leads to a 'formal' conclusion regarding the diagram. The third phase is the *application* of this conclusion and the strict acceptance of the consequences as regards the initial reality. Conversely, certain premises suggested to Paul and motivated by direct reading of the diagram are rejected (e.g. 'This street is longer than that one'). Paul treats these propositions as nonsense, because he has constructed the model himself and is fully aware of what he wanted to retain and what he wanted to ignore.

In the process we have just observed, we see the natural primitive form of axiomatization, deduction and interpretation in essence. There is obviously a vast distance between this primitive activity and the axiomatic method in action, between the operative concept of a structural correspondence in a child and a mathematician's concept of structure. But if we could successively transform this natural germ of the axiomatic process – still deeply rooted in the concrete – into a method of thinking and solving problems by gradually raising the level of abstraction of the diagram constructed and used, the teaching of the axiomatic method would find one of its natural bases in the naïve methodology of the child himself. One of the absolutely necessary conditions of this transformation is the pupil's realization that mathematical structures reflect systems of relations revealing themselves in reality in a manner not only *schematizing*, but if necessary *extrapolating* real data and that, thanks to this essential transmutation, they are *polyvalent**.

Paul is not aware that his diagram, or any diagram, can be interpreted differently, for in the situation of his little problem he does not need to take this into consideration. Neither does he need to extrapolate real data. On the contrary, exact compatibility of such data, concerning the structure in question, with his diagram is the absolutely necessary condition for the correct solution of his problem. The child usually finds himself in the same situation during his initiation into the arithmetic of natural numbers and that is why there

*Here and subsequently the concept of polyvalence is interpreted in the primitive sense (isomorphic models of a structure are treated as different).

is no gulf between the child's natural thinking and his mathematical activity (a balance which is unfortunately already disturbed during his study of fractions). On the contrary, the secondary-school pupil finds himself faced with complicated intersection structures (geometry, field of real numbers), the elementary components (basic structures) of which obviously have their origin in the concrete, but which have become mathematical structures as a result of the *extrapolating schematization* of real data.

Failure to understand the character of this transformation often leads to a paradoxical situation in secondary mathematics teaching: on the one hand there is an inevitable confusion of abstract and concrete in the average pupil's thinking when he is deducing, reasoning and demonstrating, and on the other hand there is a sterile separation of abstract and concrete when he has to apply his mathematical knowledge to solving practical problems. The average pupil's conception of mathematics thus becomes artificial: there is a deep gulf between his natural thinking and his organized activities in education.

In analysing this situation, we see no new specific difficulties for initiation into the axiomatic method apart from those already existing in traditional teaching and which will also exist in the new teaching, because they derive from the complicated relation between abstract and concrete in mathematics. On the contrary, there are reasons for the assumption that the educational approach to this initiation might help to balance abstract and concrete in the pupil's thinking. We do not feel that the introduction of axiomatic thinking calls for teaching which is more detached from the pupil's intuitions than traditional teaching, which is more sterile in its applications. We add one essential reservation: that the problem is not reduced to the construction of a fine axiom (which is obviously very important) and to the projection of this axiom from the 'mathematical sky' into the reality of school.

3.2   Axiomatization: description and definition

In his work the professional mathematician, like the pupil, encounters situations where he has to formulate a definition himself, and other situations where he has to apprehend the meaning of a concept from a definition formulated by someone else.

This distinction must be taken into account in the analysis of the educational problem of initiation into the axiomatic method, for we can try to achieve this in two different ways: one which goes through the stage of axiomatization in class and the other which bypasses this stage and starts straight off with a ready-made axiom presented to the pupils. These two types of teaching method mobilize different activities of thought and reveal different difficulties and advantages. We shall discuss them separately.

Let us start with a survey of the first type of situation, that is, situations in which we construct a definition in general and an axiom in particular.

What interests us from the educational standpoint is the interplay of two fundamental aspects of thinking arising in the process of definition: analysis, which is expressed in the establishment of a report, and synthesis, which leads to the construction of a project. These aspects play different roles in different situations; their mutual relation decides the nature of the definition, which is apprehended by the definer either as a 'report definition' or as a 'project definition'.

For instance, Cauchy has constructed the 'report definition' of the limit of a function, for he has formally legalized a concept which, having been used by mathematicians in an operative and creative manner, was nevertheless vague from the standpoint of logic. The analysis of Euclidean geometry made by Hilbert, leading to his system of axioms, has the same character. A pupil who, after apprehending a concept intuitively and operatively (drawing, model, concrete activity) seeks a definition, performs similar work. The special character of this process lies in the fact that the person who looks for a definition *a posteriori* expresses in that definition only part of his knowledge and intuitions regarding the object thus defined. He must therefore choose and isolate from the set of properties already apprehended a subset of properties the conjunction of which is sufficient to imply all the others. This choice may be more or less free and the criteria for it may be different or even diametrically opposed (e.g. the 'natural' definitions in classical mathematics or the 'genetic' – constructive – definitions in teaching, or the 'key theorems' as definitions in Bourbaki's work). The method of *a posteriori* definition is therefore not easy, and calls for a creative effort and a broad, deep knowledge of the elementary structures used for defining more complicated structures.

Construction of an *a priori* definition involves other aspects of thinking and another type of creation. On the basis of the axioms of Euclidean geometry which are the result of establishing a report definition, new geometries have been proposed *a priori*, the non-Euclidean geometries. These were project definitions constructed by an operation on the given axioms: omission of one axiom, replacement of some axioms by others, etc. Classifications, generalizations, particularizations, variations in conditions and different combinations of known structures leading to intersection structures may become starting points for project definitions in general and project axioms in particular.

Rational educational organization of the interplay of these two aspects, which transform a description into a definition, a report of intuitions and previous knowledge into a structure project, seems to us to be the essential prerequisite for this form of introduction to the axiomatic method.

To illustrate this remark we shall consider two examples. We shall pass over the appraisal and criticism of these methods from many points of view (e.g. concerning the choice of axioms). What we are solely interested in is two different situations in axiomatization:

(a) The situation in which one separates a structure common to several non-isomorphic models already well known: the construction of an *a priori* polyvalent structure.

(b) The situation in which one tries to axiomatize only one field of prior knowledge which forms a theory as yet little elaborated, or which is little separated from reality in that it is on the border between concrete and abstract.

3.2.1 *Example: description of a structure common to several models*
From a thesis, 'Methodology of mathematics teaching', Higher Teacher Training College, Cracow

Nine fifteen-year-old pupils are to study certain algebraic concepts: various sets and definition of algebraic operations. The teacher suggests some examples of lattices, one after the other. The pupils note impatiently that 'it's always the same thing', whereas the objects, orders and operations are completely different in the examples considered. This provokes a group search for an answer which leads to the axiomatization of the lattice structure. In the course of this 'schematic description', the pupils suggest also including in the list of 'common properties' properties which are not common to all the examples considered as being 'the same': for example, distributivity of multiplication over addition – a specific property of total order. But it is soon perceived that some of the examples analysed do not obey these rules. These suggestions are therefore rejected; proposals regarding properties which can be deduced immediately from those already recognized as 'common properties' are also rejected (commutativity of operations, law of absorption, for instance). Finally an axiomatic system – the intersection of two different axioms – is obtained for the structure of the lattices. The term 'lattice' is introduced.

Thus, the description aiming at the construction of a diagram covering several models leads to the axiomatic definition as a result of (a) the symbolic description of the diagram, which facilitates deduction without going back to the initial models; (b) the conscious construction of a polyvalent diagram from the outset; (c) the term fixing the synthesis of a new mathematical object.

Thereafter the distributive lattice is defined by adding the additional axiom to the axiomatic system already established.

Three types of exercise bring out the different ways of using the axiomatic system thus established and conceived as a definition:

(a) Recognition of the lattice structure in particular cases. Question: Is this a lattice?

(b) Deduction. Question: Do the two lattice operations have similar properties to those of arithmetical operations? We find and demonstrate certain analogies

$$(a+b)+c = a+(b+c), \qquad a < b, \qquad 0 < c \Rightarrow a.c < b.c, \qquad \text{etc.}$$

and certain differences

$$a.a = a, \qquad a+a = a, \qquad a+ab = a, \qquad \text{etc.}$$

(c) Interpretation of the results of the deduction in different models, which reveals to pupils in a naïve but striking manner the economy of axiomatic thinking.

For example, to the question, 'What is

$$\text{LCM } [b, \text{HCF}\{\text{LCM}(a,b), \text{LCM}(a,c)\}] ?'$$

one pupil quickly gives with satisfaction the answer $\text{LCM}(a, b)$, using the formula $(a+b)(a+c)+b = a+b$, previously obtained for the distributive lattice.

The manner of solving these problems and the comments of pupils prove that they have understood the axiomatic system as the definition of a structure, and deduction as the only natural way of seeking that structure. How could we study the lattice except by referring solely to its definition?
One pupil asked the question, 'Could we do all mathematics in the same way?' This shows a true Bourbaki spirit.

3.2.2   *Example: gradual structuring of a field of intuitive knowledge by elementary structures determined* a priori.

We shall analyse the process of gradually structuring the intuitive geometrical knowledge of pupils aged from fourteen to fifteen (e.g. the first-year pupils in Polish secondary schools) relating to the structure of the metric plane. We begin by introducing pupils to the concepts: set, certain operations on sets, mapping of a set into a set, order in a set, distance in a set (distance in general; distances on the surface of a cube, a sphere; distance in a set of numbers, in a given set of pupils).

We make use of the fact that as the pupils come from different schools, they therefore form a new group and work with a new teacher.

The guiding idea of axiomatization which we can present to the pupil is as follows: at the start of our work in class, we must establish an intuitive understanding, which we shall subsequently use in geometrical terms and whose underlying ideas are not strange to us. We have already fixed a common vocabulary: set, operations on sets, mapping of a set into a set, order in a set, distance in a set. We shall try to express as concisely as possible, using this vocabulary, the intuitive geometrical relations which we wish to bring out.

In this way we proceed to the gradual structurization of the plane by means of set structures and topological structures intuitively grasped and previously determined. We aim always at mapping-relations: two points – distance, belonging; two points – short line; product of two sets; two straight lines (secants, parallels, direction); operations on distances; three points – distance (condition of collinearity), order in the straight line – distance, etc.

Here is an example of the process. The pupils bring out 'natural order' in the straight line (they have no idea of any order in the straight line other than the natural order), 'characterizing' it by the properties most frequently emphasized : between two points there are many other points, each point is preceded and followed by many other points.

In order to create the need to describe the structure of the metric line in a manner more appropriate to the axiom which it is desired to establish, the teacher can use the situation presented in Figure 31.

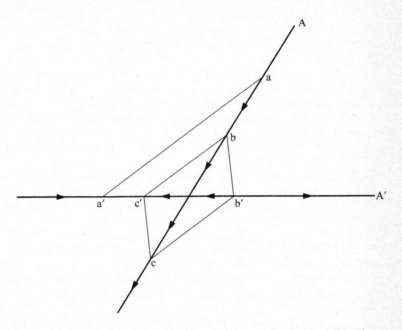

Figure 31 A mapping of line A into line A' : the segment [bc] is projected in the direction bb', but the rest of the line A is projected in the direction bc' (bb'//cc', aa'//bc'//b'c)

We map the line A into the line A', projecting the segment [bc] in the direction bb' and projecting the rest of line A in the direction bc' (bb'//cc' and aa'//bc'//b'c). We thus impose on A' the order treated as natural in A. The arrows illustrate the two orders in question.

The order obtained in A' appears 'unusual', but owing to the method used it is 'forced' to have the same properties which have so far been considered as 'characteristic' for the natural order. The concepts, 'between', 'successor', 'predecessor' on the straight line become relative. The structure described covers models we wish to eliminate; it is too polyvalent and the need for an additional condition becomes apparent.

The first observation – still intuitive – is that the 'unusual' order has been obtained by a mapping chosen 'maliciously' by the teacher, for part of the straight line A was projected in one direction and the other part in another direction. When imposing the natural order of any straight line A on any straight line A′ by means of parallel projection, we should obtain the natural order in A′ and not an unusual order. We establish a new property of the natural order: the parallel projection of one straight line on another preserves the natural order.

The second discovery is revealed during the search for the answer to the question, 'What is unusual in the order defined in A′?' Point a′ precedes point b′, point b′ precedes point c′ and, despite this, the distance a′ c′ is smaller than the distance a′ b′! This does not agree with the common aspect of natural order in the straight line, for if we imagine moving along the line in its natural order, after point a′ we *must* be 'moving away' from that point. How could we bring out this image using only our above vocabulary? We observe that point b is in its natural order between point a and point c if and only if a, b and c are different, and ac = ab + bc.

Would this description be sufficient to distinguish the 'unusual' order from the natural order in A′?

We observe that if a person understood geometrical concepts in this way, if he were in agreement with us regarding these two properties, he would be forced to admit that the order defined in A′ is not natural, since this order in A′ is not consistent with our two properties of natural order.

We continue in the same manner; we add axioms as and when necessary to establish 'common sense' and avoid possible confusion, but always using only the structures determined by the vocabulary fixed at the outset. Proofs of intuitively obvious theorems or of those encountered in previous lessons, and definitions known but re-established are not superfluous. On the contrary, they are very important for they prove that 'our description was good', that it defines the relations in question in accordance with what we wished to show.

On the other hand, 'malicious' examples suggest to us the need to add more axioms, for our description was 'not good enough' to avoid confusion in understanding the 'common sense' of the relations in question. Discoveries and proofs of new theorems, and also new definitions prove, on the other hand, that our knowledge of these relations was not and never will be complete.

At a certain moment it is decided – at the suggestion of the teacher – to consider the description as complete: 'We shall deal henceforward only with the diagram of this structure.' The report of the basic propositions is established and the list is closed. This act of decision transforms the description which has been established step by step into the definition of the metric structure of the plane which, from then on, will be the object of precise, deductive study.

3.2.3 As we have mentioned, we shall pass over the discussion on the axioms established in the previous examples. In all these methods we are interested only in the educational programme which is common to them, that is, in initiating pupils into the axiomatic method through guided axiomatization in class.

We use the term 'guided axiomatization' to designate the following educational situation: (a) the teacher envisages an axiom chosen as the basis of instruction, (b) he organizes a problematical situation or he presents directly to his pupils a problem, which becomes the starting point for a series of situations favourable to the group elaboration of the axiom in question.

The above processes have been guided by the pilot ideas clearly presented to the pupils: 'to find the same thing in different situations', 'to describe the common sense of certain terms with a vocabulary defined beforehand'.

In relation to these various ideas, the interplay of two aspects – report and project – intervening in the process of definition was organized differently. In section 3.2.1 we were presented with the typical process of *abstraction* where the two aspects – report and project – play important roles to the same extent (the report of different situations leading through analysis to the establishment of common characters and the new synthesis of these characters detached from their particular materializations, expressed in the project definition of a structure). The second example is only an attempted report of previous knowledge structured in a new way during this report.

The modern spirit of these approaches is expressed in:

(a) the pilot idea of the process;

(b) the use of modern resources (elementary mathematical structures prefabricated for the assembly in question, language and symbols of set theory);

(c) presentation of the axiom elaborated as a description defining a structure, fixed by the adequate term (vector space, lattice, metric structure of the plane);

(d) change-over to deduction, finding its motivation in the structural character of the object of the search;

(e) bringing out a certain concept – still primitive – of the polyvalence of the structure envisaged (construction of the polyvalent structure by definition in the one case, conscious restriction of the polyvalence of the initial structures by relating these structures to each other in the second situation).

The approaches outlined above do not constitute an exhaustive list of possible forms of guided axiomatization. In presenting them as examples we merely wished to emphasize the diversity of the teaching methods which can be used, and to draw attention to the numerous situations lending themselves to the organization of various profoundly mathematical activities of youthful thought which arise during this process. Such attempts, concealed in the intimacy of the classroom, still await a clear-sighted educational analysis and an objective appraisal.

Guided axiomatization in class is obviously not open free searching; it is narrowly channelled by the way the problem is formulated and as a result of situations conditioning the pupil's thinking in order to establish the axiom predetermined by the teacher. Nevertheless the pupil here participates actively in the group search for a definition, trying to specify and formalize his intuitions which are not yet far from their concrete sources.

A process requiring the same high degree of thinking activity, but in the opposite direction, is the preliminary realization of an object from a verbal or symbolic definition formulated by another person, and in particular from a ready-made axiom. We use the expression 'preliminary realization', for the comprehension of a structure is a process. During the deductive development of the axiom we gradually penetrate more and more deeply into the meaning of the structure defined. The preliminary clarification of the meaning of the definition in mathematics already requires not only a certain maturity of thought, but also technique in this process. Among the various approaches of this kind, the most primitive and spontaneous are searching for models, constructing particular examples belonging to a familiar field of knowledge and satisfying the defining conditions. This method is also used by the authors of even very advanced mathematical treatises, who often interpret the definitions formulated with logical rigour with examples specially chosen in order to facilitate the reader's understanding of these definitions. Yet it is the formal definition which should present this meaning in the clearest and most absolute manner, any particularization always introducing superfluous elements and accidental characters and, therefore, masking what is essential. The reality is nevertheless different and it may be that the meaning of a formally perfect diagram can only be grasped by its concretization. It may also happen that such realization only occurs during deduction: in the light of properties formally established almost blindly, the concept in question is apprehended afterwards.

The average pupil usually remains perplexed when faced with the text of a complicated definition. He does not know how to select the necessary operations for assembling representations belonging to fields that are familiar to him. Effective rational strategies for treating mathematical definition should, therefore, find their proper place in mathematics teaching at all levels. Learning how to decode the formal definition should be treated as an educational problem of the same importance as learning how to define. From this point of view, too, we can organize the group work on the axiom presented to the pupils beforehand, provided that (a) the axiom in question is only a very simple composition of elementary structures, well-known to the pupils, and expressed in terms and symbols already frequently used, and (b) the pupils have available several different models of the defined structure which are familiar to them. To take a typical example of this, let us consider the concept of a group. (We are thinking of fifteen-year-old pupils who do not know the term 'group' but have a general notion of the operation and the properties of an operation.)

The search in class for different models of this structure, constructed according to the programme presented in the axiomatic definition, gives an opportunity for instructive teaching approaches. Progressive corrections of the examples proposed by pupils, which often satisfy only part of the conditions, and the search for the answer to the question, 'Is this a group?', is all just normal work aimed at the comprehension of the mathematical definition in general. But since the object thus defined is a polyvalent abstract structure, these approaches become an essential mechanism for initiation into the axiomatic method, establishing the correct relations between formalism and underlying intuitions. The numerous different non-isomorphic models of a given axiom, discovered in class, guarantee the necessary equilibrium by allowing thought to move in the void of formalism with a certain familiarity and by protecting thought against dangerous obstinacy due to intuitions from a particular model. We give life to the formal diagram, which nevertheless remains an abstract object whose properties can be established only by the deductive development of its definition.

This need to give concrete life to normal emptiness is very strong among schoolchildren (and not only among them).

As an experiment, in the context of diploma work at the Cracow Higher Teacher Training College, a group of students (intelligent sixteen year olds) were presented with a variant of Bachmann's (1959)* axiom without any interpretation. They were merely told that the propositions in question concerned objects and operations of which nothing else was known. Could they deduce other information regarding these objects and operations? The students demonstrated some simple theorems, but disapproved of these 'blind' approaches, although the formal calculations according to the rules fixed *a priori* seemed easy to them. The geometric interpretation brought visible relief and in turn aroused interest in the formal treatment of the problem, for they had found satisfaction in the economy of the calculation, which 'had sense'. Once equilibrium between the concrete and the formal had been reestablished, the beauty of algebraic thinking was revealed naturally and impressively.

Note that in order to initiate students into the axiomatic method it is not of the first importance – it is not even necessary – to begin by general explanations regarding the concept of axioms. It is possible to act axiomatically without talking of axioms. The teacher would be very successful if he could bring his pupils to a level where they could describe the axiomatic process, like their mathematical practice, using the language which is familiar to them and realizing, like Monsieur Jourdain discovering he spoke prose, that they have quite naturally applied a 'scientific method' important not only in mathematics, but – according to some researchers – especially in applied mathematics (Ljapunov, 1960). The necessary condition for this realization is, on the one hand, organization of education to pass at each level through the stages of observation, mathematization, deduction and application, and on the other, construction of adequate axioms conducive to such organization.

*References for chapter 3 will be found on p. 150.

3.3   Preparatory stage

We made a sudden jump from the spontaneous axiomatizing activity of little Paul to 'guided axiomatization' in class. What should occur in between?

The tasks involved in teaching mathematics up to the age of fourteen are numerous and preparation for the axiomatic method is only one very special aspect and not the most important. But as regards the question considered here, this special aspect concerns us above all, for an attempt at more universal structurization must be preceded by restricted, limited and fragmentary structures. Differentiated activities leading to the schematization and extrapolation of real experience, realization of the relations linking the properties of abstract objects thus obtained, local deductions, etc. can all be organized by stages in primary education and in the first classes of secondary schools without necessarily establishing a global construction from the outset. All the processes of which we have given examples when speaking of 'guided axiomatization' and many similar ones may find their local realization therein: transporting a structure, discerning a structure from different situations, restricting a structure by crossing it with others, generalizing a definition or its transformation, aiming at the invariance of a particular structure (e.g. during the change-over from the plane to three-dimensional space), etc. Three conditions seem to be absolutely necessary for moving on to the higher level of systematic axiomatization:

(a) The preparatory stage must be organized from the outset so as to aim at modern structurization of concepts and operations gradually detached from reality. As soon as possible we must reach the stage of realizing, perhaps still naïvely and partially, the simplest elementary structures of set theory, algebra and topology, and of using these structures and the proper language in local structures (Dienes, 1963; Papy, 1963).

(b) The second condition concerns the development of geometric concepts. The basic operation of schematization extrapolating real data should be grasped and applied consciously by the pupil. Examples of geometrical diagrams constructed, sought and applied in order to solve practical problems can serve as introductory examples. The use of geometrical diagrams in order to give concrete shape to more abstract ideas (in solving certain arithmetical problems or as Venn diagrams, for example) would bring out the 'two faces' of the geometrical diagram: abstract for one reality and concrete for another.

(c) The third condition concerns the local deductive organization of teaching material: immediate conclusions at the beginning; equivalence of two definitions; then situations where the pupil cannot obtain additional data and is obliged to use a closed set of information to solve a problem; situations where the pupil is set the problem of establishing a property by referring only to restricted information, although he knows other data he might use; situations where the pupil imposes such restrictions himself; situations where the pupil wishes to convince the class he has found a correct solution (e.g. a geometrical construction), etc. Teaching should make the pupil aware of these processes, which he often uses spontaneously. In the end the pupil should be brought to realize that we can reason deductively only on relations, that even if at the outset we formulated key data referring to particular objects, the conclusions concern any objects satisfying the premises expressed in such data. In solving one problem in this way, we always solve a whole class of problems; whether we wish to or not, we obtain a wider conclusion than the one we were trying to obtain, for although we aimed at objects, we acted on structures. This mechanism can be brought out at each step and each level, even in solving ordinary arithmetical problems.

3.4 Axiomatic organization of the course

Axiomatic organization of educational subjects as a whole after a certain secondary-school level is obviously necessary for the initiation of pupils into the axiomatic method. It is too soon to decide what this level should or can be, since the experiments continuing at present in various pilot schools admit different levels as starting points (for example, in the Belgian pilot classes axioms are being discussed with twelve year olds, see Papy, 1963; in the Cantonal Lycée at Lausanne the notion of axioms is introduced in the second cycle) and only after completing at least one series of these tests can their results be objectively appraised.

Nevertheless it is possible to formulate some guiding ideas regarding the axiomatic organization of secondary-school mathematics – ideas based on restricted but significant observations, on educational theory and on the nature of the problem of teaching the axiomatic method.

The axiomatic method cannot be taught in the void. We must have either material to axiomatize or material to interpret intuitively a given axiomatic definition. We must also have the tools needed for axiomatization and utilization of a previously established or given axiom.

The material to which we have referred is not only the world of experience, observation, intuition and concepts half detached from their concrete sources, but also fragments of mathematics already 'locally organized' (according to the expression of Freudenthal, 1963), which are almost ripe in the pupil's minds for a more general synthesis. The tools we have mentioned are: the most elementary structures already familiar to the pupil, modern language, a certain intuitive orientation in basic logical concepts (definition, theorem, proof) elaborated during 'local organizations', and an absolutely necessary skill in elementary operations etc. That is why active initiation into the axiomatic method must not be started too soon.

Moreover, we are aiming at the axiomatic method in action. A method is always concerned with an activity. To believe that pupils can be taught the axiomatic method without having applied that method is a teacher's illusion. To conclude the elementary mathematics course by revision of the material in the last class with a view to its later axiomatic organization would be to return to the nineteenth-century conception of axiomatization as the logical organization of a ready-made and almost dead discipline. We want to present the axiomatic method to pupils as the useful creative mechanism of thinking. That is why initiation into the axiomatic method should not be started too late. It is very important to find the best moment. Experience, which is still limited, suggests that the most favourable moment is about the age of fifteen, but we must wait for more significant results.

The second question requiring analysis is the form of the axiomatic organization of educational subjects. What axioms should be used? How should they be arranged and how should they be introduced into what mutual relations? We take into consideration certain algebraic axioms (group, ring, field, vector space) and an axiomatic organization of the field of numbers, as well as geometry and probabilities.

It would be premature to answer the questions referred to above; we await the complete elaboration of certain projects covering educational subjects as a whole.

The problem of initiation into algebraic axioms – 'true definitions' for the naïve thinker – is quite simple, as we have already emphasized. As the introduction of the axiom of the theory of probabilities is scheduled for the last class in the secondary school and preceded by the realization of other axioms, it will not perhaps cause particularly serious difficulties *formally*. We have emphasized the word 'formally', for we must have no illusions that the generalization of the classic definition of probability, even if accepted easily by pupils previously introduced to the elements of analysis, will lead directly to the comprehension of the structure thus defined, as pupils are acquainted only with simple primitive examples of sets and have only a rough notion of measurement. But even if it were not possible to penetrate more deeply into the theory, the construction of the axiom in question and the establishment of its most important consequences for statistical applications would be highly instructive.

As we have only very limited information regarding experiments in this field, we have no basis for analysing this question more thoroughly, but it would be worthwhile to seek educational methods of introducing the axiom of probabilities naturally. On the one hand, as the Dubrovnik programme rightly notes, it is 'an excellent opportunity for demonstrating how to construct an axiomatic theory' (OECD 1961), and on the other hand it also provides a particularly favourable opportunity for the correct presentation of the relations of theory and practice of the experimental method and the axiomatic method, the combination of which determines the omnipresence of mathematics in modern culture.

Numbers and geometry also give rise to open questions, the first being as yet little discussed, while the second is the subject of heated debate.

As regards the first question, there are not many partisans of the axiom of natural integers in secondary education. According to the most widespread opinion, the most important operations on sets and on natural integers should be treated as basic elements, elaborated intuitively and organized locally (local deductions). The main discussion concerns the degree of precision of the successive constructions leading by stages to the concept of the field of real numbers. Movement from one stage to another should comprise (a) motivation for the enlargement of the known set of numbers, (b) definition and operations on new numbers and algebraic characterization of this structure, which is simply the axiomatization of the structure, and (c) identification of the set used at present with the subset of the set defined, by means of the isomorphism established.

Since this programme is to be carried out in primary schools and in the first cycle of secondary schools with pupils from twelve to fifteen years old, it is not possible to take the successive constructions further than the level of a still-intuitive outline organized purely deductively in certain fragments. We must not forget that we must not only make pupils *realize the algebraic properties of operations and algebraic structures which are gradually enlarged*, but also that they must acquire a *necessary skill in elementary calculations*.

Different ways may be used to lead to an outline of the concept of real numbers. Whatever the method used, the final synthesis expressed in an axiom of the field of real numbers appears necessary. This axiom might be formulated as one of the bases of second-cycle mathematics (the underlying idea of the proposed programme for the first class in Polish lycées). Using the language familiar to the pupils, the teacher would bring out the structure of the commutative, completely ordered and continuous field of real numbers, containing the subfield of rational numbers and the ring of integers. From this point on, operations on numbers should be strictly related to the axiom established as a report transformed in the definition of a structure.

The axiomatic organization of geometry is still the centre of controversy (CIEM, 1963). On the one hand, we find very interesting propositions, but they are opposed to axiomatic presentation or pass over it in silence (Freudenthal, 1963; Libois, 1963). On the other hand, many axiomatic systems of geometry have already been elaborated for use in secondary education. In this study we can do no more than mention the most typical ideas.

Three types of solution are proposed:

(a) Geometry as part of algebra.

(b) Geometry as part of the study of the field of real numbers.

(c) Independent geometry, but not isolated from algebra nor from the study of the field of real numbers, and conceived as a particular intersection structure.

Fundamental to the discussion concerning all these systems is the concept of 'unitary elementary mathematics'. What is beyond dispute is the set-theoretical basis of elementary mathematics teaching, accepted unreservedly in all modern theories. They differ in the interpretation of the term 'unitary' with reference to the construction of mathematics for the fifteen-year-old age group. We have seen that in the axioms of geometry two conceptions of this 'unification' are reflected: the conception of a single algebraic current and the conception of two currents (algebra and topology in the form of Euclidean metric space), which derive independently from the set-theoretical basis, cross several times and finally merge in the study of the elements of analysis and of probabilities.

3.5   Some problems in teaching the development of the axiomatic theory

The axiomatic construction of the course calls for a very clear-sighted teaching approach if the method is to function. It is vital to understand the methodological significance of (a) definition, (b) theorem and (c) proof.

In our experience, an understanding of the methodological role of definition is the key to an understanding of over-all construction, for correct deductive reasoning requires in the first place the disciplined use of definitions, including the axiom as basic definition. Lack of this discipline among pupils is revealed in various ways. For example, the difficulties and misunderstandings observed in traditional teaching of deductive geometry largely derive from the incomprehension of the methodological significance of the definition, as the pupils do not refer to the characters expressed in the definition but to an intuitive over-all image going further than the letter of the defining text. Our research has proved that pupils do not use definitions very consciously.

In reverting here to these questions which are familiar to every teacher, we wish to emphasize that the familiar but disciplined use of definition in the axiomatic organization of the course must be the subject of a particularly clear-sighted teaching approach. In his approach, the teacher must be concerned, for example, with the formal and intuitive interpretation of definition as equivalence; with analysis of the defining conditions and indication of the significance of each of these conditions separately in the light of counter-examples; with continuous organization and re-organization of the concepts introduced, in respect of their classification and their mutual relationships which new theorems and definitions continually reveal; with the realization of the equivalence of definitions and effective use of that equivalence.

All this requires a great deal of time, which is why we cannot press forward too quickly in the axiomatic theory, despite the modern construction which is particularly favourable to the acceleration of the process and may give rise to dangerous illusions among teachers.

Similar remarks apply to theorems and their proofs. There must be time to go systematically and continuously into the very concept of proof on the one hand, and the establishment of a proof strategy on the other. The problem has two aspects:

(a) Comprehension of the methodological significance of proof and comprehension of the criterion of verification in the axiomatic theory are the *sine qua non* of initiation into the axiomatic method.

(b) Proof plays an extremely important part in the comprehension of defined concepts and theorem content.

Many definitions are properly understood only when applied in reasoning. Many theorems are understood better – or even only – in the light of their proof.

3.6 Problems of rigour

In considering initiation into the axiomatic method, we cannot pass over the problem of rigour. Three aspects call for educational analysis : (a) precision in formulating definitions, theorems and proofs, that is, precision of language, (b) rigour in reasoning and (c) consequence in the axiomatic development of theory. We shall discuss each of these problems in turn.

The justified and necessary reaction against the imprecise definitions and pseudo-proofs of traditional teaching brings with it the danger of going to the other extreme of being obsessed with formalism, fascinated by logical rigour and of identifying axiomatic thinking with formalist thinking. We sometimes find beginners whose fear of letting imprecision creep into their teaching is a great danger.

The average teacher, even with a modern outlook, cannot have the scientific perspective available to a research worker. He follows modern trends in a restricted and limited field and he may easily, unintentionally, reduce a creative methodological idea to a mass of details treated in an exaggerated manner. For all our educational approaches we should impose as a safeguard the principle that we must not be more 'purist' in our teaching than are the mathematicians in their customary routine practice. Though it may seem paradoxical, this principle leads to a moderate conception of rigour in the initiation of pupils into the axiomatic method.

What is required above all is precision in formulating the definitions and theorems, precision which can be understood and accepted consciously by the average pupil. That is why we must find means of expression which, while preserving the correct mathematical sense, are not lacking in echoes of the intuitive images and lively colours of ordinary language. Some laxity of language consciously accepted in class, some simplifying conventions introduced openly, the use of diagrams and symbols often with the character of 'road signs', all these may lighten the manner of expression without abandoning its essential correctness – a procedure also to be found in the routine practices of mathematicians.

The question is, therefore, to evolve optimum precision of language in mathematics teaching. Modern language facilitates verbal description, for it is possible to use terms, which were unknown in traditional teaching, to designate structures briefly. This may be seen, for example, in the formulation of modern axioms. But modern language for use in teaching, evolved for the greatest educational benefit, is still in its infancy. Traditional language is a historical fact resulting from evolution; a change in this language would be a new historical fact established by a *coup*. But this revolution cannot be achieved by directly transferring the language of mathematical treatises to school textbooks; it calls for a great deal of educational work based on concrete experience. Here we must draw attention to the very interesting and very convincing suggestions which can be found on nearly every page of Papy's books. There we see a new language *in vivo*, elaborated in a creative manner, making simultaneous use of verbal, symbolic and non-verbal means of expression with remarkable inventiveness (Papy, 1963).

All such approaches require time and it is, therefore, not possible to develop axiomatic theory in education rapidly. In teaching, such development consists not only of a statement of a fragment of the ready-made theory, but above all of initiation into the method of true intellectual activity. During this development it is necessary to create pauses for reflection on the distance travelled, or on local organizations within a global organization. For this purpose it might be necessary to dispense with a proof from time to time. Three situations may occur in the course based on the axiomatic principle: (a) 'complete' proofs, (b) outline proofs and (c) open omission of proof with information given by the teacher. The first and second may contain proofs or outline proofs evolved by the pupils themselves, and proofs with which they are made acquainted through the exposition of a pupil or the teacher, or through reading.

All these forms exist in the professional mathematician's practice. It would be impossible for him to prove in detail all the theorems he uses and in addition to 'learn' all these proofs in the manner required of the pupil. He may know only an outline of the reasoning in question; he may also content himself with information provided. There are no grounds for applying a more rigorous system in teaching. We must accept the fact that some fragments of an axiomatic theory can and should be presented to pupils in the form of information, that some proofs can be omitted or merely outlined, provided the situations are absolutely clear. Pupils must realize that we have dispensed with the presentation or search for the proof in question, but that the theorem requires a proof that has already been established by mathematicians; they must also realize when they have been given only an outline proof and must distinguish this outline from a 'complete' proof.

Of course this postulate can be questioned, since non-formalized – even very subtle – reasoning is only an outline of a proof (that is why we put the word 'complete' in inverted commas). But non-formalized proofs considered as 'complete' are used daily by mathematicians who aim at optimum precision. This optimum precision depends on many different aspects and is defined only approximately by common sense, a certain 'honesty' and experience. The same situation occurs in school, where optimum precision cannot be defined absolutely beforehand. It is 'honest', for example, to leave some gaps in a proof that can be easily completed by the pupils themselves; it is not 'honest' to conceal serious gaps which cannot be completed in class, but it is 'honest' to leave them, explaining frankly to the pupils the reasons for the omission. For some fragments of the course which are in the nature of information, we save time which is needed for learning the method.

3.7 Confrontation: the traditional and modern conceptions of the axiomatic method in teaching

According to our plan outlined at the beginning, we must consider both the difficulties observed in traditional teaching concerning the concept of axiomatic theory and the sources of these difficulties. Some of these difficulties arise from the erroneous presentation of the ideas in question, and will not occur in the modern presentation. More radical difficulties will have to be taken into account in the modern conception.

Attempts to initiate pupils into the axiomatic method in traditional teaching were – and still are – concerned only with elementary geometry. This situation is not favourable to the correct development of the methodological ideas in pupils' thinking for many reasons. The following four reasons seem to be particularly conclusive:

(a) As the pupil is not acquainted with similar processes in other fields of school mathematics, he is convinced that deductive construction is necessarily connected with geometry, and that it is merely the 'geometric method'.

(b) Efforts are made to introduce the axiomatic concept with examples concerning a field which is not favourable to this exercise. The classical axioms of geometry are complicated and difficult to express simply, concisely and precisely, particularly since traditional teaching uses only very few symbols and does not make use of the simplifying language of sets.

(c) These complicated axioms – the only ones in traditional teaching – concern a structure deeply rooted in the concrete and explored with a technique which is obviously necessary and has many educative values, but which is singularly likely to confuse intuitive and formal aspects (geometrical drawings and models). In this situation the methodology of geometry may appear to the average pupil as artificial and ambiguous.

(d) The presentation of the concept of axioms and the meaning of proof in the axiomatic theory is not correct, as it introduces fundamental misunderstandings from the beginning.

The existence of educational and mathematical confusion in the teaching of traditional geometry is seen in the obstinate search for teaching methods which might 'convince' the pupil of the 'necessity' for deductive verification of theorems.

Even the space devoted to this question in methodological works proves that the situation is not natural, that deductive reasoning appears to the pupil as a process imposed from outside: 'We do this in mathematics.'

Analysis of the typical suggestions regarding motivation of the method reveals even deeper confusion.

We shall not discuss these typical 'prescriptions' and 'motivations' in detail here, but shall merely make some general remarks regarding the three groups formulated most frequently.

The first group – independently of the methodological and philosophical positions of their authors – endeavour to shake the pupil's confidence in his conceptions based on experience and observation in geometry and to show the 'superiority of reasoning over experience'. This argument is an obvious subterfuge used to extricate the teacher from a very awkward situation. In this connexion we find, for instance, the 'prescription of illusions'. The pupil is presented with a drawing provoking an optical illusion. He checks his observation by measurement, for example, and finds with surprise that the drawing has deceived him; hence the conclusion, 'reasoning is superior to experience.' This conclusion is an obvious subterfuge, for the pupil discovered his mistake by measuring and could not correct his optical illusion otherwise.

Another striking example of this type of confusion is the 'prescription of sophisms'. We draw, for instance, a scalene triangle ABC, the perpendicular bisector of AB and the bisector of $\angle ACB$ in such a way that their point of intersection is inside the triangle (distorted drawing), which makes it possible to 'prove' that the triangle is isosceles. We draw the 'conclusion' that the drawing has deceived us and that we must reason independently of the drawing. This 'conclusion' could be immediately questioned by a pupil capable of opposing the authority of his teacher, for it would be sufficient to draw the diagram accurately in order to avoid the confusion; the only natural conclusion would therefore be that one must draw accurately.

Another 'prescription' lays stress on the 'weaknesses' of experience: it would be impossible to verify the theorem in question on 'all possible figures', as measurement gives only approximate results, constructions are inaccurate, etc. Hence the conclusion, 'Reasoning is superior to experience.' This is another subterfuge. If the experimental method consisted in verifying all possible cases, if generalizations on the basis of approximate measurements could not be made, the experimental sciences would not exist. The argument we have just mentioned is evasive for it tries to get out of difficulty without bringing what is solely valid here: the object of the mathematical research, the abstract diagram, which cannot be studied experimentally because of its very character.

The suggestions of the second group try to relate to the object of research. A strict distinction is made from the outset between the 'thought figure' and the 'drawn figure' or the 'object with the form of that figure', or between the 'thought operation' and the 'concrete operation' (drawing), and it is proposed to show from the outset the 'thought' figures and operations as proper objects of study. In this situation it is easier to establish in beginners a concept of verification 'by reasoning'. But it would be illusory to identify this concept with the notion of proof in an axiomatic theory. For the average pupil, 'to prove' means 'to convince' and to convince a reasonable person it is sufficient to show that what appeared non-evident is evident in the light of reasoning. To achieve this result it is sufficient to reduce the theorem to an intuitive premise; to reduce everything to axioms by force smacks of eccentricity.

The 'prescriptions' and 'motivations' of the third group relate to this spontaneous interpretation of proof. In discussion with the pupils the social aspect, relativity of evidence, is emphasized. The teacher at first plays the part of the habitual opponent. The pupils gradually become involved in this intellectual battle. Some of them acquire a taste for it and soon become habitual disbelievers, finding difficulties where there are none. Gradually the pupil who is doing the proof and who has to defend himself begins a dialogue with himself. The debate with the others is transformed through this interiorization into more and more precise reasoning. The pupils become accustomed to the method. But we must not fall into further illusions: becoming accustomed to a certain procedure and understanding the methodological significance of it are not the same thing, as may be seen absolutely clearly from the results of our research. The pupils – even in the higher classes – have two different concepts of 'truth' in geometry and two different concepts of 'proof': natural and scholastic ('required by the programme', as one fifteen year old put it). The traditional presentation of the method is not conducive to eliminating this duality.

An analysis of textbooks and works on the methodology of traditional mathematics teaching enables us to establish a classification of the most frequent conceptions presented to pupils in connexion with the 'deductive method'. Let us first of all consider the typical explanations.

(a) A priori *evidence*

(i) Fundamental concepts – completely clear concepts, which we cannot define; axioms – absolutely evident theorems, which we cannot prove.
(ii) Primitive concepts – such simple concepts that they require no definition; axioms – such evident theorems that they require no proof.

(b) *Evidence based on experience*

Primitive concepts – concepts reflecting certain objects existing in real space; axioms – simple propositions based on observations which by continual repetition have become more strongly imprinted on the mind than others.

(c) *Method and logical order*

It is not possible to explain the meaning of a concept without reference to another concept. It is not possible to prove the theorem without basing one's reasoning on other theorems. In order to avoid the *regressio ad infinitum* we must accept certain concepts without definition as primitive concepts and certain theorems without proof as axioms. We are usually told that these fundamental concepts are established by free choice, but also by taking into consideration evidence based on experience or on intuitive representation.

Less frequently we are told that the choice is determined by simplicity and convenience in the development of the theory. We may also be referred to the idea of pre-existing simplicity, even in recent textbooks.

(d) *Implicit definition*

(i) Axioms – propositions, accepted without proof, expressing characteristic properties of primitive concepts, of which we know nothing else.
(ii) Axioms – the most important information, without which it would be impossible for us to use primitive concepts.

The above explanations obviously reflect the various stages of development of the concept of the axiomatic method. Interpretation (a) reflects the idealistic conception of Proclos, interpretation (b) the realistic conception of Pasch. According to Proclos, axioms and postulates are clearer than the deduced theorems which are devoid of such clarity. Two thousand years after Proclos, Pasch writes of primitive concepts as follows: 'die Kernbegriffe wurden nicht definiert, keine Erklärung ist imstande, dasjenige Mittel zu ersetzen, welches allein das Verständnis jener einfachen, auf andere nicht zurückführbaren Begriffe erschliesst, nämlich den Hinweis auf geeignete Naturgegenstände' (Pasch and Dehn, 1926, p. 15).

As regards axioms: 'Kernsätze gründen sich auf Beobachtungen, die sich unaufhörlich wiederholt und sich fester eingeprägt haben als Beobachtungen anderer Art' (p. 16).

Regarding certitude: 'Die Unanfechtbarkeit der Beweise, durch die Lehrsätze auf die Kernsätze zurückgeführt werden im Verein mit der Evidenz der Kernsatze selbst, die durch einfachen Erfahrungen verbürgt sein sollen, gibt der Mathematik den Charakter höchster Zuverlässigkeit, der man ihr zuzuschreiben pflegt' (p. 92).

These two conceptions were, and still are, reflected in traditional teaching and its language, where the term 'evident' is used in the sense of Proclos' idealistic doctrine or of Pasch's realistic doctrine, the confused concept of evidence being the source of many misunderstandings. For the pupil, most of the theorems proved are no less evident (sometimes they are more evident) than the axioms themselves. Axioms are no more directly suggested by experience than other theorems. In this situation the explanation of the meaning of the axiom based on evidence cannot be comprehensible. The question why we must prove evident theorems, why we must use in the reasoning only the properties expressed in the definitions, etc., cannot, therefore, be answered in a manner which would be regarded as reasonable by the average pupil.

If we compare the pseudo-realistic conception, which is a popular version of Pasch's programme, with the concept of the axiom conceived as the definition of a structure, we see that the modern conception is more conducive to the correct presentation to the pupils of the mutual relations of experience and abstract thinking in geometry. The pseudo-realistic explanation conceals the fact that if the axioms of geometry reflect our experience concerning real space this is not a mechanical reflection occurring independently of the organizing activity of human thinking, stimulated by real problems which it has to solve at once.

The modern conception of structure is closer to reality. If from the outset in the 'inductive synthesis' we could make the pupil conscious of this operation of schematization extrapolating and transmuting real data into an abstract diagram, he would better understand the object of his study in geometry and the axiomatic method.

Interpretation (c) endeavours to bring out the hypothetical and deductive character of geometry. But while this character can be easily grasped by the beginner locally, the same cannot be said of the over-all theory. Interpretation (d) refers to implicit definition, but this concept is not, and cannot be, achieved logically in teaching classical geometry. It is said that axioms are 'propositions, accepted without, proof expressing characteristic properties of primitive concepts, of which we know nothing else', but we use from the outset drawings and models in a manner exceeding their symbolic role. The expression, 'of which we know nothing else', is in contradiction with the procedure itself, which relates continually to observations, images or spatial intuitions.

In mentioning the above four sources of difficulties in traditional deductive geometry we realize that we have outlined only certain selected aspects of the problem. Nevertheless it seems to us that this superficial and fragmentary survey enables us to formulate conclusions which would perhaps be useful in the elaboration of the new teaching of the axiomatic method.

(a) The axiomatic method should be introduced on the example of the simple, polyvalent axiom, having models familiar to the pupils. The roles of definition, theorem and proof in the general axiomatic construction might be brought out without confusion.

(b) It would be necessary to find ways of presenting the axiom as the definition of a structure which is the proper object of the study conceived as the search for a more and more detailed description of that structure, which possesses certain properties expressed in the theorems. The formal criterion of verification would be solely acceptable in this situation; the relation between the concrete, from which this structure was derived, and its abstract character could be presented clearly and correctly.

(c) More complicated theories, or those more deeply rooted in the concrete, such as geometry, could be studied axiomatically thereafter, the pupils being previously initiated into the method by means of a simpler example and already knowing some elementary structures necessary for the modern structurization of intuitively familiar fields.

As regards geometry, we are of the opinion that great care must be taken from the teaching standpoint to ensure equilibrium between the topological and algebraic structures used in the description of classical space, and reasonings based on algebraic calculations' and 'qualitative reasonings' (Krygowska, 1962, 1963).

References

BACHMANN, F. (1959), *'Aufbau der Geometrie aus dem Spiegelungsbegriff,* Berlin: Springer.

CIEM (1963), *L'Enseignement mathématique,* 2nd series, vol. 9, no. 1–2.

DIENES, Z. P. (1963), *An Experimental Study of Mathematics Learning,* Hutchinson.

FREUNDENTHAL, H. (1963), 'Enseignement des mathématiques modernes ou enseignement moderne des mathématiques', *L'Enseignement mathématique,* 2nd series, vol. 9, no. 1–2, pp. 28–44.

KRYGOWSKA, A. Z. (1962), 'L'enseignement de la géométrie dans la mathématique unitaire d'aujourd'hui', *Mathematica et Pedagogica,* no. 23.

KRYGOWSKA, A. Z. (1963), 'Sur la nécessité d'une conception pédagogique dans la réforme de l'enseignement des mathématiques, *Bulletin de l'Association des Professeurs de Mathématiques,* no. 232.

LIBOIS, P. (1963), 'Espaces et figures géométriques', *L'Enseignement mathématique,* 2nd series, vol. 9, no. 1–2.

LJAPUNOV, A. A. (1960), 'O fundamente sovremennoj matematiki', *Matematičeskie Prosveščenie,* Moscow.

OECD, (1961), *Synopses for Modern Secondary School Mathematics.*

PAPY, G. (1963), *Mathématique moderne,* Brussels and Paris: Didier.

PASCH, M., and DEHN, M. (1926), *Vorlesungen über neuere Geometrie,* Berlin: Springer.

4 Psychological and Educational Research Bearing on Mathematics Teaching

Prepared by E. A. Peel, Professor of Educational Psychology, University of Birmingham

4.0 The field

'The days when a teacher of mathematics could shut his eyes to psychology, and dismiss it as well-meaning advice of which he had no need, or as opinion which he did not share, are gone.' (Fletcher, 1964, p. 2.)* This is heartening reading but let us educational psychologists not over-state the significance of educational and psychological research for the study of mathematics teaching, learning and understanding. As Cronbach observed, the teacher 'developing a new curriculum expects the psychologist to know when a child can be taught certain subject matter or how one can best present some idea.' Cronbach then warned that this 'trust in psychology is a source of embarrassment, for we not only lack the answers to most of these questions but we find that such questions are incapable of being given a general answer' (Rosenbloom, 1964, p. 19).

However, this does not mean that we are unable to offer some helpful comment to the teacher of mathematics, particularly when psychology is concerned with human learning and thinking, and educational research is directed towards problems in mathematics and nearly allied fields. But we must remind ourselves that research in educational psychology is relatively recent, whereas, although the craft of education may not be the oldest in the world, it is near to being so. Furthermore, the educational psychologist cannot work effectively without the mathematician. As in the developing technique of programmed instruction, progress is best made by a team composed of the specialist teacher and the educational psychologist.

In this chapter the discussion will be primarily concerned with intellectual and cognitive aspects of the learning of mathematics. Even where the topic of motivation is touched upon it will be in terms of the concept of curiosity which itself relates very closely to the tendency to form hypotheses and to explore intellectually.

One can analyse intellectual and cognitive activity in a systematic way by considering differences in two dimensions: differences between individuals at a given age or time, and differences in the same individuals between different times, as in learning, development and thinking.

*References for chapter 4 will be found on p. 171.

Differences between individuals at a given time lead us to study mathematical ability by the use of mental and scholastic tests.

Although these differences are important, studies along the time dimension, whether of short duration as in thinking, problem solving, concept formation, or of longer periods as in learning, intellectual development and curricular problems, are much more significant for the teacher of mathematics.

This rationale of two kinds of difference – between different individual pupils at a given time, and between the same pupils, or an equivalent sample, at different times – provides a systematic framework which leads to research in the following five major fields:

(a) Intellectual ability and individual differences in mathematical aptitude and attainment.

Examples: What is the mean and range of mathematical performance at particular ages? Are there mental factors at certain ages which can be associated or identified with mathematical abilities?

(b) Experimental study of the growth of thinking, particularly with reference to number, spatial relations, geometry, classification, the development of mathematical concepts and operations and the nature of mathematical experience.

Examples: How do the mathematical ideas of children develop? How does their visual and haptic (touch, kinaesthetic, motor) perception of geometrical forms mature? How do they build up arithmetical operations?

(c) The nature of concepts, productive thinking and problem solving.

Examples: Are there psychologically different ways of solving problems? What is the sequence of mental operations in forming a concept? What are the qualities of productive thought in mathematics?

(d) Mathematics learning with reference to methods, programmed learning, learning sets (learning to learn) and the spread of learning.

Examples: What are the conditions for learning mathematics? How can mathematical tasks be broken up to improve learning of mathematical ideas? Can we teach thinking?

(e) Curricular studies aimed at revising and improving the mathematics curriculum.

Examples: What should be introduced? How should the new mathematics be taught?

4.1 Intellectual ability with special reference to mathematics

Studies of general and mathematical abilities do not have the most to offer teachers of mathematics, but historically such research was the first to develop a clear attack on mathematical problems and it has attracted many teachers of mathematics, who were also interested in educational psychology, influenced by the Galtonian tradition. These include Jenkins (1939), Lee (1955), Saad (1957) and Wrigley (1958).

The method consists first of carrying out a job analysis of mathematical activity which leads to the construction of a battery of psychological and educational reference tests which are given alongside tests of mathematics to a group of pupils. The matrix of correlation coefficients between all tests is analysed by standard techniques of correlational analysis to yield mental 'factors' which account for the original data and have to be interpreted in terms of the test material used. Reviews of studies of mathematical ability are given by Vernon (1950, pp. 38–42, 46–8, 116–18) and Wrigley (1958). In general there appears to be a hierarchy of mental abilities headed by general intelligence followed next by a division into two basic group abilities: those considered the basis of the comprehension of words, connected prose, number and other symbolic systems, usually described as verbal–educational; and those conducive to visualizing and thinking spatially in two and three dimensions and also in problems of movement, often labelled spatial–kinaesthetic. These two basic group abilities may be further subdivided into more specialized intellectual powers and so on.

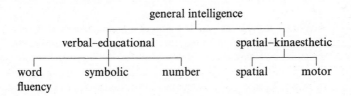

Where does mathematical ability lie in this hierarchy? The answer is not easy to give.

The findings and theories offered are not at all conclusive on the nature of mathematical ability. We do not on the whole obtain a clear-cut picture, save that general intellectual ability is important (a trite observation to make to any experienced teacher) and there is a group factor we might call mathematical ability. Attempts to analyse this in greater detail reveal number, verbal, spatial, thinking elements intricately mixed up with material content elements.

Many of the factorial researches to date have produced a rather confused picture because thinking categories have been mixed up with content categories (arithmetic, algebra, geometry, trigonometry, mechanics, etc.) and also with attainment measures. If we are to investigate whether the hierarchy of factors suggested by Burt (1949) and implied in Piaget's (1953) theory of intellectual development do hold for mathematics, we might restrict the analysis to arithmetic, algebra and geometry separately, as was done in 1956 by Kline, who investigated ability in algebra. He used eighteen algebra tests, including tests of fractions, quadratics, factoring, radicals, exponents, symbolizing and word problems, and twenty reference tests of a psychological and educational kind. He found four marked factors. These he called verbal comprehension, deductive reasoning, algebraic manipulative skill and number ability.

Even when psychological reference test material derived from Piaget's researches (see section 4.2) is incorporated into factor analyses of mathematical ability (Evans, 1965), its sensitivity seems to be obscured by the correlational methods used.

The attempt to analyse mathematical ability in terms of mental factors is a worthwhile exercise in psychology, but what is its value to the teacher of mathematics? It suggests that understanding and progress in mathematics is related to these more or less innate propensities. But the teacher should neither accept too readily these findings nor lean too heavily on the assumption underlying the thinking which promotes these studies. Over emphasis of mental abilities may lead to a relative neglect of the changes possible from good teaching.

The other side of the study of individual differences in mathematics provides evidence of the mean performance and the range of performance of groups of pupils in various branches of mathematics learning and understanding. Saad (1957, 1960) revealed a greater extent of errors and misunderstanding in the arithmetic, algebra and geometry taught in middle grammar-school forms than most teachers would expect. Storer (1956) found similar results when he investigated the errors made by middle grammar-school pupils in algebraic fractions, and demonstrated that they are more extensive than normally assumed by educationists. Many of the errors suggested wrong transfer and generalization on the basis of false analogy and incomplete structuring. Land (1963) revealed a similar weakness in the mathematics attainments of school leavers and in 1956 the Educational Testing Service, Princeton, observed that 'many students who are apparently capable of doing well in mathematics courses fail to do so.'

4.2   Studies of the growth of pupils' thinking

There is no doubt that educational and psychological research into the growth of pupils' thinking, much of it carried out and inspired at Geneva under the direction of Piaget, Inhelder and their co-workers, has the greatest significance for teaching mathematics. This applies both to the studies of children's general intellectual development and logical development, and also to the more specific studies of the growth of number and mathematical concepts. There have been several major publications describing the method, results and underlying thinking in this field, but of particular interest to the teaching of mathematics are Piaget (1950), Piaget (1952), Piaget and Inhelder (1956), Inhelder and Piaget (1958), Piaget, Inhelder and Szeminska (1960) and Piaget and Inhelder (1964). A study of the test situations utilized by the Geneva workers and the reactions of the children which abound in these publications might well be studied by all teachers of mathematics interested in the contributions that psychology might make to their subject.

In the study of children's concepts of number Piaget (1952) first investigates the way in which they arrive at the invariance of wholes and conservation of quality, and then the problem of one-to-one correspondence leading to cardinal and ordinal meanings of number is very carefully probed; finally he studies the way in which children combine classes and numbers additively and multiplicatively. The study of the relationship between class and number is peculiarly appropriate nowadays when the teaching of sets in primary and secondary schools is becoming increasingly widespread.

The study of the child's conception of space (Piaget and Inhelder, 1956) brings out an important sequence in the growth of his spatial ideas which link very closely with basic structures recognized by mathematicians, one of these being topological structure. In their book on the growth of the child's spatial concepts, the authors show that topological space is first appreciated and that projective and Euclidian space only appears later. The authors make use both of haptic* and visual perception and their results have been confirmed by other workers outside Geneva.

The monograph on the growth of the child's conception of geometry (Piaget, Inhelder and Szeminska, 1960) attempts to do for geometrical elements – angles, lines, etc. – what is done in the earlier book for number.

The Growth of Logical Thinking (Inhelder and Piaget, 1958) marks a first serious attack on the nature of intellectual growth during adolescence and, although it is primarily concerned with thinking in the field of science, much of the material does relate to thinking in mathematics, particularly in its emphasis on the importance of structure.

Lastly, of great interest to primary teachers is the more recent publication, *The Early Growth of Logic in the Child* (Piaget and Inhelder, 1964). Here the investigators are concerned with how the child comes to classify and order within the class, and in many ways its findings are very similar to those obtained by Vygotsky (1962). The capacity to group and order the environment in a logical way is something which the child acquires only slowly in the first few years and he demonstrates his difficulties both in arriving at criteria for grouping and also in recognizing the structural properties these criteria possess.

In England, Lovell (1961) carefully repeated many of the earlier experiments on children's concepts of number, material, space and time, and substantially confirmed the broad findings of the Geneva school.

These books offer the reader most valuable information about the empirical side and the sensitive probing which has been carried out at Geneva into thinking related to mathematics, but the books are so numerous and extensive that it is not always easy to get a clear-cut picture of the hypotheses being tested and the theoretical conclusions emerging from the work.

There is one further publication, *Logic and Psychology* (Piaget, 1953), which sets out clearly for the more sophisticated reader most of the main features of

*Haptic perception refers to the recognition of shapes by touch and manipulation only, without the aid of vision.

Piaget's system, but this is not a monograph for those inexpert in his mathematical logic. Piaget gave a first-hand account of his system at two symposia held at Cornell and Berkeley, and fortunately the reports of these symposia have been published as *Piaget Rediscovered* (Ripple and Rockcastle, 1964).

Piaget's four personal papers in the symposia include one on development and learning, which sets out the essence of his entire system, and another on development of mental imagery, which appears to be particularly significant for mathematics since he sees mental imagery as being integrally related to the nature of knowing. Two aspects of knowing are differentiated: the figurative and the operative. The figurative deals essentially with fixed states and the operative with transformations leading from one state to another. The operations involve transformations which are part of a total structure. The third paper, on mother structures and the notions of number, is of central interest to the mathematics teacher. Piaget points out that studying the development of knowledge in children resolves problems inherent in understanding human knowledge, particularly scientific and mathematical knowledge. He reminds his readers that the three mother structures of mathematics distinguished by the Bourbaki group – algebraic structures, relations of order and topological structures – have their counterparts in the evolution of children's thinking. In his fourth paper he is concerned with the relations between the notions of time and speed in children.

Turning back to his first paper on development and learning, I want to summarize what he has to say on the nature of experience. His formulation of this problem is the clearest that has yet been made and unequivocally pinpoints the central problem in the teaching of mathematics. Experience is of two kinds: first, physical, whereby the child learns and constructs the actions and operations by which he organizes his environment. These range from simple counting to grouping, classifying, subdividing, composing and the like, and form the conceptual and operational basis of his interpretation and control of his physical environment. But this is not all there is to experience. The actions and operations by which the child organizes his environment have their own properties. This is called the logico-mathematical aspect of experience and is illustrated by the case of the child who learns that counting a set of objects leads to the same result whether he counts from front to back, back to front, or whatever the configuration in which the objects are arranged. Similarly, the logico-mathematical experience underlying the physical act of grouping and classifying is what we know as the algebra of sets. Yet again we have the difference between the perceptually based concept of the circle and the mathematical properties and theorems which define a circle. Saad (1960) investigated the mathematical understanding of grammar-school pupils from fourteen to sixteen years old and found many instances of describing by a spatial picture instead of by mathematical properties.

Keats's (1955) ingenious experiment to show how far concrete reasoning had to precede formal thought also illustrates the distinction between the act of carrying out a concrete operation and the formal properties of such an act.

Thus he had problems like

$$8 - 7 + 7 = \Box ?$$

which could be solved concretely, by the process of taking 7 from 8 and adding 7, and problems like

$$A - B + B = \Box ?$$

which can only be solved by recourse to the principles of inversion and reciprocity. Of course a child may solve $8 - 7 + 7$ formally by reference to these principles, but $A - B + B$ and $A \circ B \times B$, where $\circ$ is an operation and $\times$ is its inverse, cannot be solved concretely.

Similarly he had concrete inequalities such as:

(a) Harry runs faster than Jim.
     Harry runs slower than Sam.
Now underline the correct answers:
Jim runs faster than Harry.   (right, wrong, can't say)
Sam runs faster than Jim.   (right, wrong, can't say)

(b) L, H and E are boys.
     $\circ$ means taller than, faster than, darker than;
     $\times$ is its opposite.
     L $\circ$ H
     L $\times$ E
Now underline the correct answers:
H $\circ$ L   (right, wrong, can't say)
E $\times$ H   (right, wrong, can't say).

Whether Keats's pupils solved the 'concrete' problems in numerals, actual names and concrete operations by a concrete process or a formal one is immaterial to the point being made here. This is that the actual operation of adding, subtracting and comparing have properties which include those of inversion and reciprocity.

In essence mathematics concerns the properties of the operations by which the individual orders, organizes and investigates his environment. These properties constitute logical and mathematical structure.

The distinction between physical and logico-mathematical experiences, differentiating between actions and operations on the one hand, and their properties, logical and mathematical on the other, seems to lie at the root of the precepts advocated by several contemporary experimenters in the teaching of mathematics, although in fact they may not use the same names to describe the distinction.

Thus Skemp (1961) made an attempt to extend what Piaget did for the study of children's number awareness to their mathematical thinking. Skemp begins by assuming that concept and operation are the basic ingredients of mathematical thought and then distinguishes between concept formation and the use of operation on the one side (physical experience?) and their manipulation reflectively on the other (a knowledge of the properties of the concepts and operations?). This latter he called reflective activity and regarded it as the essential feature of mathematical learning and thinking. He then devised tests of concept formation and in the case of operations with those of combining and reversing. The test material consisted of shapes, patterns and two-dimensional geometrical figures and his pupils ranged from fourteen to fifteen years of age. He correlated the scores in the different tests with performance by the pupils on a GCE mathematics test. His hypothesis postulated that reflective activity is as essential for mathematics as classifying activity is for arithmetic. The results showed a clearly more significant correlation between mathematics and the reflective scores than between mathematics and the scores on the formation and use of concepts.

The parallel between this thinking and that exemplified in the instance quoted from Keats seems apparent. One may debate as to how far Skemp's test for reflective activity, which in the case of concepts involved merely finding double-attribute concepts, as for example in identifying the property of triangles with curved sides from an array of figures with three, four or five sides, some of which had curved and some straight sides, is in fact different from that used for simple classification, wher a one-attribute concept was used, as in curvilinearity as against rectilinearity.

Both writers show that the earlier concrete, physical experience must be developed before one can move on to the second experience, that of logico-mathematics, which is concerned with the properties of the criteria of the first experience. The point is that, unless there is experience in existence, any attempt to describe its properties is going to be rather arid and fruitless.

The work of Dienes is also based on this principle, as is shown clearly in his monograph, *Concept Formation and Personality* (Dienes, 1959). Here he attempted to determine the psycho-dynamics of the process of concept formation and to discover in what ways the ability to form abstract concepts connected with other aspects of the personality. He worked with ten-year-old children and devised two ingenious tasks from which he was able to trace and score how the children formed mathematical concepts (using apparatus). The first task involved arriving at concepts of: elements of a group, product of elements, identical and different elements, and transformation of one identity to another. The second involved the 'inequality of integers' in a binary choice system.

His major hypothesis is that concept formation by different individuals depends on their powers of insight. Insight is used in the sense described by the Gestalt psychologists and refers to the discovery of essential structures as set out by Wertheimer in 1945:

(a) the speed with which successive insights tend to be made;

(b) the emotional intensity of the insights;

(c) the number of separate insights, or the existence of or lack of connexions between different insights.

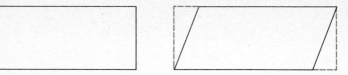

Figure 32 The area of a parallelogram is found by relating it to the area of a rectangle

What Wertheimer meant by structure is well thought out in the following instance.

After children learned to find the area of a parallelogram, beginning with the rectangle (Figure 32), Wertheimer discovered that 'it does happen that, having found or having been shown how to get the area of the parallelogram, children who are asked to find the area of the trapezoid, or of any of the following figures, are not at all helpless, but after some deliberation, sometimes with a little help, produce fine, genuine solutions of the kind that follow.'

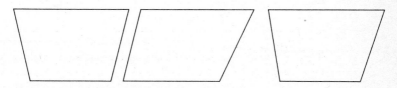

Figure 33 Trapezoids whose areas are to be found

In all the cases illustrated in Figure 33 it is possible to solve the problem by changing the figures sensibly (A-responses) or to apply the learnt operations, or some of them, blindly and unsuccessfully (B-responses).

A-responses are shown in Figure 34. The subjects change the figures into rectangles by shifting the triangles. They will not give B-responses (Figure 35).

Dienes was also able to separate formal analytical from constructive judgements. Girls were found to be more constructive, boys more analytical.

This material requiring intellectual action was correlated with various personality assessments in order to attempt to answer the second part of the task undertaken in the research. The connexion between intellectual activity and emotional drive was found to be more intimate in the case of boys.

Not the least value of the research is the insight Dienes provides for us about the pupil's capacity to understand novel ideas – and the path he opened up for modelling, teaching and testing these concepts. What Dienes appears to be doing here, and in his later applications to the actual teaching of mathematics (Dienes, 1960; Land, 1963, pp. 49–57), is to model the properties of the actions and operations as well as to build up these actions, operations and concepts in a concrete way. Thus he not only forms the concepts and operations

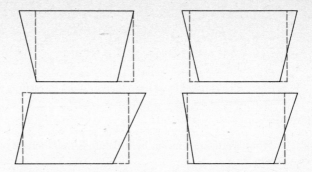

Figure 34 A-responses: the shapes are altered to produce rectangles of equal area, by adding and taking away triangles of equal area

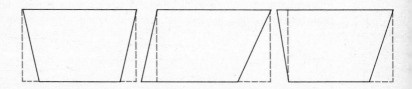

Figure 35 B-responses: the blind and unsuccessful application of a learnt rule

concretely but also models their logico-mathematical properties in various ways so as to arrive at true mathematical experience. Others have brought out these same differences between physical experience and logico-mathematical experience in other fields of thinking and also in studies of more advanced mathematics.

In American circles the work of Bruner (1961) (see also Morrisett and Vinsonhaler, 1965, and NSSE, 1964, ch. 13) lies nearest to the thinking of Piaget and his colleagues, and of Dienes. Bruner is essentially concerned with improving the quality of the mathematical thinking of pupils and, like the other developmentalists, insists that mathematical processes should be discovered through concrete experience in the earlier stages of learning Wong (1965) is making similar attacks on the problems of mathematics teaching in Malaya.

Peel (1960, pp. 72–4) compared the ways in which a group of young adolescents aged from eleven to thirteen years learnt and operated a new number system (to base six) with the methods used by adults. The results support the findings of Keats and Skemp. Many of the schoolchildren were able to apply the new number system successfully merely 'by first translating into the decimal system, obtaining the answer in this system and then retranslating by means of the key which they extended to meet their requirements'. Many adults, on the other hand, are able to 'think' in the new system, being able to generalize the essential relationships, and then combine them and reverse them (reflectively as Skemp would say), showing a grasp of the logico-mathematical properties of the relative steps. Peel's (1960, p. 100) code experiment demonstrated a similar difference between children in the age range from nine to thirteen years and seventeen or eighteen year olds.

In all these researches the change-over from concrete to logico-mathematical experience seems to take place during the period between eleven and fourteen years of age, the exact age of the transition depending partly upon the difficulty of the concept: eleven or twelve for spatial material, thirteen for symbolic and verbal, and even older for such ideas as momentum, limits and infinity.

There have not been many studies of the growth of thinking in coordinate geometry and calculus, but a useful exception is the research by Reynolds (1961). He prepared questionnaires on some items in coordinate geometry, algebraic formulae, equations and identities, limits and infinity to be answered by pupils in first, third, fifth and sixth forms of five schools. The aim was to discover the way in which the children's concepts of these topics developed.

At different stages, restricted or vague ideas are revealed on the conception of the distance of a point from a line, the basic ideas of coordinates and axes, the significance of the graph of an equation, and on variables. In formulae there is great difficulty in expressing ideas in symbols, a limited idea of area and perimeter, and confusion on the features distinguishing equations, identities and formulae. The younger children show some general appreciation of large finite numbers and of non-ending processes, but in the latter there were contradictions and impasses. The older children have broader ideas on limits, infinity and comparisons of infinite quantities, but it is only in the sixth form that non-ending processes are constructed to deal with

$$\lim_{x \to 0} \frac{1}{x}.$$

From the analysis of the results, different emphases and approaches are given for teaching coordinate geometry and formulae. They are based on the provision of a variety of experience in a concept, before formal work, and on linking closely the growth in symbols with the growth in ideas. It is intended that the understanding of concepts shall be present before skilled manipulation be done. A plea is made for the specific teaching of ideas in limits and infinity, and suggestions for their teaching are given. All the topics dealt with are brought together in an approach to the calculus.

4.3 Concept formation, productive thinking and problem solving

The difficulties inherent in forming mathematical concepts find their parallel in other subjects and in the simplified experiments carried out in psychological laboratories.

The three aspects of a concept, its extension, its intensive property and its name or symbol, present problems in learning mathematics.

The act of classifying lies at the basis of concept formation. Thus the grouping together of coins, counters and discs of all kinds constitutes the extensive aspect of a concept, and the explicit formulation of the property common to all the objects in this class makes up its intensive aspect. As Saad (1960) has shown, this latter can range widely in secondary-school children from the property of being 'round' to the articulate geometrical formulation of 'a path in a plane which is always the same distance from a fixed point in the same plane'.

It is quite common to find, even with adults, that people may discover the extensive part of a concept before they are able to formulate the rule or intensive property which characterizes the extension. This may be demonstrated by the Vygotsky (1962) block test, which consists of twenty-two blocks varying in colour, shape, height and size, there being five colours, six shapes, two heights and two sizes. On the bottom of each block, not seen by the subject, are printed one of four nonsense syllables 'lag', 'bik', 'mur', 'cev', these being apportioned as follows:

'lag' on all tall large figures,
'bik' on all flat large figures,
'mur' on all tall small figures,
'cev' on all flat small figures.

The game consists of the experimenter turning up a block and asking the subject to put together all those blocks he thinks will have the same 'name'. When he has done this the experimenter then turns up one of his wrong choices and asks him to try again. Then he turns up another 'wrong' choice and so on.

The upturned blocks remain with their names showing. Eventually the subject should finish up with four piles classified by the twofold categories listed.

A common result of the experiment is to find that the person tested has been able to form the four groups but is not immediately able to say what is the exact basis of the grouping.

The test reveals in young children that the power to classify logically does not come into being ready made. It is preceded by grouping first in heaps, the basis of whose selection is highly subjective and even representational, and then into complexes, based on concrete and factual criteria, as by using colour in spite of the different names, and by making half-objects. The criteria of action for logical classification only appears later.

There is a rough parallel between the extensive and intensive aspects of a concept and the ideas of generalization and abstraction. When we talk about generalization, whether in science, mathematics or in the humanities, we are in fact thinking of the widening of the extensive part of the concept to include new cases etc. This may in turn have an effect on the intensive aspect or rule.

In one sense this rule has been abstracted and hence we may think of the intensive element as being equivalent to abstraction. But abstraction is used in other senses by the mathematician. One such meaning is as follows: generalization carries with it the idea of logical inclusion (of sets within sets etc.), whereas abstraction implies the logical membership relation. Yet again many people use the two terms of generalization and abstraction as being interchangeable.

The third element of a concept, its name or symbol, produces many deep-seated problems in the learning of mathematics. Dienes reminds us firmly of the tendency in the young learner to detach the symbol too readily from what it symbolizes and the subsequent tendency to concentrate too much on symbol manipulation. Teachers and textbooks in mathematics very often contribute to this same process of separation of the symbol from the concept it symbolizes. It should be noted that the choice of a symbol is often quite arbitrary and that this also makes for separation.

Concepts have been described as the organizers of experience. They are first formed and then they are utilized to guide explanation, inquiry, productive thinking and problem solving in situations which arise independently of those leading to the formation of the concepts. The formation and utilization of concepts are not always clearly separable, but in the main, in explanatory thinking, productive thinking and problem solving, it is the *use* of concepts which is most important.

Keeping the distinction in mind between formation and use, let us now turn to study creative thinking and problem solving. In his discussion of productive thinking, Peel (1960, ch. 7) describes and evaluates the research carried out by Wertheimer, by Duncker (1945) and by Luchins (1942).

Wertheimer used exclusively mathematical problems such as finding the areas of geometrical figures and summing progressions, and in teaching these made full use of the ideas generated by the pupils whom he prompted and probed in order to discover the way in which they arrived at mathematical structures significant to them. As a result he made the idea of structure an essential part of his exploration of thinking. Thinking consists of 'envisaging, realizing structural features and structural requirements; proceeding in accordance with and determined by these requirements; thereby changing the situation in the direction of structural improvements, which involves: that gaps, trouble regions, disturbances, superficialities, etc., be viewed and dealt with structurally'.

Similar research intended to test the relative efficiency of the analytical and intuitive approaches to problem solving were reported from Florence by Marzi (1962). This work stems from the experiments of Bartlett (1958). The constructive–intuitive method leaves jumps, whereas the analytical one 'makes use of disjunctions, conjunctions, associations and successive efforts as the necessary "steps" towards the same and only solution of the problem'. The results enabled the investigators to discuss the following points:

How is previous knowledge used?

The importance of conventional procedures.

The detection of a mistake does not automatically imply that it will be corrected.

The importance of the concepts of 'key-move'. (See the note (p. 159) on Wertheimer's trapezoid problem. There the key move was the recognition of the addition and subtraction of *equal* areas.)

How are intuitive 'jumps' made possible?

Where does the analytical process lead?

Duncker's (1945) well-known research on problem solving revealed two extremes in problem solvers: those who used mechanical methods and those who reached a solution organically. In the first, a less pertinent type of heuristic is used than in the second, where the end point guides the solver to rephrase the problem successively in an 'organic' way. By the first type of heuristic the pupil places the problem in a 'field' of possible theorems and tries these out in a too general and relatively purposeless way. Peel (1960, pp. 158–65) gives several examples from science and mathematics illustrating the differences between organic and mechanical solutions. In an organic solution the thinker begins from the original problem and successively restates it by asking what it means and what is necessary. Each successive restatement is more precise in terms of the data available and takes the thinker to a final solution. Mechanical solutions, on the other hand, begin by asking what is given and then by casting about for theorems which might apply (Duncker, 1945, p. 45).

It is often difficult to distinguish between organic and mechanical thinking, since both usually lead to the same result. But it is possible sometimes to set up a problem in which mechanical thinking leads to a wrong solution.

Here is an instance from arithmetic (Peel, 1960, pp. 163–4):

I go for a car ride travelling one hour at 40 m.p.h. and for the next hour at 30 m.p.h. What is my average speed over the journey?

Usually we get the mere working

$$\frac{30+40}{2} = 35 \text{ m.p.h.,}$$

although we suspect a mechanical answer and we cannot distinguish between organic and mechanical working out. There is a significant omission of any reference to the real meaning of speed and in particular average speed, as being equal ultimately to total distance divided by total time. The above answer represents a mechanical transfer of the use of averages without asking what averaging speeds involves.

However, if we change the problem slightly we can contrive that a mechanical solution gives a wrong answer! This is how it is done. Let the problem now read:

I go for a car ride travelling outwards for 120 miles at 40 m.p.h. and then back by the same route at 30 m.p.h. What is my average speed over the journey?

The mechanical reply by taking over the idea of averaging without any real insight into the limiting restrictions imposed by averaging 'speeds' is as follows:

$$\frac{40+30}{2} = 35 \text{ m.p.h.,}$$

which is wrong!

The organic solution would go something like this:

My time outwards is $\frac{120}{40} = 3$ hours.

My time homewards is $\frac{120}{30} = 4$ hours.

My average speed over the whole journey means the same thing as

$$\frac{\text{My total mileage}}{\text{My total time}} = \frac{240}{7} = 34\tfrac{2}{7} \text{ m.p.h.}$$

The problem of the effect of familiarity–unfamiliarity on problem solving was taken up afresh by Hindam (1960) by extending the concept of familiarity far beyond its usually accepted meaning (Sutherland, 1941) relating to vocabulary and content, to include 'method, steps, sequence of elements, relevance of materials, use of "key" words, use of diagrams and so on'. Tests of significance showed marked differences in favour of familiar material. Examples used by Hindam include the following:

Familiar
When birds migrate they fly at a faster speed than in ordinary flight. The ratio of the migration speed to the ordinary speed of a swallow is about 6/5. If the migration speed is 30 m.p.h., find the ordinary speed.

Unfamiliar
In the triangle ABC the ratio of the sides AB, BC is 6/5. If AB = 30 inches, find BC.

A cake was cut into four pieces. Mother had $\frac{1}{2}$, Patricia $\frac{1}{8}$, John had half as much as his mother and father had the rest. How much did father have?

A Tiger Lillet cocktail is made from four ingredients: $\frac{1}{2}$ Van der Hum, $\frac{1}{8}$ dry vermouth, half as much maraschino as Van der Hum and the rest is Lillet. How much is Lillet?

The role of familiarity was investigated further by giving pupils problems in certain specific fields such as money and travel. One group of children was prepared by a talk on money, currency and exchange followed by exercises. It performed significantly better in a money-problem test than a control group which had had exercises only (Peel, 1960, pp. 166–8).

At this point the distinction between problems and exercises needs to be made (Peel, 1960, pp. 169–70). It is a distinction not always clear to the young teacher. A problem arises in a situation when the person having to respond has no ready-made response available. On the other hand, exercises are set to promote and test a habitual response it is desired to reinforce. The trouble is that the 'mechanical' way of attempting to solve problems tends to make them

don't use
exercises or
let problems be
too much of the same
thing

degenerate into mere exercises. This tendency is particularly encouraged if the series of problems is too narrowly devised. They lose their quality as problems and become a series of exercises. The thinker becomes 'set' in his way of thinking and mode of response. Luchins investigated this problem by inducing a 'set' in arithmetic problems involving the transfer of liquid between water jars of different capacity. He then interposed problems which could be solved more satisfactorily by other routines and found that the 'set' prevented this alternative thinking. As Peel (1960) writes:

In problem solving the pupil needs to be free from 'set' to consider the problem in its own terms. Exercises in textbooks may, unless they are varied, induce restrictive sets which will prohibit the organic thinking so desirable in genuine productive thinking. On the other hand, the thinker cannot proceed from nothing. Some learned or previously experienced facilitation must form part of problem solving. The teacher's task is to maintain the equilibrium between problems and exercises (pp. 170–71).

We need to extend this type of inquiry to the experimental study of development in problem solving and mathematical thinking at the later adolescent level in the branches of algebra and geometry, relating this to theories of concept formation and apprehension. At present it seems as if Piaget's concepts of operation and operational structures give a better insight into the way of mathematical higher-level thinking than the 'organic' explanation of the Gestalt school. The latter does not appear to be sensitive enough. We therefore need more analyses along Piagetian lines of such situations in mathematics as utilized by Wertheimer and Duncker.

Related recommendations have been recently advocated by Crutchfield and Covington (1963) as a result of their attempts to teach problem solving. Using programmed-learning techniques they presented thirteen lessons in which aspects of thinking, problem solving and crime detection were involved. In their own words:

Inasmuch as our aim was to train for a *generalized* problem-solving skill, the problems did not pertain to specific curricular content, but dealt rather with a variety of mysteries and puzzling occurrences, such as the theft of a statue from a museum, and a case of strange goings-on in a deserted house.

Each lesson posed a single mystery problem which the child was to solve. The lesson was constructed so that each child, by being given successively more clues and information, was finally led to discover the solution for himself. At various points in the story the child was required to restate the problem in his own words, formulate his own questions, and generate ideas to explain the mystery. Immediate feedback was given to his responses in the form of examples of other ideas or questions that he might have thought of in the given situation. These examples were primarily ones which fifth-graders would find novel and uncommon, and which would open new lines of investigation or new ways of viewing the problem.

It was assumed that presenting numerous examples of this type would tend to broaden the child's limits of acceptance as to what constitutes important questions and fruitful ideas.

Each lesson was part of a continuous theme and required forty-five minutes.

The children were then given the Duncker X-ray problem* with other problems, and it was found that of ninety-eight children taking the auto-instructional programme, 35 per cent solved the X-ray problem, whereas, among a matched control of ninety-seven children not so instructed, only 13 per cent were able to solve the problem.

Among the general properties of thinking worked into the programme by Crutchfield and Covington were the following:

(a) the necessity of identifying and defining the problem appropriately;
(b) the importance of asking questions and of taking time for reflection rather than leaping to conclusions;
(c) looking closely at details, looking for discrepancies;
(d) the necessity of generating many ideas;
(e) the necessity of looking everywhere for clues;
(f) not being afraid to come up with silly ideas.

4.4   Learning mathematics

Whereas the research discussed in sections 4.2 and 4.3 on the development of children's mathematical thinking is comfortingly close to what the mathematician or teacher of mathematics experiences, this new field is bewilderingly diverse, stemming not from a few simple basic observations about the structure of thought but from the minute and varied unit of behaviour we symbolize as the stimulus–response.

Any situation, as for example in the exercise: 'Simplify $a+4a-2b+b$', acts as a stimulus to which the learner responds by providing the answer. The whole happening may be regarded as a unit of behaviour. More is involved, however, than just the stimulus S and the response R. Intervening is the previous learning, experience, attitudes, insights, mental structure, schemata, etc. So we have

$$S\longrightarrow \left\{ \begin{array}{l} \text{insight} \\ \text{attitudes} \\ \text{learning} \\ \text{structure} \end{array} \right\} \longrightarrow R.$$

This research starts from a study of behaviour, of the analysis of the behaviour observable when a person learns a piece of mathematics or solves a problem. Such an approach to the teaching of mathematics expresses a deep-seated philosophy in American psychological circles, that everything is teachable provided we can make a satisfactory breakdown of the units and grade the stages appropriately. Furthermore it is not restricted to simple response learning. The ideas are extended to concept formation (see p. 163) to

*Given X-rays which at sufficient intensity will destroy cancerous tissue, but also healthy tissue as well, how would you arrange for the destruction by radiation of an *inoperable* stomach tumour without destroying the healthy tissue which surrounds it?

cover all aspects of mathematical learning and thinking. The range of this activity can be gathered by glancing at the 1964 Yearbook of the National Society for the Study of Education entitled *Theories of Learning and Instruction* (NSSE, 1964).

The interest in behavioural analysis has found its most explicit and forceful form in the large amount of work carried out on programmed learning. There are in fact more programmes in mathematics than in any other subject (NCPL, 1965). Furthermore, most of these programmes are American in origin. Detailed current accounts of the progress made in programmed instruction in mathematics are available in Glaser (1965) and the chapter written by Evans on 'Programming in mathematics and logic' gives the interested person all that he needs in this field.

It is beyond the scope of this outline of educational and psychological research relevant to the teaching of mathematics to go into detail about programmed learning, and the reader is referred to a short standard text by Leith, Peel and Curr (1964) for descriptive and critical comment on this mode of learning. What may be said, however, is that good programmed learning is constructive learning. The programmer endeavours to put the learner in a problem-solving situation. 'Some instruction in the defining of terms and conventions may be necessary but apart from this the frames should promote constructive thinking by calling for problem-solving responses.' Mathematics lends itself to this idea of progress by constructive thinking on the part of the learner. It is logically coherent and a programme can be very delicately planned.

As to the two main modes of programming, linear or branching, the former is generally to be recommended for beginners, less able learners and where the field is entirely novel, but the latter better serves the interests and progress of the mature learner working at a more sophisticated level.

It is extremely difficult to know what to select for the mathematician from this detailed and piecemeal attack on mathematics learning. Much research on programmed learning inquires into the effects of organizing the programme in different ways, dealing with change of format, feedback of information, sequencing items, size of steps, mode of response, etc. Perhaps the greatest value to the mathematics teacher is that constructing a programme and at the same time observing the best experimental conditions brings home to him the need for accounting for every step in an ordinary piece of mathematics teaching and learning.

A noteworthy instance of the application of the method of programmed learning to the analysis of mathematical learning is that of Gagné and Paradise (1961) who extended the idea of the 'learning set' to the solving of simple linear equations in algebra (see also Morrisett and Vinsonhaler, 1965). It has long been known that learning a series of similar but not identical tasks brings about more than the acquisition of so many discrete skills. The learner acquires in addition a generalized readiness to learn similar and even different but related material. We say that the learning has generalized to produce a 'set' for learning related and more general tasks. Gagné started by analysing the steps required to solve a simple algebraic equation in one unknown, working right back from the final step to the beginnings of the process, asking the question, 'What would the individual have to know in order to be able to perform the new task, being given only instructions?'

Thus at some stage in solving linear equations he would have to collect terms, he would have to add similars, he would have to transpose, etc.

Gagné built up a programme in which each of the sets in the hierarchy leading to final solution was taught and he then asked himself the question how far learning a lower-order set made for improved learning of a higher-order one. He found in fact that his hypotheses were confirmed, that the lower supporting set was required to be mastered before the next one could be achieved. As a piece of psychological thinking and experimentation, the work of Gagné and his associates is a noteworthy advance, but experienced mathematics teachers may feel that this analysis is one that they carry out in any case and is an essential part of the process which requires little demonstrating.

An important question on learning sets is how deep or broad the learning should be. Leith and Clark investigated the learning of differently based number systems. They took three experimental groups. Group A learned in four systems to bases five, seven, eight and nine, group B in two systems only to bases seven and eight, and group C took learning only in the base eight system. Group A took each of the four programmes once, group B took each of its two programmes twice and group C took its base-eight programme four times, thus giving in all the same amount of learning for each group. They were tested on their ability to add and subtract in a base-six number system. The research workers found that group B was slightly better than group A, and group C was significantly lower than both.

The problem of learning by discovery has been highlighted by the behavioural approach to learning, and in America one finds two clearly defined groups of protagonists and antagonists. Thus Beberman (University of Illinois Committee on School Mathematics) and Kersch and Bruner are strongly in favour of discovery methods, whereas Ausubel and Suppes hold the opposite point of view, which depends more upon statement and instruction by the teacher and application by the pupil.

One difficulty is that it is hard to say what discovery is, and what it achieves. Kersch claims that it leads to better understanding, that it enables the learner better to extend his learning for discovering new principles and applications and, thirdly, that it promotes interest.

Experiment might help to resolve the question and the over-all picture is that an intermediate method, called guided discovery, seems to lead to optimum results. Thus Gagné and Brown (1961), in teaching conceptual learning, devised three types of learning programme where (a) the rule was stated first and then a linear programme brought about identification and application of the rule, (b) the rule had to be discovered by the learner from instances and (c) a programme of guided discovery was used in which instances were worked with guidance for particular cases and the learner extended the rule to other cases. Guided discovery was found to be best, followed by discovery and followed lastly by rule and example. Similar results have been obtained by other workers in the field of elementary mathematics.

Suppes, a leading teacher of mathematics, is also one of the most convinced behaviourists. He has published several papers and monographs setting out the possibilities of the behaviourist model for mathematical learning and the foundation of mathematical concepts (Morrisett and Vinsonhaler, 1965) but his instances of mathematics learning are very simple. (The work is fully described in various technical reports nos. 80–90 issued between 1964 and 1966 by the Institute of Mathematical Studies in the Social Sciences, Stanford University.)

He has also pioneered the teaching of mathematical logic and set concepts to younger children. His results indicate that symbolic logic, if not too abstractly presented, is not too abstruse for elementary-school children of the age range from ten to twelve and that this age might represent the most propitious time for introducing formal and propositional logic. His experiment on teaching the concept of sets has led him to conclude that the notions of set and set operations are more easily comprehended than those of number.

4.5   Curricular studies

Various studies of the curriculum and suggestions for bringing it up to date reflect the findings of educational psychology and educational research to some extent. These studies are strictly not research investigations since there is no proper control, but none the less the ideas and content and methods of teaching are tried out in the school setting and the modifications made to the various curricula spring from this classroom experience. Of British writing, Fletcher (1964) shows the strongest influence of psychological studies in children's thinking, particularly of those stemming from Piaget. This book, written by a group of leading mathematics teachers, states that they are concerned 'with new mathematics, new ways with old mathematics, contemporary applications of the subject, and the psychology of teaching it' (p. 2).

They begin by pointing out that mathematics does not start from the finished theorem, it starts from situations, and this is their first condition. There must be a period of discovery, creation, even discarding and accepting. Next follows the phase of abstraction, starting with the concrete situation, recognizing corresponding structures and using one structure to solve problems presented by the other. They point out the similarity between their emphasis on mathematical structure and the corresponding emphasis placed by Piaget on the structure of children's thinking. They are critical of learning mathematical tricks and their introduction shows how closely their thinking lines up with that of Dienes and with Piaget's idea of logico-mathematical experience. This book is written by teachers of mathematics who would not make any claims to be educational psychologists.

On the other hand, *New Approaches to Mathematics Teaching* (Land, 1963) is written by a group of people who are primarily educationists, at the same time most of them being mathematicians. The book is scarcely concerned with details of mathematical curricula, but more with putting the points of view and research findings of the group of authors who include Skemp, Dienes, Land and Wrigley. Many of the psychological ideas have already been discussed in sections 4.2 and 4.3 and the point of mentioning this book at this stage is to show how close the thinking of educational psychologists and mathematicians is on the need for a reform both of the mathematics curriculum and methods of teaching it.

4.6 Summary

Five fields of psychological and educational research and thinking have been outlined by reference to the more outstanding work.

Of the first four fields discussed, the contribution from those working on problems of the growth of thinking is by far the most significant. Studies of concept formation, productive thinking and problem solving have the next most to offer. A fusion of these two approaches would seem to hold most promise for future research. Learning research based on variants of the stimulus–response paradigm is beginning to attack school mathematics learning problems, but has yet far to go to be of substantial help in the classroom situation. The long-established tradition of research into mental abilities seems to offer the least, especially if the mathematician is expecting help in specific problems.

The last field of curriculum study is one in which professional mathematicians have played the major role, even when they have been concerned with the need for child-centred approaches. They confirm the need for taking account of what is known about the growth of pupil's thinking.

References

BARTLETT, F. C. (1958), *Thinking*, Allen & Unwin.
   Bartlett puts some interesting views about the qualities of different kinds of thinking such as scientific thinking, and supports them by experimental evidence. He seems to equate constructive thinking with adventurous thinking.
BRUNER, J. S. (1961), 'The act of discovery', *Harvard Educational Review*, vol. 31, no. 1.
BURT, C. L. (1949), 'The structure of the mind: a review of the results of factor analysis', *British Journal of Educational Psychology*, pp. 110–11, 176–99.
   The two parts to this contribution consist of a review of the results of factor analysis discussed in terms of Burt's theory of hierarchical structure of ability, beginning at the lowest level with simple sensation and movement, and rising through perception, association (memory), relation finding to general intellectual capacity. The interpretation is of interest in connexion with Jenkins (1939), Lee (1955), Saad (1957) and Vernon (1950).

CRUTCHFIELD, R. S., and COVINGTON (1963), lInstruction in problem solving', *American Association for the Advancement of Science Bulletin.*

DIENES, Z. P. (1959), *Concept Formation and Personality,* Leicester University Press.

A research monograph in which the author attempts to expose the psychodynamics of concept formation and to link the capacity to form concepts with orectic aspects of the personality. Ingenious tasks are devised to measure the pupil's efficiency at forming concepts. Dienes is able also to separate analytic from constructive judgements. The research is strong on the cognitive side, but the correlations between cognition and the orectic aspects are not noteworthy.

DIENES, Z. P. (1960), *Building up Mathematics,* Hutchinson.

DUNCKER, K. (1945), *On Problem Solving,* Psychological Monograph, vol. 58, no. 15, American Psychological Association.

Duncker's monograph bears on modern preoccupation with the question of heuristics in problem solving. He divides these heuristics into two extremes, mechanical and organic, but in terms of modern heuristic theory there is no essential difference between these extremes. The first is not so controlled nor solution directed, whereas in the second the solver tends to work in an organic way from the required solution. There is, however, no doubt about the difference between these two extremes in a practical sense, the second marking the problem solver who 'knows what he is about'.

EVANS, G. T. (1965), 'Growth of mathematical ability in adolescence', Ph.D. thesis, University of Queensland.

A study of high-school mathematical ability in which the author uses several reference tests incorporating some of Piaget's ideas, noticeably on the nature of formal thinking and the INRC structure. He also adopted some of Keats's tests and notions and applied Hamley's principles as well. There are some twenty reference tests in all applied with tests of achievement in secondary-school mathematics. Although the battery of reference tests was well conceived and constructed – the tests incorporating ideas which had been successfully verified in other settings – the factor analysis yielded rather disappointing results from the mathematical point of view. Evans failed to demonstrate the presence of the finer structural elements suggested by the earlier workers.

FLETCHER, T. J. (ed.) (1964), *Some Lessons in Mathematics,* Cambridge University Press.

A most helpful book on the teaching of modern mathematics, incorporating sections of binary systems, finite arithmetic and groups, numerical methods and flow charts, sets, logic and Boolean algebra, relations and graphs, linear programming, convexity, geometry, vectors and matrices. Its material presents an excellent combination of the use of concrete instances, charts and diagrams with a close attention to the fundamentals of mathematical structure. It is both a teachers' and a pupils' book. As the latter it is perhaps short in exercises. The authors include members of the Association of Teachers of Mathematics.

GAGNÉ, R. M., and BROWN, L. T. (1961), 'Some factors in the programming of conceptual learning', *Journal of Experimental Psychology,* vol. 62, pp. 313–21.

A comparison of discovery and directed learning methods.

GAGNÉ, R. M., and PARADISE, N. E. I. (1961), 'Abilities and learning sets in knowledge acquisition', *Psychological Monographs,* vol. 75, no. 14 (whole no. 518).

GLASER, R. (ed.) (1965), *Teaching Machines and Programmed Learning, vol. 2 Data and Directions,* Audio-Visual Instruction Department, National Education Association.

The chapter written by Evans, entitled 'Programming in mathematics and logic', gives a full account to date of what has been achieved in attempts to programme mathematics learning.

HINDAM, Y. H. (1960), 'The effect of familiar and unfamiliar settings on problem solving in mathematics', unpublished Ph.D. thesis, University of Birmingham.

A very comprehensive attack upon the effect of familiarity and unfamiliarity on the power to solve problems. Familiarity is taken to include not only familiarity of content and vocabulary, but also method, number of steps, relevance of material, sequence and use of diagrams. The superiority in solving problems where these various factors are present is clearly demonstrated. The fields of mathematics study are grammar-school arithmetic, algebra and geometry.

INHELDER, B., and PIAGET, J. (1958), *The Growth of Logical Thinking,* Routledge & Kegan Paul.

The first comprehensive study of the adolescent's thinking. Each chapter is given over to some aspect, investigated by setting the pupils a simple science experiment. The operations and the structure of adolescent thought are revealed. The work as a whole is perhaps of greater interest to the science teacher but there is much – particularly in the discussion of structure and hypothetico-deductive reasoning – that is significant in mathematics.

JENKINS, J. W. (1939), 'An analysis of factors entering into the results of tests based upon logical principles of mathematics', Ph.D. thesis, University of London.

KEATS, J. A. (1955), *Formal and Concrete Thought Processes,* Princeton: Educational Testing Service.

This study carried out at the Educational Testing Service, Princeton, is an ingenious effort to discover how far the concrete thinking has to precede formal thought in the field of mathematical reasoning. Keats used tests of arithmetic and algebra, including combination and dissociation of number, probabilities and inequalities. His work is particularly significant with regard to the use of the principles of inversion and reciprocity in generalized number and elementary algebra. He showed that concrete thought precedes a formal reasoning and that the change-over was very marked round twelve or thirteen years of age with the tests used.

LAND, F. W. (ed.) (1963), *New Approaches to Mathematics Teaching,* Macmillan.

A collection of papers by educationalists most of whom are interested both in mathematics and psychology. The papers put contemporary views and discuss the implications of research findings for mathematics teachers. The authors include Land, Wrigley, Dienes, Skemp and Sawyer.

LEE, D. M. (1955), 'A study of specific ability and attainment in mathematics', *British Journal of Educational Psychology,* vol. 25, pp. 178–81.

Jenkins (1939) and this work refer to factorial analyses of the results of mathematical tests and related ability tests. Both make use of the idea that mathematics is based on the concepts of class, variable, order and correlated orders within difference classes.

LEITH, G. O. M., PEEL, E. A., and CURR, W. (1964), *A Handbook of Programmed Learning, Educational Review* Occasional Publication no. 1, University of Birmingham School of Education.

A concise comment upon, and account of, programmed learning. Curr evaluates education without teachers. Peel outlines and discusses the learning principles involved in linear and branched programmes. Leith describes the writing of programmes, outlines research findings and finally sets out criteria by which a programme should be judged. There are several appendixes including an annotated bibliography and a selected list of programmes.

LOVELL, K. (1961), *The Growth of Basic Mathematical and Scientific Concepts in Children,* London University Press.

A publication setting out the re-exploration, with statistically significant groups, of many of the initial probes and theories of the Geneva school on the growth of the child's capacity to conserve number, substance, weight, time, space, length, area and volume. It re-affirms the broad theory offered by Piaget, Inhelder and their co-workers, but in detail has innovations and elaborations to offer, particularly with reference to some of the geometrical concepts. It does not offer anything startlingly fresh (beyond Piaget) but provides a much-needed confirmation of earlier ideas.

LUCHINS, A. S. (1942), 'Mechanization in problem solving', *Psychological Monograph,* vol. 54, no. 6.

This monograph is very relevant to any study of the relationship between problems and exercises. It demonstrates how difficult it is to prevent a regular series of problems degenerating into exercises. It links with Duncker (1945) in that it is also describing heuristics and the way in which they change. The material includes a well-used type of arithmetical problem and the study as a whole is relevant when one considers the uses of exercises and problems in textbooks. It is also useful in connexion with ideas about programmed learning in mathematics.

MARZI, A. (1962), 'Mathematical learning', unpublished research at the Institute of Psychology, University of Florence.

MORRISETT, L. N., and VINSONHALER, J. (eds.) (1965), 'Mathematical learning', *Society for Research in Child Development. Monograph,* vol. 30, no. 1 (serial no. 99).

This report of a conference on mathematical learning, held in 1962, provides a representative cross-section of the more forward American thinking on problems of learning and thinking in mathematics. Gagné applies his method of teaching by hierarchical sets (psychological) to learning non-metric geometry. Bruner is concerned with presenting mathematical operation in a concrete form and Cronbach sums up as an educational psychologist. Suppes reports several experiments which he maintains support a behavioural explanation of mathematics learning.

NCPL (1965), *Mathematics Programmes,* National Centre for Programmed Learning, University of Birmingham School of Education.

NSSE (1964), *Theories of Learning and Instruction,* Yearbook, National Society for the Study of Education.

In chapter 13, Bruner discusses some ideas about teaching, illustrated from mathematics learning.

PEEL, E. A. (1960), *The Pupil's Thinking,* Oldbourne.

A textbook which sets out to study the growth of the pupil's thinking in all school fields. It derives its theory in the main from the writings of Piaget, but is by no means uncritical of this theory. It contains also references to much research carried out at Birmingham by the author and his research students in the last few years. It abounds with references to learning and thinking in the mathematical field and makes a special point of discussing productive thinking, problem-solving exercises and the relationship of thinking and skill learning in elementary mathematics. It is a useful source book for many of the references given in this chapter.

PIAGET, J. (1950), *The Psychology of Intelligence*, Routledge & Kegan Paul.

The main purpose in referring to this study is Piaget's insistence on the clear distinction between the discovery theories of Gestalt's psychology and the construction theory of the Geneva school. In this book Piaget maintains that Gestalt's schemata are too rigid and fixed to account for the development of children's thinking and perceptions.

PIAGET, J. (1952), *The Child's Conception of Number*, Routledge & Kegan Paul.

This well-known and often-consulted study analyses the growth of the child's capacity to conserve quantity and to set up correspondences between cardinal and ordinal number. Lastly there is the section on the additive and multiplicative composition of number. Its experiments are most often repeated in educational research and the broad features of the theory have never been seriously questioned. The recent *La genese des structures logiques elementaires* by Piaget and Inhelder might well be read in conjunction with parts 1 and 3 of this reference.

PIAGET, J. (1953), *Logic and Psychology*, Manchester University Press.

A small book containing lectures delivered by Piaget at Manchester University, and is one of the briefest accounts of his views about the essential important phases in the child's intellectual development. It also sets out very clearly the main points of his epistimology and relates it to his psychology of childhood.

PIAGET, J., and INHELDER, B. (1956), *The Child's Conception of Space*, Routledge & Kegan Paul.

This well-known monograph traces the genesis of the child's conception of space from its topological beginnings, through the development of projective constructs (shadows, sections and perspective), to the emergence of the child's grasp of Euclidean space. The book is based on experimental studies throughout. It begins with some tests of visual perception and then goes on to drawing tests. The later sections utilize more complex lay-outs such as model villages. It is in all a very penetrating study.

PIAGET, J., and INHELDER, B. (1964), *The Early Growth of Logic in the Child*, Routledge & Kegan Paul.

The authors conduct a long series of experiments on the development of the child's power to classify material and to order it within the class. The work is of interest to the teacher concerned with the beginnings of mathematics.

PIAGET, J., INHELDER, B., and SZEMINSKA, A. (1960), *The Child's Conception of Geometry*, Routledge & Kegan Paul.

Here the members of the Geneva school subject the genesis of the child's geometrical concepts (lengths, angles, curves and solids) to the same kind of analysis which characterized the earlier study of number (Piaget, 1952) and shows a similar emergence of the conservation of geometrical constructs. It follows naturally upon the study of the child's spatial concepts (Piaget and Inhalder, 1956). The technique is experimental, combined with detailed analysis of verbatim reports of the children's reactions and constructions.

REYNOLDS, J. (1961), 'The development of certain mathematical concepts in grammar-school children between the ages of 11 and 18 years', unpublished M.Ed. thesis, University of Nottingham.

This research follows the methods of Saad but applies them to study the pupil's understanding of certain particular concepts in mathematics, including limits and infinity. Among other findings he reports that the abstract notion of a non-ending sequence or of indefinite continuity seems to be present in the first-form children, but the development of ideas relating to infinity is neither consistent nor systematic.

RIPPLE, R. E., and ROCKCASTLE, V. H. (eds.) (1964), *Piaget Rediscovered,* School of Education, Cornell University.

A report of the conferences at Cornell and Berkeley supported by the National Science Foundation and the US Office of Education. The conference was concerned with cognitive studies and curriculum development. Part 1 is made up of the four papers presented by Piaget. They form the most succinct account of the basis of the Geneva thinking and experimentation. Part 2 is made up of papers by educational psychologists on cognition and learning in relation to schoolwork and includes articles by Ripple, Cronbach, Smedslund, Wholwill, Peel, Suchman and Easley. All these papers have some significance for mathematics teachers. Part 3 consists of a series of curriculum project reports which includes a paper by Kilpatrick on cognitive theory and the SMSG project, in which mathematical structure plays the key role. Their compatibility between mathematical structure and Piaget's theory is noted. Easley writes about the Illinois Mathematical Project.

ROSENBLOOM, P. C. (ed.) (1964), *Modern Viewpoints in the Curriculum,* McGraw-Hill.

Cronbach writes as an educational psychologist on the nature of learning (pp. 19-35). Apart from his clear summary of what curriculum planners may expect of educational psychology, there is a short evaluation of the new mathematics programmes by Moise of Harvard which is of interest to mathematicians.

SAAD, L. G. (1957), 'Understanding in mathematics', Ph.D. thesis, University of Birmingham.

This contains a factorial analysis of mathematical ability, as well as an analysis of understanding of mathematical concepts and principles.

SAAD, L. G. (1960), *Understanding in Mathematics,* Birmingham University Education Monograph, Oliver & Boyd.

(See also Saad, 1957.) Saad prepared tests of concepts and principles inherent in secondary-school arithmetic, algebra and geometry and analysed the responses by frequencies of correct and incorrect answers, and also gave a detailed account and discussion of different kinds of misunderstandings. The research revealed many weaknesses in middle-secondary-school mathematical understanding. These misunderstandings can be accounted for by Piaget or Gestalt theory (see Peel, 1960).

SKEMP, R. R. (1961), 'Reflective intelligence and mathematics', *British Journal of Educational Psychology,* vol. 31, pp. 45-55.

The beginning of an attempt to carry out an analysis of algebraic concepts and operations in order to do for algebra what Piaget did for the study of children's number concepts. Skemp suggests that his test of 'reflective activity' correlates more highly than 'conception formation' and 'use of operation' with mathematics marks.

STORER, W. O. (1956), 'An analysis of errors appearing in a test on algebraic fractions', *Mathematical Gazette,* vol. 4, no. 331, February.

An account of a study of secondary-school algebra, in the middle forms, and contains a break-down of the errors in mathematical thinking and computation. They can also be interpreted in terms of Gestalt theory.

SUTHERLAND, J. (1941), 'Aspects of problem solving', *British Journal of Educational Psychology,* vol. 11/12.

One of the earlier studies on the effects of familiarity of vocabulary for efficiency in solving problems. It demonstrates clearly the advantages of background familiarity.

VERNON, P. E. (1950), *The Structure of Human Abilities,* Methuen.

A comprehensive account of the pattern of human mental powers gathered both from the American and British schools of factorial analysis. The evidence for general intellectual ability, more specialized group abilities, primary mental abilities, school and vocational abilities and attainments is discussed. It is a good assembly and commentary upon the main experimental evidence available and is written succinctly and clearly.

VYGOTSKY, L. S. (1962), *Thought and Language,* MIT Press.

WONG, R. H. K. (1965), 'The new approach in mathematics teaching', *Bulletin of the Faculty of Education, University of Malaya,* vol. 1.

WRIGLEY, J. (1958), 'The factorial nature of ability in elementary mathematics', *British Journal of Educational Psychology,* vol. 28, pp. 61–78.

Two parts of this paper are of interest, the summary of previous work, and the results of the author's own experimental study and the factorial analysis of the results. These confirm previous findings that general ability and group abilities make up mathematical capacity.

Part Two
The New Mathematics

5 A Selection of Syllabuses

In this period of extensive educational reform the planning of school programmes in mathematics should be based on recent advances in scientific knowledge about child development in particular and about the process of human learning in general. If carried out on this basis, experiments with the construction of modern mathematics syllabuses can do much to aid the reform of mathematical education. Such experiments should cover a wide range of mathematical topics so as to contribute to an objective selection of those most appropriate to a given age group in a particular type of school, and to their distribution within syllabuses.

The examples of new syllabuses which follow represent a sample from different countries of different social and educational structures. They are examples of courses designed for secondary education: the age group from twelve to eighteen years. Figure 36 shows the age correlation of different grades in the different national syllabuses presented in this chapter. Some are experimental in nature, others have a wider application. Certain syllabuses are formulated in general terms, others provide further details and teaching instructions; some appear more restrictive for the teacher, others give greater freedom. Despite these differences, the emphasis in each syllabus is on the early introduction of the basic mathematical concepts.

This common core of basic concepts was the object of several recommendations of the Unesco symposium in Budapest.

The basic concepts of mathematics should be taught to all children at the beginning of their course. This common core will be the basis on which further lines of development and specific complementary studies are built up.

Many experiments have shown that it is possible to use the language, elementary concepts and operations of sets, and the concepts of relation and functions at the age of twelve (or even earlier). One reason for using these concepts is that they facilitate the later study of elements of topology and analysis.

Experiments have also shown that it is both possible and desirable to introduce, as early as the age of twelve, the concepts necessary for the proper presentation of the structure of vector spaces (equivalence, translations, vectors, the concept of group, . . .). This would permit the study and use of vector spaces from the age of fifteen.

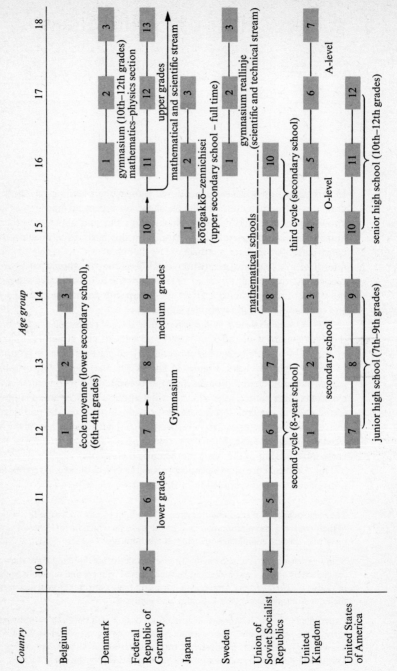

Figure 36

Investigation was urged into the ways and methods of presentation of certain topics in the context of modern mathematics.

Ultimately the operational value of a syllabus is closely related to the competence and training of the teachers responsible for using it in the classroom. The role of pre-service and in-service teacher training in support of the reform of mathematical education is the subject of chapter 7.

5.1 Belgium

General secondary education comprises six years of schooling in two cycles: lower secondary, from sixth grade to fourth grade (pupils from twelve to fifteen years), and upper secondary, from third grade to first grade (pupils from fifteen to eighteen years). The lower secondary school (école moyenne) comprises the three years of the first cycle. In these schools, mathematics is taught in four weekly periods of fifty minutes each during the thirty weeks of the school year.

The new programmes for lower secondary schools were prepared by the Centre Belge de la pédagogie de la mathématique and adopted on an experimental basis in the State schools and in certain State-supported schools. The programme for the sixth grade went into general use in 1968.

5.1.1 Sixth grade *(twelve and thirteen years old)*

(a) Sets

(i) *Sets.* Examples; elements of a set; Venn diagrams; the empty set; the set with one element. Names and objects; equalities. The symbols $=$, $\in$, $\varnothing$; the notation $E = \{x \mid P(x)\}$ and variants of it.

(ii) *Parts of a set.* Parts or subsets of a set. Inclusion, symbols $\subset$ and $\supset$. The set of subsets of particular sets.

(iii)*The algebra of sets.* Intersection, union, difference (optional: symmetric difference). Commutativity, associativity of $\cup$ and $\cap$. Distributivity of each of $\cup$ and $\cap$ over the other. (Some contra-examples, such as the non-associativity of $\setminus$ and $\cup$ taken together.)

(iv) *Partition.* Examples of partitions of a set; definition.

(b) Relations and graphs

(v) *Relations and graphs.* Illustrations of relations; graph of a relation; the relation, the set of couples; relation from the set A to the set B; the product $A \times B$; the reciprocal of a relation; the image of a set by a relation. Relative properties of $\times$, $\cap$ and $\cup$.

(vi) *Properties of certain relations.* Reflexivity; symmetry; transitivity; asymmetry.

(vii) *The composition of relations.* Examples; associativity of compositions; the reciprocal of a composition.

(viii) *Functions.* Functions; mapping; bijection; composition of functions; transformations and permutations of a set (optional: injection, surjection).

(ix) *Equivalence.* Examples; equivalence and partition.

(x) *Order.* Examples; definitions; total order. The symbols $\leqslant$, $\geqslant$, $<$ and $>$.

(c) Natural numbers. Integers

(xi) *Natural numbers.* Idempotent sets; elementary ideas of the cardinal number of a set. Finite and infinite sets. Cardinals of finite sets. Problems connected with the cardinal of the union, intersection and product of a couple of sets. Discovery of the definition of addition and multiplication of natural numbers using set operations. Clarification and multiplication of the elementary properties of addition and multiplication from set operations.

(xii) *Systems of numeration.* Binary and denary numbers.

(xiii) *Elementary study of* $\mathbb{Z}$, $+$,.. Elementary properties. Equations. Numerical and literal exercises.

(d) Geometry

(xiv) *Plane; point; straight line.* The plane, an infinite set of points. The straight line, proper subsets of the plane. Set of straight lines in a plane. Incidence properties using Venn diagrams. Parallelism; the symbol $/\!/$. The direction of a straight line, the partition of a plane.

(xv) *Parallels and perpendiculars.* Straight lines and perpendicular directions, the symbol $\perp$. Relations between $\perp$ and $/\!/$.

(xvi) *Directed straight lines.* The two reciprocal total orders of the straight line. Orientation of straight lines. Open and closed half-lines. Open, closed and half-open (open–closed) segments. Discovery of the definition of convex sets.

(xvii) *Parallel projections.* Examples and definition. Image of a part of a plane by a projection. Parallel projection of a straight line A onto a straight line B and its reciprocal. The parallel projection of a directed straight line on another directed straight line, both intersecting and not; special case: the projection of a directed straight line onto a parallel line; parallel directed straight line of similar and opposite sense.

(xviii) *Equipollence and translation.* Equipollent couples. Equipollence is an equivalence. Projection of equipollent couples; the little theorem of Thales. Midpoint of a segment; parallelogram theorems. Properties of equipollences; cross-equipollences. Translations or vectors. Examples of translations;

images of parts of the plane by a translation; images of straight lines, half-lines, segments, couples of points by a translation.

5.1.2   *Fifth grade (thirteen and fourteen years old)*

(i) *The group of translations or vectors.* Composition of translations. Commutative group of translations of the plane. Notations of vector spaces. First principles of vector calculus.

(ii) *The group* Π^0, $+$. New representation of group of translations or group of vectors. Subgroups of Π^0, $+$. Sum of parts of Π^0, $+$. Algebra in Π^0, $+$; equations; problems.

(iii) *The totally ordered group* D^0, $+$, $\leqslant$. Every straight line D^0 containing 0 is a subgroup of Π^0, $+$. Study of the order group D^0, $+$, $\leqslant$. Sum of segments; first ideas of the approximation of a sum.

(iv) *Summary of the idea of a group.* Idea of a group from examples already seen; new examples, particularly the cyclic group. Calculus of any group. Addition and multiplication; notations. Integral coefficients and exponents. Equations in a group.

(v) *Real numbers.* Graduation of a line; Axiom of Archimedes. Binary and decimal subgraduations. Terminating and non-terminating binary ('bicimal') and decimal numbers. Axiom of continuity; first appearance of concept of real number.

(vi) *Theorem of Thales.* General form of the theorem. Ratio of parallel vectors.

(vii) *Enlargements (and shrinkings).* Images of parts of the plane by an enlargement. Ratio of an enlargement. Enlargements of non-zero ratio preserve linearity, incidence, parallelism, midpoint, ratio of parallel vectors, the set of segments. Composition of enlargements with the same centre; the commutative group. Group of enlargements and translations (alternatively called the group of dilatations).

(viii) *Addition of real numbers.* The ordered additive group of real numbers. Equations and inequations; approximation; absolute value.

(ix) *Multiplication of real numbers.* For enlargements of rational ratio and the same centre: the ratio of the product of two enlargements equal to the product of the ratios. Definition of multiplication of real numbers by the generalization of the preceding property. The associativity and commutativity of non-zero real numbers. Equations in $\mathbb{R}_0$.

(x) *Multiplication of vectors by a real number.* Mixed associativity. Double distributivity. Linear combinations and projection.

(xi) *The real ordered field* $\mathbb{R}_0$, $+$, $.$, $<$. The structure of the ordered field. Calculation in the field. Notable products. Problems.

(xii) *Fractions.* Fractions with real terms. Rules and exercises for calculating with fractions. The field of rational numbers.

(xiii) *Linear equations with one unknown in the real field.* Problems.

(xiv) *Inequations.* Approximations; first elements of a calculus of errors.

(xv) *Plane vector space.* Vectorial calculation. Linear vector equation. Bases and coordinates. Problems.

(xvi) *Central symmetries.* Images of a part of the plane by a central symmetry. Centres of symmetry of parts of the plane. Compound of two or more central symmetries. Group of central symmetries and translations.

(xvii) *Parallel symmetries and orthogonal symmetries.* Images of parts of the plane; in particular, straight lines. Preserved properties. Axes of symmetry of parts of the plane.

5.1.3   *Fourth grade (fourteen and fifteen years old)*

(i) *The relation 'divide' in $\mathbb{Z}$ and the set of natural numbers.* Prime divisors and primary factors of a number. Subsets and subgroups of $\mathbb{Z}$, $+$. All the subgroups of $\mathbb{Z}$, $+$ are cyclic. HCF and LCM of a subset of $\mathbb{Z}$. Bezout's relation.

(ii) *Linear equations.* Vector, parametric and Cartesian equations.

(iii) *Functions $\mathbb{R}$ over $\mathbb{R}$ and polynomial functions.* Examples. Cartesian representation. Addition and multiplication of functions. Ring of mappings of $\mathbb{R}$ upon $\mathbb{R}$.

(iv) *Algebra of real polynomials in one indeterminate.* Algebra of polynomials. Division by $x - a$. Division with a remainder. Simple exercises of factorization.

(v) *Square root of a real positive number.* Square roots and approximate square roots.

(vi) *Systems of linear equations of one, two and three unknowns.* Gauss's method. Problems.

(vii) *Systems of linear equations and inequations of one and two unknowns.* Solution of simple systems. Problem; geometric interpretation.

(viii) *Group of displacements and group of isometries of the plane.* Orthogonal symmetries; translations, rotations and turns as composed by them. Compound of an orthogonal symmetry and a translation parallel to the axis of symmetry. Commutative group of rotations about a given centre. Group of displacements, group of isometries.

(ix) *Distance.* Distance; circles; open and closed discs.

(x) *The group of angles.* Angle (directed) of a rotation; angle (directed) of a couple of half-lines; angle (not directed) of a pair of half-lines. Calculations with angles.

(xi) *Cosine and scalar product.* Cosine of an angle; cosine determines an angle. Scalar product and its invariance in isometries. Pythagoras' theorem. Elementary trigonometrical formulae.

(xii) *Triangular inequality.* The Cauchy–Schwartz inequality. Triangular inequality. Convexity of a disc. Intersection of a straight line and a disc or a circle. Approximation in the plane.

(xiii) *The relation of congruence and the relation of isometry.* The set of congruent parts of the plane. The set of isometries of the plane. When are two couples of points congruent (or isometric)? The same problems for two triplets of points.

(xiv) *The group of similitudes of the planes and the subgroup of direct similitudes.*

(xv) *Area and the measure of area.* Areas of simple parts of the plane. Calculation of areas using vectors and trigonometry.

5.2 Denmark

5.2.1 *The new mathematics programme in the Danish gymnasium*

The authorized curriculum in mathematics pertaining to the mathematics–physics line in the Danish gymnasium (grades 10–12, the age group from sixteen to eighteen years) is outlined in section 5.2.2.

After seven years of elementary school, many of the Danish pupils are transferred to the three-year *realskole*. Two or three years later, a small selection (at present about 6 per cent of all children) is admitted to the three-year gymnasium. About half the pupils enrol in the mathematics–physics section. In this section there are six lessons per week in mathematics and physics throughout the three years; the rest of the time is devoted to geography, biology, foreign languages and the humanities.

Traditionally, the Danish teacher has considerable freedom in arranging his courses. Consequently, the authorized curricula are merely lists of topics. Usually they are accompanied by official recommendations and comments by school authorities, examples of which are given in section 5.2.3.

5.2.2 *The subject list in mathematics for the mathematics-physics section of the Danish gymnasium.*

(a) *General concepts from set theory and algebra.* Set, subset, complement, union, intersection. Equivalence relation, ordering relation. Mapping of a set into and onto another (the concept of function), one-to-one mapping, inverse mapping (inverse function). Denumerability. Binary composition; group, ring, field.

(b) *Numbers*. The natural numbers. Axiom of induction. Primes. Greatest common divisor, Euclid's algorithm. The ring of integers, equivalence classes modulo an integer. The field of rationals, its denumerability. The field of real numbers, its continuity, upper and lower bound, non-denumerability, infinite decimal fractions. Absolute value. The field of complex numbers.

(c) *Combinatories*. Combinations and permutations, binomial formula. The concept of a finite probability distribution. Examples of determination of probabilities by means of combinatories.

(d) *Equations and inequalities*. Equations and inequalities of first and second degree with one unknown. Equations and inequalities of first degree with two unknowns. Simple examples of other equations. Second-order equation and the binomial equation in the complex field.

(e) *Plane geometry*. The rectangular coordinate system. Change of co-ordinates. Vectors and their coordinates. Vector algebra, including scalar product. Analytic representations of a line. Area of a triangle and parallelogram. Definition and analytic representation of parabola, ellipse, hyperbola. Mapping of the plane onto itself; parallel displacement, rotation, reflection, multiplication and composition of these mappings; orthogonal affinity.

(f) *Solid geometry*. The rectangular coordinate system. Vectors and their co-ordinates. Vector algebra, including scalar product. Parametric representation of a line. Analytic representation of the plane. Distance and angle. Equation of the sphere, spherical coordinates, spherical distance between two points (the cosine relation). Polyhedra, Euler's theorem, the regular polyhedra. Volume of a prism, pyramid, right circular cylinder and cone, sphere. Surface area of right circular cylinder and cone, sphere; area of spherical triangle. Congruence and symmetry.

(g) *Elementary functions*. The linear function of one variable. The linear function of two variables. Polynomials in one variable, including their factorization, greatest number of roots, determination of rational roots in polynomials with integral coefficients. Rational functions of one variable. Logarithmic functions, logarithmic scale, use of slide rule and logarithm tables. Exponential functions, power functions. The trigonometric functions, addition formulae, logarithmic formulae; application of trigonometric functions to oscillations and to computation of unknown sides and angles in a triangle. The linear function of one complex variable and its geometrical interpretation.

(h) *Calculus*. The concept of limit. Continuity and differentiability of a real function of one real variable; continuity and differentiability of a vector function of one real variable (tangent vector). Differentiation rules. Taylor's formula (approximating polynomials), differentials. The definite integral as a limit of sums. The indefinite integral. Integration rules, including integration by parts and integration by substitution.

(i) *Applications of the calculus.* Determination of the range of a function and intervals of monotonicity. Simple examples of determination of asymptotic properties of functions. Drawing of graphs of given functions, and drawing of curves determined by a simple parametric representation. Velocity vector, speed, acceleration vector. Determination of areas and volumes by integration. Examples of applications of the calculus in probability theory. Examples of applications of the calculus to numerical problems and to problems in physics and other subjects. Examples of simple differential equations.

(j) *A subject chosen by the teacher.*

5.2.2 Comments on the subject list

General remarks. The subject list does not indicate a chronological arrangement of the material. It is left to the teacher to decide what he finds appropriate from a pedagogical and systematic point of view. Also, correlation with the instruction in physics and other subjects has to be taken into consideration.

The teachers are recommended occasionally to comment on the origin of important notions and their historical development.

When dealing with examples, say from physics, the teacher is supposed to show the student that the use of mathematics is in accordance with definitions and theorems, even if the language of physics appears shorter than is customary in mathematics.

(a) *General concepts from set theory and algebra.* Set theory is primarily thought to be employed as a means of clarifying the fundamental concepts and reasonings, and as a basis for a precise and up-to-date mathematical mode of expression. The set-theoretical concepts should be defined at moments when the discussion of other subjects makes this natural. General set-theoretical concepts should be illustrated by varied examples, both new ones and examples from material taught in grades 8-9.

The elements of logic are not mentioned in the list, but it is recommended that set-theoretical considerations be used to illustrate some of the basic logical rules. If this is done, in connexion with equations and inequalities for example, the pupils will gain a better understanding as well as manipulative skill.

A function should be defined in the general form, as a mapping from one set into another. The use of this notion of a function throughout in the teaching of the various topics in the mathematics curriculum will have a great unifying power.

An extended course in abstract algebra is not intended. The fundamental concepts, rule of composition, group, ring and field shall form the basis for a description of the algebraic structure of the number system. Through examples from different fields of mathematics, the algebraic concepts can illuminate the connexion between subjects which otherwise seem wide apart.

(b) *Numbers.* The students should realize the fundamental role played by the axiom of induction; in particular, its application to proof by induction should be made clear.

Concerning prime numbers, only the theorem that the set of prime numbers is infinite, and the theorem about unique factorization in primes are required.

A precise description of the algebraic structure, ordering and continuity of the system of real numbers should be given, but no construction of the system of real numbers from the system of rational numbers should be included.

The students should acquire skill in working with absolute values. In exercises, absolute value should appear in equations, inequalities and in connexion with functions.

(c) *Combinatories.* The students will have to become acquainted with the general concept of a finite probability field. The treatment should not be restricted to fields where all points have the same probability. It is here a question of presentation of a simple mathematical model and the application of the terminology attached to this model.

(d) *Equations and inequalities.* Some types of equations of which only examples should be given are: a system of three linear equations with three unknowns; a system of two equations with two unknowns, one equation of first degree, the other of second degree; equations in which the unknown appears under a square root; exponential equations and trigonometrical equations with one unknown. The examples of these kinds of equations should be simple.

(e) *Plane geometry.* Change in coordinates must comprise parallel displacement and rotation of the coordinate system. In analytic geometry, the vector concept should play a central part. The expression, 'analytic representation of a line', refers to coordinate – as well as vector – equations, parametric representation and normalized equations.

The treatment of conics can be restricted to derivation of the equations of the parabola, ellipse and hyperbola based on a geometric definition of these curves. Special properties of conic sections (theorems about tangents etc.) can be dealt with in exercises.

As indicated in the list of subjects, the mappings in question (parallel displacements, rotations, etc.) are meant to be considered as mappings of the entire plane onto itself and not as mappings only of single figures. However, an account should be given of how characteristics of the figures, the sizes of distances, angles and areas, for example, are transformed under the mappings (invariant and non-invariant characteristics); especially the fact that a circle is mapped onto an ellipse by an orthogonal affinity should be demonstrated. In this connexion, the parametric representation of the ellipse can be mentioned.

(f) *Solid geometry.* Fundamental theorems about parallelism and orthogonality of lines and planes are presented (without proofs) to an extent necessary for the introduction of orthogonal coordinates and the treatment of polyhedra.

The analytic representations of planes must include coordinate – as well as vector – equations and also normalized equations.

Exercises in applications of spherical coordinates should include problems concerning geographic and astronomic subjects.

Regular polyhedra should be considered in detail only in the cases of the tetrahedron, the cube and the octahedron.

(g) *Elementary functions.* In connexion with linear functions of two variables and their level lines, one can treat problems about maxima and minima of such functions restricted to domains determined by linear inequalities (linear programming).

Besides the function-theoretical description of polynomials, it must be demonstrated that the set of polynomials forms a ring, and the analogy between integers and polynomials should be stressed.

Practice in the use of the slide rule should concentrate on its principle and elementary applications. Not too much time should be spent on technical points of the use of the slide rule.

Presentation of the application of trigonometric functions should include the fact that a linear combination of pure oscillations with the same period is a pure oscillation.

(h) *Calculus.* During the last thirty years, the treatment of calculus in the Danish gymnasium has reached a high level. Not only manipulative skill but a careful introduction of basic notions and rigorous proofs were aimed at.

It is implicitly recommended that rigorous considerations should not be over-emphasized.

In connexion with the concept of limit, standard theorems about limits of sums and products, etc. should be mentioned. Proofs can be confined to only one or two of these theorems.

The selection of proofs of the basic theorems on continuous functions is left to the teacher's discretion.

The students should be given the opportunity to carry out approximate computations of the values of certain functions on the basis of Taylor's formula.

(i) *Applications of the calculus.* Calculations of volume by integration should comprise computation of the volume of rotational solids and pyramids.

The use of frequency functions as a basis for determination of finite probability fields is understood to be based on a postulate which states that in every particular case there exists a function with the property that the probability distribution corresponding to an arbitrary finite division of the set of real numbers in subintervals can be determined by integration of this function over the subintervals. Thus, the presentation can be kept inside the frame of the theory of finite probability fields, and the problems will actually be exercises in integration, formulated in the language of probability theory.

The treatment of simple differential equations may be limited to the mention of the equations

$$\frac{dy}{dx} = f(x) \quad \text{and} \quad \frac{dy}{dx} = g(y) \neq 0.$$

Simple calculations of moments of inertia and centres of gravity can be included as examples of applications of infinitesimal calculus to physics.

(j) *A subject chosen by the teacher.* Content, extent and mode of treating the optional subject should be adapted in such a way that the students are not faced with more difficult problems here than those arising from the other mathematics lessons.

Some examples of the fields from which the optional subjects may be taken are history of mathematics, number theory, matrices and determinants, theory of groups, set theory, Boolean algebra, differential equations, series, probability theory, statistics, theory of games, topology, projective geometry, theory of conics, non-Euclidian geometry, geometry of high dimensions, geometrical constructions, descriptive geometry.

The optional subject may also be chosen in connexion with the corresponding part of the physics course. As examples of suitable subjects, probability theory and kinetic theory of gases, differential equations and oscillatory circuits may be mentioned. Finally, the optional subject may be organized in connexion with subjects other than physics, for example, probability theory and heredity.

The existence of an optional subject in the mathematics curriculum is new in Denmark. A couple of months in grades 11 or 12 will be devoted to the optional subject. Of course, both modern and classical subjects will be chosen, but it is expected that many teachers will choose the theory of probability as their teaching subject. In the list of non-optional subjects, probability does occur, but only on a very modest scale. Of course the teacher is free to choose between an axiomatic and a non-axiomatic treatment of probability, but certainly an axiomatic treatment will be used by some teachers. (This will probably be easier to carry through if the treatment is restricted to discrete sample spaces.) In this case, the pupils will get a very useful impression of a simple axiom system and an example of a mathematical model.

5.3 Federal Republic of Germany

5.3.0 *Example of a general programme for the teaching of mathematics. Association for the Advancement of Science and Mathematics Instruction*

Modern developments in mathematics have brought out certain unifying concepts, which bring the various branches of mathematics into one coherent whole and lead to an insight into the relations between theoretical mathematics and its practical applications. Mathematics is concerned with patterns and structures, with sets of objects and the structures which may be defined on them, with the links between structures by relations and functions, mappings and transformations. The patterns themselves appear as models of abstract structures which are described by means of appropriate systems of axioms and logical sequences. This conception of scientific mathematics calls for the adaptation of the school mathematics curriculum.

To teach mathematics it is important to think of the basic objects as sets, to apply given structures to them, to understand the building of mathematics as a mental construction of patterns beginning with the simplest, and to develop skill in the use of the tools of logic. It is best to begin with data based on intuitive knowledge, progressing by the analysis of the data, by limited ideas of order, by induction, idealization and abstraction. This will avoid the mistakes which may arise from too great an emphasis on deduction in the early stages.

Besides the emphasis on the structural treatment of mathematics, we must not neglect the algorithmic point of view, the importance of which, for applied mathematics, is steadily increasing as computers become larger and more powerful. The importance of the algorithmic treatment is not limited to their numerical solution, as it also leads to a fuller understanding of the principles involved. With the help of simple examples, the underlying principle may be discussed, leading to greater skill in solving problems.

Objects. Mathematical objects may be: numbers, points; pairs, triples, n-tuples of numbers or points; straight lines, planes, geometrical figures; vectors, matrices; relations, functions, mappings (single valued), sequences as functions on the set of natural numbers; sets of objects etc.

Sets. Examples of sets are: number sets, for example, natural numbers $\mathbb{N}$, integers $\mathbb{Z}$, rational numbers $\mathbb{Q}$, real numbers $\mathbb{R}$, complex numbers $\mathbb{C}$; point sets, for example straight lines, planes, curves; sets of ordered number pairs (pair sets, functions), of n-tuples in product sets, of vectors in vector spaces, of subsets of a set, etc.

Structures. Structures are recognized very early (and later on classified by systems of axioms' on sets, for the elements of which certain qualities, operations and relations are defined: for example, algebraic structures (semigroups, groups, rings, fields, vector spaces), structures of order (simply ordered, well ordered) and topological structures.

Mappings (functions). From the most general standpoint mappings are unique coordinations by which each element of a set A (domain, original set) is coordinated with exactly one element of a set B (range, image set); they are special relations from A to B. Mappings are often connected with certain structures defined on A and B, for example, the monotone functions of the real analysis with structures of order, the continuous functions with the topological structure of the set $\mathbb{R}$. Mappings of algebraic structures are called homomorphic ones or homomorphisms if they preserve the original structure; in the case of one-to-one mappings they are called isomorphisms. In geometry the translations, reflections, rotations and generally the congruence mappings are the characteristic mappings (automorphisms) of the Euclidean plane which preserve the original structures. By analogy, the mappings of similarity, affinity, projectivity, etc. are the automorphisms of other corresponding geometries.

Logical notions. Adequate logical and linguistic insight into mathematical patterns and the relations between them lead to the following notions, amongst others: object and its symbol or name; proposition (statement) and its truth value (true, false); variable (place holder, empty place), term, propositional function; equation, inequality; basic set (domain), solution set; fulfilment of propositional functions (compliable, non-compliable, general validity); relations and operations within the logic of propositions, for example, 'negation' $\neg$, 'and' – conjunction $\wedge$, 'or' – disjunction $\vee$, 'if . . . , then . . .' $\Rightarrow$, 'equivalent' $\Leftrightarrow$; notions of deduction, conclusion and equivalence; quantifiers ('for every x' – $\forall x$, 'for at least one x' – $\exists x$); axioms for the description of the properties of structured patterns, patterns as models of systems of axioms, relations with the notions of deduction and conclusion.

The following arrangement of the mathematical topics is based on systematic treatment. It does not mean any methodical or didactic order; it intends no co-ordination of single classes or forms, and it does not indicate the separation of geometry, algebra and analysis in the classroom.

5.3.1   *Programme for the lower forms (fifth, sixth and seventh school years)*

General aim of instruction. The initial aims are competence in arithmetic, knowledge of simple applications of arithmetic in various situations, and familiarity with basic constructions in geometry.

Besides these pragmatic aims, teaching in the lower forms should introduce important mathematical ideas. By applying the simple notions and symbols of the theory of sets and of the logic of propositions (statements), the principal qualities of the structured set $\mathbb{N}$ of the natural numbers – and in relation to these, the qualities of the integers and of the rational numbers – should be elaborated (for instance, structure of order, simple algebraic structures). That is why the teacher should always have in mind the main ideas of the structures mentioned in the previous section and make them effective in the arrangement and presentation of the material. The first basic geometric ideas should be developed from intuitive experimentation with special geometric figures including their mappings. This should be deepened by 'local ordering' (Freudenthal) of the concrete geometrical facts (i.e. connecting and classifying the elaborated geometrical statements).

(a) *Algebra and arithmetic.* (i) The set $\mathbb{N}$ of natural integers. Equality and order on $\mathbb{N}$ (the relations $=$, $<$, $\leqslant$). Simple notations of the theory of sets and their symbols (e.g. $\in$, $\notin$, $\subset$, $\subseteq$). Representation of the natural integers on an axis. The operations on $\mathbb{N}$ $(+, -, ., :)$ and the appertaining rules of arithmetic (commutativity, associativity, distributivity). The number 0. Mental arithmetic. Letters as place-holders (variables) for elements of $\mathbb{N}$. Simple equations and inequalities of the form

$$a + x \lesseqgtr b \quad (a, b \in \mathbb{N};\ b > a),$$

$$a \cdot x = b \quad (a, b \in \mathbb{N};\ a \mid b).$$

Subset $\mathbb{P}$ of prime numbers, prime factors; notation with powers. Rules of divisibility; greatest common divisor; least common multiple. Decimal and binary system.

(ii) Equations of the form $a \cdot x = b\,(a, b \in \mathbb{N})$. Enlargement of $\mathbb{N}$ to the ordered set $\mathbb{Q}^+$ of positive rational numbers (fractional numbers or fractions). Fractional calculus (additional leading idea: the multiplicative group in $\mathbb{Q}^+$). Equations and inequalities as in subsection (i), but $a, b \in \mathbb{Q}^+$. Decimal fractions and their use. Decimal notation of linear, square and solid measure, as well as of monetary matters. Preparation of the concept of function.

(iii) Calculating with proportions and some applications (e.g. rule of three, interest account). Rounding off numbers. Tables and slide rule as auxiliaries in arithmetical problems. Equations of the form $x + b = c$ and $a \cdot x + b = c$ $(a, b, c \in \mathbb{Q}^+)$. Enlargement of $\mathbb{N}$ and $\mathbb{Q}^+$ to the ordered set $\mathbb{Z}$ of integers and to the ordered set $\mathbb{Q}$ of rational numbers respectively (additional leading idea: $\mathbb{Z}$ as ordered ring; $\mathbb{Q}$ as ordered field). Simple equations and inequalities, transformation of terms, sets of solutions). Graphic representation as additional preparation for the notion of function. Simple questions of the theory of combinatories with aid of set diagrams, tree diagrams and graphs.

(b) *Geometry*. (i) Models and nets of cuboid and cube. Rectangle, square. Experimental introduction of basic objects (point, couple of points, line segment, ray, straight line, plane) and basic concepts (rectangular, parallel, equidistant, distance). Linear, area and solid measure. Estimating and measuring. Geometric representation of numbers (e.g. by vectors on a straight line).

(ii) Cylinder and circle. Knowledge of compasses and ruler. Experimental cyclometry. Angle, measure of the angle, direction of rotation. Experimental introduction into mappings (reflections on straight lines and points; translations and rotations; enlargement). Symmetry. Composition of mappings (preparation for the concept of groups) in the sense of the first phrase under 'Geometry' in section 5.3.2.

(iii) Quadrilaterals and their symmetries. Plane and spatial lattices. Translations represented by vectors. Congruent mappings (leading idea: properties of groups). Basic geometrical constructions. Triangle. Deduction of the theorems of congruence in the sense of motion geometry. Simple constructions of triangles. Nets of simple solids.

5.3.2   *Programme for the middle grades (eighth, ninth and tenth school years)*

General aim of instruction. The initial aim of the instruction at this level is to make the students familiar with the following subjects: use of algebraic terms: solution of equations; comprehension and representation of functions, mappings; applications of numerical methods; intuitive and constructive treatment of geometric figures; understanding of some relations between geometry and reality, between geometry and algebra (e.g. linear systems and vectors); elementary methods of mathematical definition and proof. The pupils should develop insight into the deductive structure of geometry, and to mathematize concrete situations. This faculty can well be trained initially by inductive methods and then by gradual abstraction which leads to basic notions of structural mathematics. These notions represent the fundamental categories of mathematization.

In this connexion we need to develop the algebraic properties of the different number sets, using gradually but expressively such notions as set, relation, operation, group, ring, field, order, isomorphism, in concrete examples. Applying the principle of permanence as a structural leading idea (i.e. extension of given number sets without alteration of certain structural principles), the gradual development of the number sets should include some simple properties of the real number set $\mathbb{R}$ (irrationality). The transformation and equivalence of algebraic terms, including their dependence on the basic range, should be treated on a broad basis in accordance with the equivalence principle for substitutions in algebraic expression.

One of the most important tasks in the middle grades is the exact definition of the function and the notions connected with it (e.g. the notion of a variable). We begin with sets of ordered pairs and with the idea of coordination of sets, using the terminology of mapping in a general way. In geometry we move towards a deductive system, in the sense of a pre-axiomatic order of intuitive geometrical facts, and reduce this to a closed system of basic geometric notions and principles. Here, too, the concepts of coordination (i.e. mapping, transformation) and the transformation group, the treatment of which partly leads to a vectorial approach, have proved to be very productive. The connexion between geometry and numbers, and the approach to the notion of limit (e.g. incommensurability and irrationality; nests of intervals in connexion with roots, calculation of circles, infinite geometric series) are of essential importance for the mathematical instruction in the middle grades.

With regard to logic we have to train the abilities of exact reasoning and speaking. The formation of statements in the 'if ..., then ...' form, the distinction of necessary and sufficient conditions, an understanding of the deductive proof (being at the same time a preparation for the insight into the axiomatic method) and of the negation of 'and' and 'or' connexions, all belong to this stage. Essential logical auxiliary topics in the middle grades are statements and forms of statements (propositional functions) with 'place holders' (variables), functions and names of functions, interpretation and evaluation of the solution set of forms of statements (propositional functions; equations and inequalities) by substitution, the consequential relation between forms of statements as a basis for computing with equations. The analogy between logical connexions and those of set theory should be elaborated, that is, the analogy between the 'and' connexion and the notion of intersection; the 'or' connexion and the union of sets; negation and the complement of a set; the logical conclusion and the subset notion; logical equivalence and the equality of sets.

(a) *Algebra and arithmetic.* (i) Comprehensive elaboration of the concept of sets and simple relations and operations of sets ($\subset$, $\subseteq$, $\cap$, $\setminus$, $\cup$, $\times$). Building up the basic sets $\mathbb{N}$, $\mathbb{Z}$ and $\mathbb{Q}$ (leading idea: axioms of an ordered field). Algebraic terms with place holders, equations and inequalities as propositional functions. Dependence upon the (finite or infinite) basic domain, exercises in substitution (also as preparation for the theory of functions). Equivalence of algebraic terms in the sense of equality with respect to substitutions, and of transformations with the aid of the axioms of fields (transformation rules). Linear equations and inequalities (variables as place holders); transformation rules; resolutions and set of solutions. Compatibility, incompatibility, with the basic domain. Building up an elementary theory of functions; the function as a one-to-one correspondence or mapping of one finite or infinite set onto another. Domain of a function, range of a function, set of pairs, functional equation, graph, arrow diagram, scale, table. The linear function and the function of reciprocal proportionality. Discussion of terms such as $|x|$ and $[x]$. Sets of solutions of systems of two linear equations. Resolving methods and their applications, also by use of graphs, vectors, determinants*, matrices*.

(ii) Outlook to systems with more than two linear equations (see also linear combination of vectors* under the heading 'Geometry and linear algebra' in section 5.3.3). Systems of linear inequalities with two variables. Representation by sets of points in Cartesian coordinates. Sets of solutions (also as intersection and union of sets of points); applications to simple problems of linear planning*. The pure quadratic equation $x^2 = g$ and its insolubility in $\mathbb{Q}$ if g is not a perfect square. The concept of an irrational number. The set $\mathbb{R}$ of real numbers and their characterization by nested rational intervals. Elaboration of structural properties for the sets of numbers $\mathbb{N}$, $\mathbb{Z}$, $\mathbb{Q}$ and $\mathbb{R}$, with explicit use of the concepts of order, group, ring, field, isomorphism. The quadratic function $x \to ax^2 + bx + c$ in the real domain and its zero points (set of solutions of an equation). The root function $x \to \sqrt{x}$, as inverse of $x \to x^2$ ($x \geqslant 0$).

(iii) Enlargement of the theory of functions by introduction of new terms: power function $x \to x^m$ with integral and rational exponents. Roots as

*Topics marked with an asterisk are recommended for the middle grades leading to the mathematical and scientific branch of the gymnasium. The topics not so marked represent the minimum for all gymnasia.

powers. Calculating with powers under the necessary restriction to non-negative bases. Exponential and logarithmic functions. Calculating with logarithms, slide rules and tables. Arithmetic sequences and series, also of higher order*, as functions defined on $\mathbb{N}$. Principle of induction*, finite and infinite geometric sequences and series. First introduction to the concept of limits. Applications (e.g. periodic decimal fractions, problems of commercial arithmetic).

(b) *Geometry*. (i) Development of plane Euclidean geometry from the concept of mapping, later on also by use of the concept of congruence. Transition to an adequate deductive system; if possible, separation of affine concepts (straightness; parallelism, order) and metric concepts (orthogonalism, equidistance, angle*). Methods of deduction (proof). Exercises with geometric constructions; straight lines and angles with circles. Systematic discussion of affine and congruent mappings (leading idea : group). Investigation of affine relationships based on the problem of straightness; parallelism (possibly including similarity*, see subsection (ii)) and on the congruence relation developed from its equivalence properties with aid of orthogonalism and equidistance. Symmetry of figures from the point of view of group theory (systematics of quadilaterals), additive group of vectors, etc. Solid geometry* (parallelism and orthogonalism, translations, rotations, reflections). Cube and cuboid representation by oblique images, as well as by parallel projection* to front and ground plans.

(ii) Similarity geometry (possibly already in subsection (i)). Enlargement as affine mapping in plane and space. Continuation of vector algebra (composition of vectors and scalars, linear dependence). Ray theorems. The group of similar mappings. Area of straight-sided figures. Reducing areas; shearing as area-preserving affine mappings. Rules of Pythagoras. The problem of relations between geometry and numbers: incommensurability. Area and volume on the basis of common content postulates*. Surface and volume of cube, cuboid and parallelepipeds. Theorems of chords, secants and tangents of the circle, as well as of the area of the circle.

(iii) Cyclometry and introduction to the concept of limits. Building up trigonometry, if possible in connexion with vectors: definition of the trigonometric functions, sine, cosine and tangent, at the unit circle, immediately defined for any real argument. Simple relations between these functions. Periodicity and symmetry. Sine theorem and cosine theorem; applications. Stereometry (prism, pyramid, cylinder, cone, sphere). Representation in orthogonal and oblique parallel projection* (with exception of cone and sphere).

5.3.3   *Programme for the upper grades (eleventh, twelfth and thirteenth school years)*

General aim of instruction. The concept of number must be consolidated and, especially, generalized by insight into the topological closure of real numbers. Later on this insight must be deepened by the introduction of the field of complex numbers, being the smallest upper-field of real numbers. The theory of functions will be intensified through analysis developing the concepts of neighbourhood, accumulation point, point of convergence, limit, continuity, differentiability, etc.; these notions lead to an understanding of basic problems in infinitesimal calculus and its most important applications. The idea of vector space in geometry and linear algebra effects a synopsis and uniform mastery of different mathematical topics according to basic principles of order and to a precise mathematical language. Geometry further on deals with groups of transformations, especially the affine one, possibly the projective ones as well.

Beyond that, mathematical education in the upper grades should contribute to an understanding of the axiomatic way of thinking and deal with problems of basic mathematical research, at least in a special topic to be chosen by the teacher. The mutual interaction between pure and applied mathematics should be shown as often as possible. The 'mathematization' of given situations, in physics, sociology or biology, for example, should be represented by means of selected characteristic examples.

Mathematics in the upper grades should occasionally deal with philosophical, cognitive and socio-historical problems of a basic nature.

A deeper insight into these problems should be developed in the final year by giving the teacher a great amount of freedom with regard to the subject matter, methods and didactics; for this purpose, section 5.3.4 presents a list of optional topics.

(a) *Algebra and calculus.* (i) Real sequences as functions on the set of natural integers. The idea of neighbourhood. Properties of sequences: monotony, boundary, cluster point, divergence, convergence, Weierstrass's theorem of bounded monotone sequences. Limits. Convergence point, calculating with limits. Nested intervals. Limits of functions. Continuity and disconuity (e.g. $x \to |x|$, $x \to [x]$ and their compositions with simple conventional functions). The derivative and the problem of the tangent. The concept of differentiability of functions. Rules of derivation (sum and product). The rational integral functions (zero points in the real domain, symmetry properties, derivatives, primitives). Polynomials and first insight into the field of complex numbers. Trigonometric functions, sine and cosine (addition theorem, derivative, primitives). Physical applications (velocity, acceleration, oscillations*). Recommended: Rolle's theorem, mean-value theorem. Examinations with aid of the derivatives: Newton's approximation theorem*. Relative maxima and minima. Point of inflection (necessary and sufficient conditions). Discussion of curves, also with the aid of intuitive auxiliaries of motion geometry; practical applications of maxima and minima.

(ii) Continuation of the differential calculus; differential and differential

---

*Topics marked with an asterisk are provided for the mathematical and scientific branch of the gymnasium, which starts with the eleventh school year. The subjects not so marked represent the minimum course for any type of gymnasium.

quotient. Rules of derivation (quotient, chain rule). Rational fractional functions and their derivatives. Applications and discussion of curves. Root functions, including derivatives and primitives. Inverse functions and the rules for the derivatives of inverse functions*. Exponential and logarithmic functions including derivatives*. Primitives of exponential functions*; logarithmic functions as primitives*. Introduction to integral calculus; for example, through the problem of area calculation. Riemann sums and integrability of piecewise monotone and bounded continuous functions. Primitives and integral function. Definite and indefinite integrals. The first two principal theorems of integral calculus. Basic integrals. Applications to computing areas, volumes* and physical problems* (e.g. 'work').

(iii) Algebraic equations. The field of complex numbers*. Extension of infinitesimal calculus* by a deepened study of at least two topics mentioned in section 5.3.4(a). Probability theory; fundamental concepts based on set theory. Calculating with probabilities. Stochastic models*. Some problems of statistics* (e.g. normal distributions, samples). One example of the strictly axiomatic treatment of a mathematical discipline (see section 5.3.4(c)).

(b) *Geometry and linear algebra.* (i) Linear combination of vectors (see also 'systems of linear equations' in subsections 5.3.2(a) i and ii). One-, two- and three-dimensional vector spaces. Relations between point spaces and vector spaces. Coordinate systems. Formulation of the metric in $\mathbb{R}^2$ and $\mathbb{R}^3$ with the aid of vectors and coordinates.

Scalar product and vector product (as far as not mentioned in subsection 5.3.2(b) iii). Analytic geometry of lines, planes, circles and spheres* in vector and coordinate representation, separating the affine and metric points of view.

(ii) Systematic treatment of the affine mappings of the plane; invariants and fixed elements. Affine mappings of the circle. Conics in normal position as graphs of special equations of the second degree; applications, constructions. Simple affine and linear mappings* (common methods for the generation of the conics; affine and metric invariants).

(iii) Continued development of analytic geometry in at least one of the topics mentioned in section 5.3.4(b). Geometry on the sphere, mainly as a model of a non-Euclidean geometry. One geometrical example of the strictly axiomatic treatment of a mathematical discipline (see section 5.3.4(c)), as far as not treated in subsection (a) iii.

5.3.4   *Optional topics*

The sections mentioned below may be understood as an addition to, and a deepening of, the obligatory topics above.

(a) *Algebra and analysis.* (i) Integration by substitution, integration by parts, decomposition into fractional parts.

(ii) Power series, inclusive of residual examination.

(iii) Physical applications (e.g. centre of gravity, moment of inertia).

(iv) Simple differential equations.

(v)   Curves in parametric forms.

(vi) Questions of differential geometry (rectification, lateral area, osculating curve, curvature, space curves).

(vii) Euler's theorem and hyperbolic functions.

(viii) Fundamental theorem of algebra.

(ix) Theory of games. Mathematical treatment of problems of sociology.

(x)   Elementary theory of numbers.

(b) *Geometry**. (i) The general equation of the second degree and classification of conics.

(ii) Problems of solid geometry.

(iii) Plane projective mappings (invariants, subgroups, etc.).

(iv) Cyclotomic equation including the resulting problems of constructions.

(v)   Conformal mappings.

(vi) Symmetry groups. Congruent mappings of geometrical figures onto themselves.

(vii) Intuitive topology.

(c) *Axiomatic questions*. (i) Characterization of the field of real numbers by basic properties.

(ii) The field of complex numbers.

(iii) Group, ring, field.

(iv) Axiomatic building of geometry; for example, by reflection geometry (Bachmann) or equipollence (Papy).

(v)   Finite geometries.

(vi) Non-Euclidean geometry.

(vii) Boolean algebra and applications (e.g. logic and logic machines).

(viii) Theory of probability (axiomatic treatment).

5.4   Japan

5.4.0   *The programme of high-school mathematics.*

In Japan the curricula for courses of study are laid down by the State. Mathematics for upper secondary schools (kōtōgakkō-zennichisei) consists of five sections: mathematics 1, mathematics 2A, mathematics 2B, mathematics 3 and applied mathematics. Mathematics 1 is a compulsory subject for all tenth-grade students, with a choice of one from mathematics 2A, mathematics 2B and applied mathematics. Those who have completed mathematics 2B are usually advised to take mathematics 3 next. The syllabuses for mathematics 1, mathematics 2B and mathematics 3 are given below. These courses have been in use since 1962 and will be revised in 1973.

5.4.1   *Mathematics 1 (fifteen and sixteen years old)*

(a) *Polynomials, fractions, quadratic roots.* Fundamental laws of calculation. Division of a polynomial by a polynomial, Viète's theorem. Fractions and their calculation. Quadratic roots.

(b) *Equations and inequalities.* Quadratic equations, discriminant. Imaginary numbers. Simultaneous equations (both linear; one linear and one quadratic). Inequalities, fundamental properties. Solution of linear and quadratic inequalities.

(c) *Figures and their equations.* Coordinates. Equations of straight lines; their application. Equations of circles.

(d) *Functions and their graphs.* Quadratic functions and their graphs. Trigonometric functions and their graphs. Exponential functions and logarithmic functions. Logarithmic calculation.

(e) *Figures in space.* Fundamental elements in space and the relation of them. Three perpendiculars theorem. Coordinates in space, equation of a sphere. Elements of descriptive geometry.

(f) *Mathematics as a deductive system.* Axioms, definitions and theorems. Direct proof and indirect proof. (Introduce the elements of set theory.) (This topic may be treated either geometrically or by algebra.)

5.4.2   *Mathematics 2B (sixteen and seventeen years old)*
(a) *Elements of combinatories.* Permutation and combination. Mathematical induction. Binomial theorem. Relate to elements of set theory.)

(b) *Sequences and series.* Arithmetic and geometric sequence. Infinite geometric series; convergency.

(c) *Trigonometric functions, application to complex numbers.* Addition formulae. Trigonometric identities.

(d) *Coordinates and figures.* Elements of conics; ellipse, hyperbola, parabola. Transformation of coordinates. Polar coordinates, parameters.

(e) *Differential calculus of integral functions.* Differential coefficients, differentiation. Derivatives, applications.

(f) *Integral calculus of integral functions.* Indefinite integrals, definite integrals. Integration, applications.

5.4.3   *Mathematics 3 (seventeen and eighteen years old)*

(a) *General properties of functions.* Limit, continuity, differentiability. Theorem of the mean. Convex and concave.

(b) *Differentiation of elementary functions.* Differentiation of algebraic functions. Trigonometric, exponential and logarithmic functions. Applications. Approximate functions (first and second degrees).

(c) *Integration.* Integration by substitution, integration by parts. Some examples of indefinite integration. Definite integrals. Applications.

(d) *Probability.* Definition, theorem of addition and multiplication. Binomial distribution.

(e) *Statistics.* Descriptive statistics, mean and deviation. Statistical probility, law of large numbers. Elements of normal distribution. Elements of test theory.

5.5 Sweden

5.5.0 *The gymnasium reallinje syllabus (scientific and technical stream)*

There are five weekly lessons of forty minutes each during the three years. The students are from sixteen to eighteen years old. About 15–20 per cent of all students in this age group are expected to follow this syllabus.

5.5.1 *First year*

(a) *Elementary set theory.* Set, subset, union, intersection, complement. These concepts are intended to be used in many different contexts in the sequel.

(b) *The concept of a function.* Range, domain. Set concepts to be used.

(c) *The rational numbers.* The basic rules for addition and multiplication; absolute value. Revision of the different properties of the sets of natural, whole and rational numbers.

(d) *Linear equations, inequalities and systems of equations.* The presentation is clarified by the use of set concepts.

(e) *Real numbers.* Their continuity property.

(f) *Square roots; the second-degree equation.* A short course.

(g) *Powers with real exponents.* An axiomatic introduction is suggested.

(h) *Approximate values.* Absolute and relative errors; calculations with approximate values; linear interpolation. Of use in physics and other subjects requiring mathematics.

(i) *Vectors in the plane.* (Addition, multiplication with scalars; coordinates.) A vector is defined as a set of parallel directed line segments of equal length. The basic rules.

(j) *The orthogonal coordinate system.*

(k) *The linear function.* Including the usual treatment of the equation of the straight line.

(l) *Logarithms.* Little time is allowed for numerical calculations, which are meant to be done by slide rule.

(m) *The slide rule.* The construction of the slide rule. Used in calculations from the very beginning of the course.

(n) *Trigonometric functions.*

(o) *Computers.* A short introduction.

(p) *Derivatives.* An intuitive introduction for physics.

(q) *Descriptive statistics.* Graphical illustrations; mean, median, standard deviation; the summation symbol; use of calculating machines.

5.5.2 *Second year*

(a) *Scalar product of vectors.* Defined by using trigonometry.

(b) *The triangle theorems.* Sine and cosine theorems. Easy problems.

(c) *Rational functions.* The factor theorem; discussions of signs. Treatment of what is needed for the calculus.

(d) *Limits.* The basic ideas about an $\varepsilon - \delta$ treatment. The use of neighbourhoods is recommended.

(e) *Continuity.* The properties of continuous functions are given without proof.

(f) *Derivatives.* Derivative of sum, product and quotient; derivative of rational and trigonometric functions differential.

(g) *Composite functions.* Definitions, continuity and derivative.

(h) *Derivative monotonicity*; *maxima and minima.* The mean-value theorem is used and practical applications given.

(i) *Higher derivatives.* Convexity. A short course.

(j) *Integrals.* Relation between integral and primitive function; integration of rational and trigonometrical functions; areas. Definition using set concepts. The mean-value theorem is used.

(k) *The logarithmic function.* Natural logarithms; derivative. Definition using the integral

$$\int_{1}^{x} \frac{dt}{t}.$$

(l) *Inverse functions.* Existence and continuity; derivative; cyclometric functions.

(m) *Exponential functions.* Derivative. Defined via the logarithmic function.

(n) *Power functions.* Derivatives; conics.

5.5.3 Third year

(a) *Complex numbers.* Calculation; de Moivre and Euler formulae.

(b) *Differential equations.* Linear equations with constant coefficients of first and second order.

(c) *Methods of integration.* Partial integration and integration with substitution. Only simple problems treated.

(d) *Approximation with polynomials.* Maclaurin formula. No infinite expansions.

(e) *Vector functions.* Derivative; curves in parametric form.

(f) *Vectors in space.* Orthogonal coordinate system. Extension from two to three dimensions. Equations of line, plane and sphere.

(g) *Volumes and areas.* Calculations of volumes with integrals. Area of curved surfaces (sphere, cone and cylinder).

(h) *Sequences and series.* Convergence and divergence; the geometric series. A short course.

(i) *Combinatories.* The principle of multiplication; permutations; the binomial theorem, proof by induction. Set concepts will be used.

(j) *Theory of probability.* The classical concept of probability; finite sample spaces; mean, variance and standard deviation; infinite sample spaces; the binomial and normal distribution; instances of statistical inference including confidence intervals. This course applies much of what is learnt earlier.

In the new Swedish gymnasium, special effort is made to teach the students to work more and more by themselves. In the last two years, there will only be one homework per week in each subject.

In at least two subjects, the teaching will be arranged in the following way. The students will receive an assignment for two to four weeks at a time. During this period, some of the lessons will be devoted to preparation, while the rest of the lessons will be voluntary. The student will then work on his own with the theory, and solve problems, asking the teacher for aid if necessary.

5.6 Union of Soviet Socialist Republics

5.6.0 Proposed new syllabus of mathematics

Soviet schools have ten grades, divided into three cycles of three, five and two years. The proposed syllabus for the second and third cycles are given below. (The latter proposal is provisional.)

Children enter schools after the completion of their seventh year, thus they have an average age of about eight over grade 1, about eleven over grade 4, etc.

The number of weeks during a school year is thirty-three, each with six forty-five minute periods for mathematics (at least in grades 4 to 8). This amounts to 198 periods in a year. The syllabus gives the suggested order of topics (except for some which are spread over the school year or are taught in connexion with certain other topics).

Details are given below of the topics in grade 4. In the other grades only the main topics are listed with some indications here and there of what they cover. From the second term of grade 5 algebra and geometry appear as separate subjects and the six weekly periods are distributed between them according to the following plan:

	Grade 5	Grade 6		Grade 7		Grade 8	
	Term 2	Term 1	Term 2	Term 1	Term 2	Term 1	Term 2
Algebra	4	4	4	4	3	4	3
Geometry	2	2	2	2	3	2	3

The topic 'natural numbers' for example, is taught during the first three months of the school year (September, October, November) roughly.

After grade 8 the proposed distribution of the topics for the grades is not given. (The number in parentheses after a topic indicates the number of periods allocated to that topic.)

5.6.1   *Grade 4 (average age over the school year about eleven)*

(a) *Natural numbers* (74). Decimal system of numeration. Roman numerals. The number ray. Operations ('the four rules') with natural numbers. Equality, equation. Weights and measures.

(b) *Integers* (40). Positive and negative numbers; zero. The number line. Distance of two points on the number line. Diagrams in usual representation (preview for Cartesian coordinates). Operations with integers. Evaluation of numerical expressions. Solution of equations based on the properties of equalities.

(c) *Decimal fractions* (60). Fractions. The extension of the decimal notation. Operations with decimal fractions. Measuring lengths, areas, volumes. Approximations, rounding.

(d) *Fundamental concepts of geometry* (24 spread over the school year).

5.6.2   *Grade 5*

(a) *Algebra.* Algebraic formulae; introduction of powers (30). Cartesian coordinates; linear functions, simultaneous linear functions with two unknowns (30). Polynomials (40). Divisibility of numbers and polynomials (48).

(b) *Geometry.* Axial symmetry (20). Triangles (30).

5.6.3   Grade 6

(a) *Algebra*. Rational numbers and algebraic expressions (80). Functions and variables; inverse proportionality (22). Practical calculations (30).

(b) *Geometry*. Parallel lines; central symmetry (26). Quadrilaterals; displacement.

5.6.4   Grade 7

(a) *Algebra*. Simultaneous linear equations, systematic treatment (50). Slide rule (20, distributed in connexion with other topics). Real numbers; powers and roots; Pythagoras' theorem, quadratic equations (45).

(b) *Geometry*. The circle; rotation (40). Inscribed and circumscribed polygons (13). Areas of polygons (30).

5.6.5   Grade 8

(a) *Algebra*. Quadratic functions, equations, inequalities (50) (the concept of inequality is developed through grades 4–8). Simultaneous equations, extension for non-linear equations (20). Functions and graphs, with applications (30). Recapitulation (15).

(b) *Geometry*. Similarity (45). Trigonometrical functions, for angles 0–180° only (25). Recapitulation (13).

5.6.6   *Provisional list of topics for higher grades (9 and 10)*

(a) *Algebra and elementary functions*. Power functions (10). Number sequences (16). Functions and their graphs; the derivative (40). Vectors (6). Trigonometric functions (60). Exponential and logarithmic functions (30). The integral (15). Probability and statistics (25). The extension of the number concept (10). Recapitulation (19).

(b) *Geometry*. The method of coordinates (26). Fundamental ideas of solid geometry (40). Polyhedra (19). Solids generated by rotation (25). Volumes (30). Solution of problems; recapitulation (25).

5.6.7   *Provisional list of topics for higher grades of schools specializing in mathematics*

(a) *Algebra and elementary functions*. Linear and quadratic functions and inequalities (20). Elements of linear algebra (14). Powers with rational exponents (26). Exponential and logarithmic functions (20). Complex numbers (20). Polynomials; algebraic equations (30). Sets and logic; combinatories (16). Probability and statistics (26). Number sequences, limits (20). The general concept of functions, limits of functions, continuity (20). The derivative and its applications (59). The integral (40). Differential equations (14). Series of numbers and of functions; approximations of functions (25). Applications to physical processes (20). Vectors (10). Trigonometrical functions (56). Solution of problems; recapitulation (30).

(b) *Geometry*. The method of coordinates (47). Problems about triangles (15). Fundamental ideas of solid geometry (40). Polyhedra (24). Solids generated by rotation (20). Lengths, areas, volumes (30). Solution of problems; recapitulation (25).

5.7 United Kingdom

5.7.0 *Syllabus of the School Mathematics Project: preliminary remarks*

'O-level' is an abbreviation for 'ordinary level' and refers to examinations usually taken after the fifth year of secondary school (which begins at 11+) that is, at about the age of sixteen. Another examination called A-level (advanced level) is usually taken two years later by pupils continuing their studies. The syllabuses on which teaching is based during the five years preceding, or the two following, O-level examinations are completely within the competence of the various schools and teachers. In England, no such thing as a 'national syllabus' or 'state syllabus' exists. The syllabuses for examinations are not uniform either, but their range is much more restricted; they are all variants of two or three syllabuses. The one presented here may be regarded as an example of a modern mathematics examination syllabus used in England at present.

5.7.1 *The syllabus for O-level examination*

Arithmetic problems involving the important units of weight, measure and money. (Quantities will not be expressed in more than two units.) Fractions, decimals, ratio, percentage. Numbers: prime, composite, rational and irrational; simple sequences and their generalization. Approximations and estimates, significant figures, decimal places, limits of accuracy. Scales of notation other than denary. (The number a to base b will be expressed as a_b, with b always in denary.) Expression of numbers in the form $a \times 10^n$, where n is a positive or negative integer and $1 \leqslant a < 10$. The use of the slide rule.

Length, area and volume; mensuration of common plane and solid figures; circles, sphere; parallelogram, triangle, trapezium; prism (including cylinder); pyramid (including cone).

Angle. Graphs of sine and cosine functions; applications to simple problems. Tangent function of acute angle. Solution of triangles by reduction to right-angled triangles, the use of Pythagoras' theorem; simple applications to three-dimensional problems.

The notation and idea of a set; union, intersection, complement, subset; null and universal sets. Venn diagrams including their use in simple logical problems. Relations between the numbers of elements of sets, their unions and intersections. (Approved symbols: $\in, \cap, \cup, \mathscr{E}, ', \varnothing, \{ \,,\, \}, \{ \ : \ \}, \supset, \subset, n(A)$.) The use of symbols to represent numbers, sets, transformations and operations.

Conditional and identical equations; rearrangement of formulae; inequalities and their manipulation. The solution of simple and simultaneous linear equations and inequalities in not more than two unknowns. Solution sets in various universal sets, for example integers, rational and real numbers. Applications of inequalities; the use of graphs in linear programming. Factorization of $ax + bx$, $a^2 - b^2$, $a^2 \pm 2ab + b^2$. The fact that

$$xy = 0 \Leftrightarrow x = 0 \text{ or } y = 0.$$

Simple manipulation of algebraic fractions.

Rectangular Cartesian coordinates in two and three dimensions. The equation of the straight line in two dimensions and the plane in three dimensions (involving not more than two variables). Polar coordinates in two dimensions.

Informational matrices of any shape, their addition and multiplication where appropriate. Position vectors of points as 2×1 or 3×1 matrices. The idea of linear transformations in two dimensions and their matrix expressions; the combination, by premultiplying the position vectors by square matrices, of the transformations of reflection in the lines $x = 0$, $y = 0$, $x = \pm y$, and rotation through multiples of $90°$. The unit matrices. The formation of the inverse of non-singular 2×2 matrices. Application of matrices to the solution of simultaneous linear equations in two unknowns.

Proportion of variables related by simple power laws, $y \propto x^n$, where $n = -2$, $-1, 1, 2, 3$, and $y \propto \sqrt{x}$. The forms of the corresponding graphs, and also of $y = ax + b$ and $y = a^x$. Knowledge of such terms as linear, inverse square, exponential.

Gradient of graphs by drawing, estimation of area under graphs, by square counting or trapezium rule (other methods may be employed but no greater accuracy is required). Applications to easy kinematics, involving distance–time and speed–time curves; the idea of rate of change.

Interior and exterior angle sums of polygons, criteria for parallelism. The operations on Euclidean space of reflection, rotation, translation and their combinations, and the operation of enlargement. The ideas of shearing and stretching.

Similarity and congruence. Symmetry with respect to reflection in lines and points, and rotation. Applications of similarity including areas and volumes of similar figures, scales and simple map problems. The transformations connecting directly or oppositely congruent figures.

Loci in two or three dimensions, considered as sets of points. The circle, including the property that the angle at the centre is twice the angle at the circumference on the same arc, and tangents (but not the alternate segment property).

The ability to draw, read and understand simple plans and elevations (candidates will not be required to produce technically correct plans and elevations). Nets of solids. The angles between a straight line and a plane, and between two planes.

The earth considered as a sphere; latitude and longitude, great and small circles, nautical miles, distances along parallels of latitude and along meridians.

Simple probability; problems involving the intuitive application of the sum and product laws may be set, but general statements of the laws will not be required.

Graphical representation of numerical data by bar chart, histogram, frequency polygon and cumulative-frequency polygon, pie chart. Calculation of the mean (including the mean of grouped data). (The change-of-origin method need not be used.) Estimation of the median and quartiles; inter-quartile range.

5.7.2 The syllabus for A-level examination

Elementary trigonometry. Circular functions of angles of any magnitude; the addition formulae and their consequents; circular measure.

Elementary algebra. Factor theorem for polynomials; relation between roots and coefficients of algebraic equations; partial fractions (not involving more than one quadratic factor).

Coordinate systems. Cartesian, plane polar.

Functions. As mappings and as graphs; range and domain. Special functions: odd, even and periodic functions. Inverse functions. Particular functions and their graphs: algebraic; trigonometric; logarithmic and exponential, hyper-bolic cosine and sine.

Limits of sequences of numbers. Convergence of simple infinite series (qualita-tive treatment with no formal definitions or tests). Terms of a convergent sequence as successive approximations to the limit. Iterative processes.

Derivatives (of real functions of one real variable only). Differentiation of algebraic and trigonometric functions, of products and quotients, of inverse and composite functions. Second and higher derivatives. Maxima and minima; applications of differentiation to physical situations.

Tangent as a linear approximation. Approximations by the first few terms of Taylor's series; application to standard functions (for example, binomial series, circular functions). Newton's approximation to a root of an equation. The notion of integration as summation, with applications (for example, to area, volume, mean values). Numerical methods of integration; trapezium and Simpson's rules.

The fundamental theorem of integral calculus. Its application to evaluation of integrals. Standard integrals; integration by parts; simple substitutions.

The idea of algebraic structure and of binary operations: groups, isomorphism. Equivalence relations: equivalence classes, partitioning of sets.

Vectors. Coordinates in three dimensions. Scalar products. Lines and planes. Transformation matrices.

Systems of linear equations in three unknowns; geometrical interpretations and applicability of matrices.

Matrices. Square matrices: echelon form; solution of 3×3 equations by reduction to echelon form. Non-square matrices (3×2 and 2×3): applications to geometrical transformations.

Vectors which vary with time. Two-dimensional applications to displacement, velocity, acceleration, relative velocity. Motion of a particle in a plane using vectors: Cartesian and parametric coordinates.

Complex numbers. Their sums and products. Geometric representation as (i) points, (ii) displacements (iii) rotations and enlargements. The form $r(\cos \theta + j \sin \theta)$, the notation $|z|$, the triangle inequality.

The formation of differential equations for physical situations. Simple applications involving elementary knowledge of: Newton's laws of motion; force, momentum, impulse; conservation of momentum; work and energy; d.c. and and a.c. circuit theory. (Absolute units of force only will be used. Questions may be set on other applications, in which case the questions will be self-contained requiring no prior knowledge).

Solution of differential equations. First-order separable variables, linear first-order with constant coefficients with simple particular integrals which can be found by inspection. The step-by-step solution of

$$\frac{dy}{dx} = f(x, y).$$

Computing. Flow diagrams; conditional jumps. Compound probabilities; the binomial distribution. Measures of spread: standard deviation. Continuous distributions. The normal distribution (use of tables of the error function). Distribution of the mean of large samples. Tests for significance.

5.8   United States of America

5.8.0   *University of Illinois Committee on School Mathematics (UICSM)*

A description follows of the content treated in grades 9–12 of the secondary school.

5.8.1.   *Grade 9*

The arithmetic of the real numbers (Unit 1). Addition, multiplication, subtraction and division of real numbers; basic principles for real number (commutative etc.); comparing real numbers; use of $>$ and $<$; the number line; absolute value.

Generalizations and algebraic manipulation (Unit 2). Variables and algebraic expressions; generalizations and proofs; transformation of expressions; theorems and basic principles for transforming expressions.

Equations and inequations (Unit 3). Graph of a sentence; using geometric language (interval, segment, ray, half-line) to name loci; solution of equations and inequations; equivalent equations; formula and 'word' problems; expanding and factorizing expressions; solution of quadratic equations; square roots; approximations.

Ordered pairs and graphs (Unit 4). Graphing on pictures of the number-plane lattice and the number plane; intersections and unions of sets; factors of numbers and of expressions (domain of factorization); positive integral exponents; scientific notation.

5.8.2 Grade 10

Geometry (Unit 6). Segments and angles as sets of points; measures of segments and angles; congruence of segments and angles; supplementary, complementary, vertical and adjacent angles; perpendicular lines; triangles and their properties; geometric inequations; parallel lines; quadrilaterals; similar polygons; trigonometric ratios; rectangular coordinate systems; proofs by analytic geometry; circles and their properties; measures of regions; appendix: the rules of reasoning.

5.8.3 Grade 11

Relations and functions (Unit 5). Relations; principles for sets; relations and geometric figures; properties of relations; function as a special kind of relation; functional notation and ways of referring to functions; composite functions ($f \circ g$); functional dependence; variable quantities; linear functions (graph, slope, intercept); proportionality and variation; quadratic functions and quadratic equations; systems of equations.

Mathematical induction (Unit 7). Development of properties of positive numbers and positive integers from basic principles; mathematical induction; recursive definitions; properties of the set of integers; divisibility; Diophantine problems.

Sequences (Unit 8). Sequences; continued sums ($\sum$ notation); difference sequences; arithmetical progressions; continued products ($\prod$ notation); integral exponents; geometric progressions; combinations and permutations; the binomial theorem; prime numbers.

Elementary functions: powers, exponentials, and logarithms (Unit 9). Existence and uniqueness of principal square roots and cube roots; least-upper-bound principle; principle roots; rational numbers; rational exponents; exponential functions; logarithmic functions; some laws of nature; natural logarithmic function; monotonicity and continuity; irrational numbers, infinite sets and density of the rationals in the reals; solid geometry; functional equations.

5.8.4   *Grade 12*

Circular functions and trigonometry (Unit 10). Definition of cosine and sine in terms of winding functions; 'analytic trigonometry'; laws of cosines and sines; applications; inverse circular functions; solution of equations.

Complex numbers (Unit 11). Complex numbers as ordered pairs of reals; arithmetic of complex numbers; conjugates; quadratic equations; systems of quadratic equations.

Currently, the UICSM is engaged in a research programme which has as its ultimate goal the development of curriculum materials for grades 7–12. This activity is being supported by the National Science Foundation. In this development, careful attention is to be paid to applications of mathematics to various branches of science. Project efforts have been concentrated on the development of seventh-grade and tenth-grade materials.

5.8.5   *Description of the seventh-grade programme*

The seventh-grade materials will consist, in the main, of two parts. The first part is to contain extensive work with the arithmetic of rational numbers. Since traditional teaching techniques seem unsuccessful in enabling students generally to attain a reasonable proficiency in working with common and decimal fractions, the UICSM feels that a major effort to develop new pedagogical devices in this area is in order. In the proposed development, the rational numbers are treated as operators on lengths. Beginning with natural operators, such as 3 which maps a length L onto a length $3(L)$, that is, three times as long as L, and continuing with the intuitively obvious notion that each such operator has an inverse, we develop all of the usual arithmetic operations. This is done in a way that enables the student to develop his intuitions for understanding the nature of these operations.

The second of these parts is devoted to an intuitive development of geometric concepts. In this approach, the student is not, of course, required to give formal proofs of theorems, though he is expected to give plausible arguments for any assertions he might make. The objective with regard to geometry in grades 7, 8 and 9 is to develop, on an intuitive level, all of the basic notions of school geometry. It is this phase of the student's early secondary mathematics training which will lay the foundation on which the formal study of geometry in the tenth grade will be built.

The first trial (1964/5) of the seventh-grade course has been with children of below-average ability.

5.8.6   *Description of the tenth-grade programme*

The tenth-grade geometry programme has a twofold purpose. First, in the assumption that the student has been allowed to develop his intuitions about three-space in grades 7, 8 and 9, we propose to formalize these intuitions by deducing them from carefully selected postulates. This first purpose is a standard one. The departure from the realm of traditional geometry developments in the United States appears in our second purpose. In order to realize the first purpose we define certain distance-preserving mappings of Euclidean three-space onto itself. It is our second purpose to allow the student to see how the construction of a particular set of postulates, dealing with these mappings, is effected from perfectly plausible intuitions about points, lines and planes in three-space. It is through this second purpose that we hope to give the student some insight into the manner in which mathematics is created.

A brief description follows of the chapters prepared by UICSM staff members, from a developmental mathematics outline written by Vaughan for use with experimental classes. (Note that rules of logic are interspersed throughout the mathematics development.)

Chapter 1: *Introduction.* Intuitive discussions about force table (physics), velocities, and reflections in mirrors; intuitions about orientation on a line, on a plane, and in space.

Chapter 2: *Sets, functions and slides.* Review of concept of functions; certain mappings (slides, i.e. translations) of set $\mathbb{R}$ of reals onto $\mathbb{R}$ defined; slides on $\mathbb{R}^2$ and on $\mathbb{R}^3$ defined; properties of composing slides; inverses of slides; distance-preserving defined; noting properties common to slides on $\mathbb{R}$, on $\mathbb{R}^2$ and on $\mathbb{R}^3$.

Chapter 3: *An intuitive introduction to translations of $\mathscr{E}$.* Translations of $\mathscr{E}$; introduction to an algebra of points and translations.

Chapter 4: *An introduction to logic.* Generalization; role of postulates; deriving a theorem from postulates; conditional sentences; rule of *modus ponens*; replacement rule for equations; the deduction rule; converses; biconditional sentences.

Chapter 5: *The algebra of points and translations.* Instances of generalizations; alternate choice for postulate 2; the bypass postulate; postulates about $\mathscr{T}$ (the set of translations on $\mathscr{E}$); fixed points; subtraction of translations from points and from translations.

Chapter 6: *Commutative groups.* $\mathscr{T}$ is a commutative group; significance of commutative-group postulate; examples of commutative groups; noncommutative groups; isomorphism; examples of subgroups.

Chapter 7: *Continuing the algebra of points and translations.* Extending the theorem list; a convenient rule of manipulation.

Chapter 8: *Extending the algebra and logic.* Admitting real numbers as operators on translations; logical conjunction and alternation; rule of the dilemma; denying an alternative; exportation and importation.

Chapter 9: *Vector spaces.* Review of the group concept and scalar multiplication; $\mathscr{T}$ as a vector space; applied problems (velocities and forces).

Chapter 10: *Linear dependence and independence.* Linear combinations in a vector space; sequences; linearly dependent sequences; linear independent sequences; double denial; *modus tollens*; linear dependence and independence of translations.

Chapter 11: *Lines in* $\mathcal{E}$. Collinearity; definition of line; rule of contradiction; determining a line through two points; direction of a line and of a translation; sense of a translation; parallel lines; skew lines; translations map lines onto parallel lines.

Chapter 12: *Subsets of lines in* $\mathcal{E}$. Rays and segments; half-lines and intervals; senses of rays and half-lines; parallel sets; proportionality; points of division; midpoint.

Chapter 13: *Triangles and quadrilaterals.* Triangles; points of division of sides of triangles; medians; quadrilaterals; simple, convex quadrilaterals; trapezoids; parallelograms; position vectors; centre of gravity of triangular regions.

Chapter 14: *Planes in* $\mathcal{E}$. Coplanar points; plane; plane direction; parallel planes; parallel lines and planes.

Chapter 15: *Dimension and bases.* Establishing the dimension of $\mathcal{E}$. $\mathcal{T}$ is a three-dimensional vector space; intersections of planes; bases for $\mathcal{E}$; components and coordinates; Cartesian coordinate systems; equations of lines; vector equations; parametric equations; equations of planes.

Chapter 16: *Orthogonal projections.* Properties of projections; projections of vectors; projections of points; norm of a vector; unit vectors; dot multiplications; $\mathcal{T}$ is a three-dimensional inner-product space; length of a vector; distance between points; orthogonal vectors; inner-product spaces; Schwartz's inequality; triangle inequality.

The material outlined above was taught during the year 1963/4 to two tenth-grade classes at University High School, Urbana, Illinois.

Another trial of a revised version of the first draft has been taught to three tenth-grade classes at University High School during the school year 1964/5. In addition, the original classes will be merged into a single class, and these students will study the topics listed below as part of their eleventh-grade work in mathematics.

Chapter 17: *Distance and perpendicularity.* Distance in $\mathcal{E}$; metric properties; perpendicularity of lines and planes; perpendicular bisector of a segment.

Chapter 18: *Orientation of lines and planes.* Oriented lines and planes; ortho-normal bases; unit orthogonal vectors; determinants; sense classes.

Chapter 19: *Angles.* Sensed angles; right angle; adjacent angles; cosines; acute and obtuse angles; vertical angles; angle bisectors; sines; supplementary angles; complementary angles; oriented triangles; sine law; cosine law;

projection law; angles and triangles; measures of angles.

Chapter 20: *Isometries of &.* Definition of isometry; plane reflection; proper rotations; resultants of rotations; glide reflections; twists; composing isometries.

Chapter 21: *Congruence in &.* Congruence as a distance-preserving mapping; triangle congruence theorems.

In addition to studying the above topics in the eleventh grade, the class will study exponential functions, logarithmic functions and circular functions (trigonometry).

For one who might object to the fact that this treatment of geometry spans the tenth and eleventh grades, it should be pointed out that all the major topics treated in the traditional tenth- and eleventh-grade mathematics programmes in the United States are also treated in this programme. The major difference is that, while in the traditional programme there is a sharp division between the treatment of algebraic topics and the treatment of geometric topics, this division does not exist in the proposed programme. This is due in no small part to the unifying effect of the treatment of geometric topics in the context of the vector space $\mathscr{T}$.

6 A Modern Secondary-School Syllabus in Mathematics for the Scientific Stream

Prepared by W. Servais. First published in Mathematics Today. 1964, Organization for Economic Co-operation and Development

6.0 Introduction

6.0.1 In compiling a syllabus, the first step is to choose a set of topics, which means that some topics are rejected and others adopted. Once the topics have been selected they must be arranged in a suitable progression, that is, their set must be given a partial order, since order will depend on the point of view adopted. Depending on whether one is concerned with (a) the rational arrangement of subjects, (b) the urgency of learning and using them or (c) the process by which the mind assimilates them, they would have to be arranged in a logical, a practical or a psychological order, respectively. For teaching purposes, the final order will have to reconcile all three aspects, while avoiding the worst pitfalls.

6.0.2 Nowadays we have a better understanding of mathematical ideas and theories, we are subject to greater pressure because of the steady increase in their applications, and we are more alive to the psychology of mathematics and its learning processes. This means that it has become a more complex problem to compile a mathematical syllabus but, on the other hand, we are in a better position to solve that problem.

6.0.3 By an understanding of its structures – and thanks to their versatility – mathematics has recovered its unity through set theory.

Teaching should proceed in the light of these findings and, using set theory as a basis, should build up a more unified construction, structured by homogeneous modern ideas. It should do this not only to present an authentic, albeit elementary, image of the science of mathematics, but also to develop the psychological ability to use mathematics as a tool in a broader, more deliberate and more effective way.

To achieve this it is not enough to get rid of obsolete subjects and replace them by subjects of more topical value, or to graft a few modern ideas onto an outdated syllabus. Mathematics must be taught by making active use of its structures both as means and as ends.

This means that mathematics will cease to be taught in terms of special properties and will in future be organized around a number of general themes.

Practical teaching experience shows that when it is taught in this way pupils acquire an astonishing mastery and intellectual drive which enable them to forge ahead.

6.0.4 The proposed syllabus for the scientific streams in secondary schools has been planned in this spirit. There are three areas which are of vital importance for the application of mathematics to physics, biology and the human sciences: vector spaces; elements of analysis; elements of probability and statistics.

These are the lines on which teaching must be organized if it is to meet the needs of those who use mathematics. Moreover, these themes provide the substance for a complete mathematical education.

6.0.5 Vector spaces, elements relating to continuity, limits, differential calculus and integral calculus are so universally used in science and technology that it is superfluous to emphasize their importance.

6.0.6 It is important to stress the practical and educational implications of the elements of probability and statistics:

(a) Their fields of application are extremely diverse and extensive.

(b) They represent a complex mathematical model synthesizing all the resources of the structures studied.

(c) They are an introduction to the random concept, which children often find fascinating and which has unrivalled educational value as it offers more opportunities for mental agility than any other branch of mathematics.

6.0.7 Mathematical logic is acquiring greater importance every day. It is recommended that a study should be made of it as soon as possible in conjunction with that of sets, using one to throw light on the other. In this way the notions and criteria essential for formulating statements and definitions, and for developing mathematical demonstrations will become familiar.

6.0.8 A fairly explicit syllabus has been submitted, not to make it more compelling but to give an idea of its organization and ramifications.

Experience with classes shows that this syllabus can be taught effectively in practice. It has turned out that as much time should be spent on essential notions as is required to assimilate them constructively and lastingly. In order to achieve the aims of the syllabus, it is essential not to be side-tracked by minor issues.

6.0.9 The syllabus can of course be adjusted to conditions in each particular country. Where this one is done it is recommended that (a) the three essential objectives should not be lost sight of; (b) a functional and structural arrangement should be maintained to enable those objectives to be achieved economically and effectively.

6.0.10 Some people will want to increase the number of subjects taught by adding the theory of conics, descriptive geometry, elements of projective geometry, the study of hyperbolic functions, the rudiments of differential equations, and multiple integrals.

Before these additions are made, their theoretical and practical importance for a modern secondary-school course should be properly assessed.

6.0.11 In any event, a sensible attitude must be adopted towards this, as to any other, syllabus and see that what is done is done properly, with the unhurried calm that is conducive to good results. Experience shows that where the teaching is organized functionally and based on the structures of mathematics, it is possible, in a shorter period of time, to achieve results which cannot be equalled by less-thoroughly planned methods.

6.0.12 Our experimental work has convinced us that it is possible to use the proposed subjects as a basis for a thorough mathematical education which will provide not only a sound training in essential concepts but also a body of practical, useful data.

6.0.13 A mathematical education of this kind depends not so much on the syllabus as on teaching method, for it is only good teaching that can make a syllabus meaningful. Let us make no mistake: any syllabus, however sensible and balanced it is, can degenerate into mere dogma in the hands of a dogmatic teacher.

6.0.14 A modern syllabus calls for modern teaching methods to give it life and effectiveness. To meet the requirements of a mathematics of structures, a new and effective teaching method is now being evolved based on mental structuration. It teaches mathematics by making the learner participate. The pupil is trained to mathematize a given situation by identifying its structures. He learns to schematize, assemble, inquire, deduce, calculate and interpret, by a judicious choice of methods and processes. The method makes as much use of imagination and guesswork as it does of verification and criticism. It develops ability to cope with the unknown and confidence to use the known.

In a word, it gives a dynamic and creative impetus to the pupil's thinking, which guarantees his ability to invent, adapt, master and organize.

6.1 Documentation

The programme elaborated below draws on the following sources:
(a) The Dubrovnik programme.
(b) The programme of the Commission on Mathematics of the College Entrance Examination Board.
(c) The experimental programme established by the Centre Belge de la pédogogie de la mathématique.
(d) The Scandinavian experimental programme.
(e) Work of the International Commission for the Improvement of Mathematical Instruction.

(f) The experimental programme of the Gymnasium in the Neuchâtel Canton.

(g) The Madrid experimental programme.

6.2 A modern assignment of mathematical subject matter

6.2.1 Sets

(a) Set, object, belonging, $\in$, equality. Inclusion $A \subset B$, subsets of a set $\mathscr{E}$. The set of subsets, $P(\mathscr{E})$. Empty set, Venn diagram. Determination of a subset of $\mathscr{E}$ by a condition on a variable $x \in \mathscr{E}$. Equivalence and implications of its conditions on a set $\mathscr{E}$.

(b) Algebra of sets. Intersection $A \cap B$, union $A \cup B$, difference $A \backslash B$ in liaison with the logical operations conjunction $\wedge$, disjunction $\vee$, and negation $\neg B$. Complement $\mathscr{E} \backslash A$ of a class of $\mathscr{E}$. The symmetric difference $A \triangle B$. Associativity, distributivity. Intersection and union of a family of sets. Quantifiers, $\forall x \in \mathscr{E}$, $\exists x \in \mathscr{E}$. Partitioning and covering of a set. The product set $A \times B$, the product of a succession of sets.

6.2.2 Relations

(a) Relation of a set A to a set B. Representation by a graph, by a table. The relation R as a set of ordered pairs, a subset of $A \times B$. Domain and image of a relation. Condition on two variables $x \mathrel{r} y$ determining a relation in $A \times B$.

(b) Reciprocal of a relation, composition of two relations. Relations that are reflexive (anti-reflexive), symmetric (anti-symmetric), transitive (connected). Relations of equivalence; partitioning, quotient set. Relations of order, strict order, total order, partial order.

6.2.3 Functions

(a) Functional relation of a set E to a set F. Mapping of E into and onto F. $E \xrightarrow{f} F : x \longrightarrow f(x)$. Images of subsets of E by f; $f(A)$, $f(A \cup B)$, $f(A \cap B)$. Reciprocal of a function, reciprocal images. Quotient set of E by f. Injection, surjection, bijection, functional, reciprocal function or inverse. Composition of functions.

(b) Group of permutations (bijections) of a set E.

(c) Equipotence of sets. Cardinal number.

(d) Homomorphism and isomorphism of sets structured by relations or operations.

6.2.4 The set of natural numbers

(a) The natural numbers, finite sets, denumerable sets, succession of elements of a set. Addition and multiplication defined by means of the union and product of sets. Total order of the natural numbers, consistency with addition and multiplication.

(b) Axioms of Peano. Induction.

(c) Division, remainder. Ring of residual classes modulo n.

(d) Divisor, prime numbers, factorization, primary numbers. Greatest common divisor, least common multiple. Relation to the operations $\cap$ and $\cup$ on the set of primary divisors of the numbers considered.

(e) Systems of numeration, binary and denary.

(f) *Combinations*. Arrangements with repetitions of m objects n at a time: mapping of a set of n objects into a set of m objects. Simple arrangements of m objects, n at a time: injections of a set of n objects into a set of m objects. Permutations (simple) of a set of m objects and bijection of this set onto an equipollent set. Combinations of m objects taken n at a time. Sets of subsets of n elements contained in a set of m objects. Number of subsets of a finite set.

6.2.5   *The line and the plane; dilatations*

The plane as a set of points, lines as subsets of a plane. Axioms of incidence and parallelism. Direction, parallel projection. Axioms of total order on each line, half-line, intervals, segment, convex set of points. The parallel projection of one line on another is a function increasing or decreasing. Dilatations (stretchings): bijection of the plane mapping one line onto a parallel line. Enlargements and translations. Compositions. Properties of the group. Equipollent ordered pairs, vectors, projection of equipollent vectors. Addition of vectors. Properties of a group. Addition in a plane furnished with an origin. Isomorphic groups.

6.2.6   *Groups*

(a) Examples. Additive and multiplicative groups in the set of residual classes modulo m. Tables of a group. The group of integers $\mathbb{Z}$, $+$. The group of bijections of a set. Permutations of a finite set. The group of displacements and rotations which map onto itself the set of points of a plane (one point, two points, three points, four points, five points). Studying the cases where the points are the vertices of an equilateral triangle, a square, a regular pentagon. The group of translations of the plane, the additive group of vectors in a plane. The additive group in a plane with a given origin. The group of enlargements, given the centre. The group of dilatations.

(b) Definition of a group G, $*$, internal law of composition everywhere defined, associativity, identity element, the symmetric of an element. Equations $a*x = b$, $y*a = b$ in a group. Commutative group. Additive and multiplicative notation. Symmetric of a sum or product. Multiples of powers of an element. The scalar law of a group. Cyclic groups. Subgroups.

6.2.7   *The ordered ring of integers*

The group $\mathbb{Z}$, $+$ and the additive group generated by a point on a line having a given origin. Order on the line and order on $\mathbb{Z}, +$. Multiplication of integers. The ordered ring $\mathbb{Z}, +,., \leqslant$.

6.2.8 *The line and the field of real numbers*

(a) Graduation of a line having an origin and unit point. Axiom of Archimedes.

(b) Subgraduation by successive bisections (or subdivisions by ten). Development of binary (or denary) limits. Binary (denary) unlimited sequences. Axiom of continuity. Parallel projections of one graduation on another. Theorem of Thales.

(c) Real numbers determined by binary (or denary) construction. Ratio of vectors, product of a vector by a real number. Addition of real numbers and addition of vectors. Multiplication of real numbers, and multiplication of enlargements. Distributivity of multiplication over addition. The field of real numbers, totally ordered.

(d) The rational numbers as quotients of integers, sums and products. The commutative and totally ordered field of rational numbers $\mathbb{Q}, +,., \geqslant$. Rational approximations to a real number.

6.2.9 *Numerical computation*

(a) Addition, subtraction, multiplication and division of real numbers from approximate values. Absolute errors and relative errors. The number of significant digits in a decimal development.

(b) Logarithms. Multiplicative group generated by a real number q, positive and not equal to one. Infinite geometric progressions G. Additive group generated by a real number not equal to zero. Infinite arithmetic progressions A. Isomorphism G $\rightarrow$ A: logarithmic function defined on G. Base, logarithms to base ten. If one takes $q = 1 \cdot 000\ 230\ 311\ 5$ and $r = 0 \cdot 0001$, $q^{10\ 000} = 10$ and $10\ 000r = 1$. Logarithmic computation, tables and rules. The nth roots of positive real numbers.

(c) Concepts of logarithmic and exponential functions: isomorphism of the multiplicative group of positive real numbers $(\mathbb{R}^+,.)$ and the additive group of all real numbers $(\mathbb{R}, +)$.

6.2.10 *Polynomials with real coefficients*

(a) The ring of polynomials in one or several variables over a field, over a ring. Numerical value, polynomial function of $\mathbb{R}$ to $\mathbb{R}$.

(b) The Euclidean division in a ring of polynomials with real coefficients. Division by $x - a$. Zeros of a polynomial in a given domain. Factorization.

(c) Equation of the second degree in one variable. Solution to second-degree equations. Inequations of the first and second degree in one variable.

6.2.11   *The vectorial plane and affine geometry*

(a) The commutative group of vectors in a plane $(V, +)$. Multiplication of vectors by real numbers. Structure of real vectorial algebra $(\mathbb{R}, V, +)$.

(b) Structure of real vectorial algebra in a plane with given origin. Cartesian coordinates of vectors and of points. Parametric equations and Cartesian equation of a line. System of equations of the first degree in two variables. Matrices and determinants having four elements. Inequations and systems of inequations of the first degree in two variables. Linear programming. Area of parallelograms and orientation. Transformation of coordinates of vectors and of points.

(c) General affine transformations. Translations, central symmetries, enlargements, affine axial symmetries, axial affinities.

6.2.12   *Metric Euclidean geometry of the plane*

(a) Perpendicularity of lines. Axioms. Perpendicular lines and parallel lines. Orthogonal axial symmetry. Axiom of the bisector.

(b) Group generated by orthogonal symmetries; isometries. Isometric figures. Circle. Group of displacements, rotations and translations. Axioms of rigidity. Invariance of perpendicularity.

(c) Unit vectors, isometries. Distance between two points. Scalar product. Cosine of an angle. Theorem of Pythagoras. Triangle inequality. Orthogonal basis. Trigonometric circle. Sine, cosine, tangent of an angle. Fundamental formulae of trigonometry.

(d) Similitudes of the plane. The Euclidean geometry group. Equation of a circle with orthogonal basis. Canonical form of the equations of the conics. Affine and metric equivalences.

6.2.13   *Descriptive statistics*

(a) The statistics pertaining to a population (set) divided into classes. Values and frequencies. Total frequency and composite frequencies.

(b) Statistical distribution of a variable. Histograms, frequency polygons, cumulative frequency polygons. Mode, median, mean (arithmetical). Quartiles and deciles. Interquartile range, standard deviation.

(c) Statistical distribution of two variables. Marginal and conditional distributions. Regression of the mean. Linear regression. Correlation.

6.2.14   *The plane and the field of complex numbers*

(a) Equality and addition of complex numbers, and the additive group in a plane having an origin. Cartesian form $a + bi$. The opposite of a complex number. Conjugate complex number.

(b) Multiplication of complex numbers and the group of similitudes with centre at origin O. Trigonometric form of complex numbers (polar coordinates). Inverse of a non-zero complex number.

(c) Distributivity of multiplication with respect to addition. The field of complex numbers. Linear functions of a complex variable and the group of similitudes of the plane.

(d) De Moivre's formula, the n nth roots of a complex number. Statement of the theorem of D'Alembert.

6.2.15 *Groups, rings, fields*

(a) Groups, subgroups. Intersection of a set of subgroups. Subgroups generated by a subset. Subset generators. Lateral classes, order of subgroups of groups of finite order. Normal subgroups, quotient group.

(b) Ring, field, commutative fields.

(c) Ring of polynomials of one variable (several variables) on a ring; on a field. Euclidean division in a ring of polynomials of one variable having coefficients in a field.

(d) Field of rational fractions. Homomorphisms and isomorphisms.

6.2.16 *Vector spaces*

(a) The planes and the lines of space; incidence; intersection, parallelism. Groups of displacements in space; translations and homotheties. Vectors, vector space. Space, furnished with an origin, as a vector space.

(b) Definition of a vector space and examples. Linear combinations of vectors.

(c) Subvector spaces. Intersection of a set of subvector spaces. Subspace generated by a subset.

(d) Linear dependence. Fixed families, free families. Generators of families. Bases, coordinates. Spaces of finite dimensions. Dimensions.

(e) Linear mappings. Matrix of a linear mapping with respect to a basis. Isomorphism of vector spaces of the same dimension over a field.

(f) Change of basis. Elements of matrix calculation.

(g) Linear forms. Dual spaces.

(h) Solution of systems of linear equations by elimination through the aid of linear combinations.

(i) Determinants. Application to the theory of linear equations. Orientation.

6.2.17 *Geometry of affine space*

(a) Parametric equations of a line, of a plane, of a segment. Dividing a segment into a given ratio. Cartesian equation of a plane in space. Lines and parallel planes.

(b) Affine transformations. Group. Invariance of the set of lines and of the set of planes preserving parallelism and intersection. Affine equivalence of quadratics. Particular transformations. Subgroups.

6.2.18   *Euclidean geometry of space*

Scalar product. Euclidean metric. Sphere. Perpendicular bases. Perpendicularity of lines and planes. Analytic expressions. Vectorial product ($\times$ product). Perpendicular symmetry with respect to a plane. The group of symmetries generated by perpendicular symmetries. Rotation about an axis, axial symmetry, displacement, spiral displacements. Figures invariant under these transformations. The group of displacements. The group of similitudes of Euclidean space.

6.2.19   *Finite probability spaces*

(a) Chance experiences having a finite set $\mathscr{E}$ of a simple nature. Events, subsets of $\mathscr{E}$.

(b) Elementary probability defined on $\mathscr{E}$. Probability of an event $p(A)$ of an outcome $A \subset \mathscr{E}$.

$$p(\mathscr{E}) = 1, \qquad p(\varnothing) = 0, \qquad 0 \leqslant p(A) \leqslant 1.$$

$$\text{If} \quad A \cap B = \varnothing, \qquad p(A \cup B) = p(A + p(B).$$

Independent events: $p(A \cap B) = p(A).p(B)$.

(c) Stochastic variable defined over $\mathscr{E}$. Mathematical expectation of a function of a stochastic variable. Mean, variance, distribution of a stochastic variable. Chebichev's inequality.

(d) Joint distribution of two variables defined over $\mathscr{E}$. Marginal distributions. Mathematical expectation of a sum and a product of several stochastic invariables defined over $\mathscr{E}$.

(e) Binomial distributions. Mean and variance; law of large numbers.

6.2.20   *Metric space and topology*

(a) Open interval, closed interval over the real line $\mathbb{R}$. Open disc (sphere), closed disc (sphere) over the real plane $\mathbb{R}^2$. Open ball (sphere), closed ball (sphere) over the real space $\mathbb{R}^3$. Open regions of the line, plane and space.

(b) Definition of a distance. Example of an affine distance. The corresponding structure of metric space.

(c) Topological space. The topology of open regions. Neighbourhoods, closed neighbourhoods.

6.2.21   *Continuous functions*

(a) Continuous functions of a topological space E defined over a topological space F. Continuity of a point of E, continuity of a subset of E. Examples: Identical functions over E. Constant function of E into F.

(b) Translation, enlargement, parallel projections in affine space, isometries in Euclidean metric space. Continuous bijection to a continuous reciprocal homomorphism. Subhomomorphisms of space.

(c) Composition of two continuous functions. Composition of two homomorphisms.

(d) Functions that are continuous at values in a plane furnished with an origin. Sums of continuous functions, scalar multiplication of a continuous function by a real number. Vector structure of these functions.

(e) Functions continuous at values in $\mathbb{R}$, continuity of the sum and product of continuous functions. Quotient of two continuous functions.

(f) Continuous functions of $\mathbb{R}$ (or a subset of $\mathbb{R}$) into $\mathbb{R}$. Examples: sine, exponential, logarithmic. Image of a segment by a continuous function. Ring of continuous functions of $\mathbb{R}$ into $\mathbb{R}$. Subring of polynomial functions generated by the identity function $\mathbb{R} \to \mathbb{R} : x \to x$ and constants.

(g) Limit of a function at a point. Sequence and limit of a sequence. Cauchy's theorem of convergence. Series, theorems on the important series.

6.2.22   *Differential calculus*

(a) Infinitely small or continuous functions and zeros at a point. Derivative. Rules for calculating the derivative of a sum, product and quotient of functions differentiable at a point or over a set of points of $\mathbb{R}$. Successive derivatives. Calculation of derivatives of exponential, logarithmic, sine, cosine and tangent functions.

(b) Primitives.

(c) Functions differentiable at a, functions differentiable n times at a. Calculus of differentials. Development of the limit of order n.

(d) Taylor's and MacLaurin's formulae. Development of the limits of exponential, logarithmic, sine and cosine functions.

(e) Graphs of real functions of a real variable. Tangents, increasing and decreasing functions, maximum and minimum. Concavity, asymtotes.

6.2.23   *Integral calculus*

(a) The notion of a definite integral

$$\int_a^b f(x)\, dx.$$

If c is a constant, by definition,

$$\int_a^b c \, dx = c(b-a).$$

Integral as a step function. (A numerical function f defined in an interval $[a, b]$ is called a step function, if, for any $E > 0$, there exists a function ϕ on $[a, b]$ such that $|f(x)-\phi(x)| < E$ for every x in $[a, b]$.) Upper and lower integral of a bounded function. When these two functions are equal, their common value is by definition

$$\int_a^b \phi(x) \, dx.$$

Integral of a monotonic function on $[a, b]$. Integral of a continuous function on $[a, b]$. Integral as the limit of a sum.

(b) Linearity of integrals. Chasles's formula. The law of the mean.

(c) The integral

$$F(x) = \int_a^x f(u) \, du$$

in which $f(x)$ is everywhere differentiable where this function is continuous. Primitive of a continuous function.

(d) Method of integration by parts and by a change of variables.

(e) The logarithmic function defined by

$$L(x) = \int_a^x \frac{du}{u}.$$

(f) Applications of the integral to the finding of areas, volumes, masses.

6.2.24   *Probability over the real line*

(a) Real stochastic variable defined over the set of real numbers. Probability distribution. Rectangular distribution; binomial distribution. Distribution given by an integral. Mathematical expectation of a real function of a stochastic variable. Mean, variance; dispersion; reduced variable to mean $= 0$, $\sigma = 1$. Chebichev's inequality. The normal distribution.

(b) Sampling. Estimation of a probability. Estimation of the mean. Interval of confidence of a mean and of the probability of large samples.

(c) Axiomatic definition of a probability space. A probability space is a set $\mathscr{E}$ furnished with the following structure:

(i) In the space $\mathscr{E}$, there exists a family $\mathscr{F}$ of subsets called events, which are such that: $\mathscr{E}$ and $\varnothing$ are events; if $A, B, A_1, A_2, \ldots, A_n, \ldots$ are events, then the following also are events,

$$\mathscr{E}\backslash A, \quad A \cup B, \quad A \cap B, \quad \bigcup_{i \in \mathbb{N}} A_i, \quad \bigcap_{i \in \mathbb{N}} A_i.$$

(ii) For each event A and each event B

$$A \cap B = \varnothing \Rightarrow p(A \cup B) = p(A) + p(B).$$

(iii) Over $\mathscr{F}$, there is defined a function (of real values) called the probability p such that

$$p(\mathscr{E}) = 1 \qquad p(\varnothing) = 0$$

and for all other events $A \in \mathscr{F}$

$$0 \leqslant p(A) \leqslant 1.$$

(iv) If $A_1, A_2, \ldots, A_n, \ldots$ is a succession of events such that

$$A_1 \supset A_2 \supset A_3 \supset \ldots \supset A_n \supset \ldots \quad \text{and} \quad \bigcap_{i \in \mathbb{N}} A_i = \varnothing$$

then $\lim_{n \to \infty} p(A_n) = 0.$

Note. In finite spaces, $\mathscr{F}$ is the partition of $\mathscr{E}$ and (i), (ii) and (iii) simply become the elementary probability defined on $\mathscr{E}$.

To show how the above programme becomes a unified global approach to the study, it is necessary to see when and how each item is developed. The following sections are a breakdown by years of study. Much of the material designated for ages fifteen and sixteen has already been studied in the lower cycle of secondary schools having a modern programme.

6.3   First year (fifteen and sixteen years old)

6.3.1   *Sets, relations, functions* (6.2.1–3)

Among those who have concerned themselves with the modernization of instruction, it is generally recognized that the foundation of this modernization must be the basis of science of mathematics itself: the related notions, sets, relations, functions. In those countries where new instruction has been introduced in the lower cycle of the secondary school, this foundation is taught beginning at twelve years old. We only make explicit the contents which will be in constant usage throughout the course of the upper cycle (from fifteen to eighteen).

6.3.2   *The set of natural numbers* (6.2.4)

The natural numbers are the cardinal numbers of finite sets. One studies the operations on these numbers, their representation in a binary and decimal system of numeration, and their use in computation.

6.3.3 *The line and the plane; dilations* (6.2.5)

Lines and planes are considered as sets of points. The modern concept of parallel lines (identical lines or disjoint lines in the same plane) allows a definition of parallel projection (in the plane with respect to a line of the plane) and the dilatations which are the bijections in the plane applied to all lines with respect to a parallel line.

Equipollent couples and vectors are introduced in connexion with translations. The plane furnished with an origin and the addition of points is a group isomorphic to that of the translations of a plane.

6.3.4 *Groups* (6.2.6)

The concept of group is unfolded by many examples, and an elementary study is made of the concept of an abstract group.

6.3.5 *The ordered ring of integers* (6.2.7)

The ring $(\mathbb{Z}, +, ., \leqslant)$ is studied along with the representation of integers on a graduated line.

6.3.6 *The line and the field of real numbers* (6.2.8)

The subgraduation of a line by successive subdivision by two (or by ten) and the marking of the points by this construction (binary or denary) done finitely, or infinitely, give simultaneously a construction of the set of real numbers and the line furnished with an origin.

The rational numbers are introduced as quotients of integers. In this manner, the thorny question of the real and rational is resolved.

This method of introducing the real numbers has been developed by the Centre of Mathematical Pedagogy under the direction of Papy. See *Affine Plane Geometry and Real Numbers* by Papy with the collaboration of Debbaut. In a certain way it represents the ideas expressed by Lebesgue in his *On the Measure of Magnitudes*.

6.3.7 *Numerical computation* (6.2.9)

The four operations on real numbers are carried out by approximate values. One calculates an upper bound to the errors. An elementary introduction to logarithms allows the use of tables and a slide rule.

6.3.8 *Polynomials with real coefficients* (6.2.10)

On the basis of the study made in the lower cycle, one introduces the ring of polynomials in one or several variables over a ring. A distinction is made between a polynomial form and a polynomial function. The Euclidean division in a ring of polynomials in x with real coefficients leads to factorization. Equations and inequations of the first and second degree in one variable are solved.

6.3.9   *The vectorial plane and affine geometry* (6.2.11)

The plane, in which an origin is given, has a structure of real vectors of two dimensions. The Cartesian coordinates are defined and equations and inequations of the first degree in two variables are studied with applications to linear programming. An introduction is given to matrices and determinants using only four elements. In this connexion, the area of parallelograms and the orientation of the plane are studied. The affine transformations of a plane are examined.

6.3.10   *Metric Euclidean geometry of the plane* (6.2.12)

The group of displacements and of isometries is generated by axial symmetries. One introduces the distance between two points, the angle as a couple of half lines, the scalar product of two vectors and the trigonometric ratios. The group of similitudes of a plane are studied.

6.3.11   *Descriptive statistics* (6.2.13)

The elements of descriptive statistics give opportunity to put to work the ideas acquired in numerical calculations and in graphical representation.

6.4   **Second year (sixteen and seventeen years old)**

6.4.1   *The plane and the field of complex numbers* (6.2.14)

Just as the real numbers have been introduced in connexion with the group of homothetic translations, the complex numbers are introduced in relation with the group of similitudes of the plane.

6.4.2   *Groups, rings, fields* (6.2.15)

The examples of groups, rings and fields, encountered in the preceding study, now open and bring to light a more general study of these notions.

6.4.3   *Vector spaces* (6.2.16)

Vector structure of a space having an origin serves as a base for the introduction of linear algebra which is presented in a general fashion.

6.4.4   *Geometry of affine space* (6.2.17)

The study of geometry of real affine space is made with all the resources of vectorial and analytic representation.

6.4.5   *Euclidean geometry of space* (6.2.18)

The scalar product of two vectors allows the definition of metric notions.

Orthogonal symmetries with respect to a plane generate the group of isometries and the group of displacements of space. The composition of displacement of enlargements gives the similitudes of space.

6.4.6 Finite probability spaces (6.2.19)

On the basis of concrete chance experiences, there is built a presentation of the concepts of calculus of probability limited to sets having a finite number of cases, as elementary as possible.

6.5 Third year (seventeen and eighteen years old)

6.5.1 Metric spaces and topology (6.2.20)

The Euclidean distance function enables one to define an open region of a line, plane or space. One now extends these notions to any distance. Then the fundamental concepts of topology are revealed.

6.5.2 Continuous functions (6.2.21)

The notion of continuity of a function at a point and over a set is presented in all its generality and specifically for a number of examples, in particular, exponential, logarithmic, sine, cosine and tangent. The limit of a function is defined in connexion with continuity at a point.

6.5.3 Differential calculus (6.2.22)

The definition of a derivative leads to rules for finding the derivative of a sum, product and quotient of functions having a derivative at a point or over a subset of $\mathbb{R}$. The derivatives of the exponential, logarithmic, sine, cosine and tangent functions are calculated. The inquiry into primitives is introduced as the reciprocal of derivative.

Functions differentiable at a point are introduced in connexion with the development of limits. The formulae of Taylor and MacLaurin furnish such developments. These formulae are applied to exponential, logarithmic, sine and cosine functions. The derivatives are used in the study of graphs of real functions of a real variable.

6.5.4 Integral calculus (6.2.23)

The integral

$$\int_a^b f(x)\,dx$$

is defined from the point of view of integrals of step functions (defined by step functions). The elementary properties of integrals are then given. The integral

$$\int_a^x f(u)\,du$$

of a continuous function f is a primitive of the function. These results are applied as in the classical calculus.

6.5.5 *Probability over the real line* (6.2.24)

Elementary ideas on the distribution of the probability of a real stochastic variable over the set of real numbers. With respect to sampling by large samples, the estimations and the intervals of confidence of the mean, and of the probability are explained. One uncovers the definition of a probability space.

Part Three

Steps to Reform

7 The Training and Re-Training of Mathematics Teachers

Prepared by W. Servais

There is a severe shortage of qualified mathematics teachers in every country. Even those which could still, until recently, count on a supply of good graduate teachers, are now forced to use unqualified staff in order to cope with the massive intake of pupils. In regions where a substantial proportion of mathematics teachers have never had an adequate basic training, the situation, bad enough in normal times, becomes disastrous when classes are often overcrowded and the teacher lacks a thorough grasp of his subject.

If the desired quality of mathematics teaching is to be maintained, if not improved, the vital problem is to train teachers in the content of mathematics and in teaching methods, and to keep their knowledge up to date. The two tasks, to keep working teachers abreast of new developments and to train new entrants to the profession, are of equal importance and must be carried out simultaneously. We shall consider them both, beginning with the training of future teachers, which is likely to yield more profitable results in the long term.

7.1 Training primary teachers

The responsibility for mathematics teaching lies in the first instance with teachers in primary schools and kindergartens.

Far from being negligible, the contribution of kindergarten teachers is of fundamental importance. Educational games give young children a concrete introduction to essential mathematical activities: partition of a set into classes, recognition of equivalence, seriation according to a given order, establishing a one-to-one correspondence, reproduction of drawings retaining the topological properties, etc. The significance of all these operations will be appreciated later, but their intuitive performance provides the essential basis for mathematical education. Kindergarten teachers must be able to understand the process of learning mathematics which lies before the pupils whose first steps it is their duty to guide. In Belgium, for instance, the mathematics syllabus for Froebel teachers proposed by Lenger and Servais, and adapted experimentally in 1958/9, includes the basic concepts concerning sets, relations, elementary functions and topology. However revolutionary such an initiation may appear, a little reflection will show how functional it really is, since it helps these girls to understand their courses in psychology and pedagogy, for example with regard to the experiments of Piaget.

Primary teachers have the complex task of teaching practically all subjects to children between the ages of six and twelve. They cannot be expected to be specialists in all of them. In view of the importance of mathematics, however, they must be able to teach it properly. In some countries, training courses for primary teachers include a full secondary education or are equivalent thereto. Prospective primary teachers thus have or will have the opportunity to learn the new secondary curricula. They will then have to deepen their knowledge and, if necessary, broaden it so as to be able to comprehend modern concepts of integers, fractions, negative numbers, numeration by position, linear functions (traditionally concealed under the name 'rule of three') or the simplest geometrical transformations, to mention only the most obvious. Moreover their methodology teacher, in conjunction with their mathematics teacher, should familiarize them with the principles and use of recently developed techniques of primary mathematics teaching, such as the coloured Cuisenaire rods advocated by Gattegno, the various materials and mathematical games successfully developed by Dienes, or the research of Suppes and others. It is desirable that teachers of methodology in training colleges for primary teachers should themselves be involved in the new movement.

It is questionable whether every primary teacher will be capable of teaching mathematics satisfactorily to his pupils. Some countries have realized that, with present requirements, this is an over-optimistic view. Denmark has found one satisfactory solution, described by Piene (1963)*: the curriculum for primary teachers includes a choice of a special subject. The course for those who choose mathematics includes (a) some portions of the higher secondary syllabus, (b) aspects likely to secure a better professional outlook and deeper understanding (logic, set theory, etc.) and (c) detailed treatment of certain sections of the primary syllabus. Other countries, like the United Kingdom (Mathematical Association of the United Kingdom, 1963), have a mathematics graduate (often the headteacher) in many primary schools.

This is a solution which obviously cannot yet be generally adopted, but it is considered desirable that the staff of each primary school should include at least one teacher with special qualifications in mathematics who can act as adviser.

The Mathematical Association of America (1960) strongly urged that at least 20 per cent of primary teachers in each school should have a more advanced mathematical training comparable with that required in junior secondary schools.

*References for chapter 7 will be found on p. 252.

7.2 Training secondary teachers

While practice varies according to the country, secondary-school teachers are usually trained either at the universities or at higher or secondary colleges of education. If there are two levels of training, teachers trained at the lower as a rule teach in the junior secondary classes (from eleven or twelve to fifteen), while the senior classes (from sixteen to eighteen) are taught by those who have studied mathematics at the university or equivalent higher educational establishments. These main categories may be subdivided when there are various types of secondary schools, in particular, those providing general education and technical schools.

We are not concerned here with describing the different types of preparation in various countries, but with indicating what we consider to be some of the future requirements, although these are probably still somewhat ideal.

One necessary condition must be emphasized. Every secondary-school teacher should have a broad, balanced general training. This was recognized by the Unesco symposium at Budapest which urged in its recommendations that teacher training should be founded on a full course of secondary education.

In order to teach a subject properly, one must both know it thoroughly oneself and know how to impart it effectively to others. In the case of mathematics, in which internal deductive reasoning is an essential feature, it is even more necessary to have a sound knowledge, especially when dealing with modern mathematics which has reached a degree of structuration and organic unity hitherto unknown. Learning mathematics requires the pupil to organize his intelligence even more than to acquire knowledge. The steps to such learning should be very familiar to the teacher who has to guide the pupil along them by suitable means and methods.

In order to achieve the high efficiency desired, mathematics teachers must now be given a more advanced and more thorough mathematical and pedagogical training.

7.2.1 *Mathematical training*

The level of the teacher's training must be distinctly higher than the level at which he himself is to teach.

With this end in view, the Budapest International Symposium recommended that all mathematics teachers for secondary schools should receive

specialized training in modern topics . . . to include the following fundamental topics: theory of sets and logic; abstract algebra; topology; geometry (axiomatic treatment, using vector spaces and other parts of abstract algebra and topology); analysis; theory of probability and statistics; history of mathematical thought.

The teachers for the higher classes of the secondary schools should make a more profound study of the fundamental notions and also have extra courses in specialized topics.

The essential point is not so much the extent of the technical information on a subject as the spirit in which the subject is treated. From this point of view, modern mathematical concepts are capable of throwing completely new light on the most classical subjects. In the training of future teachers, this is an advantage of which full use must be made for the benefit of education.

At each level of training, the teacher must have a proper understanding of the nature of the mathematical thought which his pupils will encounter later. It is desirable that teachers should be trained to teach at least some classes at the next level above. This would be extremely useful in a period of teacher shortage.

Details of mathematics syllabuses for teacher training are outside the scope of this book. They may, moreover, vary according to local traditions and academic facilities. CUPM (1961/2) and the Düsseldorf programme of the University of Münster may be useful for reference and comparison. In the latter programme, the senior course is divided into two parts, pure mathematics and applied mathematics. Even in topics appearing in both programmes – algebra, functional spaces, integration, ordinary differential equations, analytic functions of a complex variable – there are substantial differences in the way they are interpreted from the standpoints of pure and applied mathematics, as the former requires a more detailed treatment of structures and the latter a broadening of knowledge.

Some subjects, moreover, are quite separate: general topology, differential geometry of curves and surfaces in $\mathbb{R}^3$, study of elementary concepts (from the higher standpoint of modern mathematics), are reserved for the pure mathematics course, while the applied mathematics course deals with integral equations, partial differential equations, calculus of variations (although elements of this topic are given in the pure mathematics course), distributions, Laplace and Fourier transforms, special functions.

The Düsseldorf programme provides for a modest introduction to the calculus of probabilities at the first level and does not mention statistics. Neither does it refer to any of the new topics such as linear programming, information theory and games theory, nor to the theory of numbers. The mathematicians who met at the Budapest symposium recommended these as specialized topics for extra courses at the second level.

It may be seen that higher mathematics courses are over-loaded. Some topics may and should be developed in third-level courses reserved for post-graduates. Nevertheless it is essential that future teachers should be introduced to the important concepts, treated in a modern way, at the first and second levels so as to provide a sound basis for their training and ensure that it does not become quite out of date within a few years.

We can also understand the pressure exerted by some mathematicians to have topics hitherto regarded as appropriate to higher education included in the secondary school curriculum. For example, the participants in the Cambridge Conference on School Mathematics (1963) proposed a study of probabilities and statistics which goes further than the Düsseldorf programme;

they suggest including differential geometry of space curves, multi-dimensional differential and integral calculus, problems of limit conditions, Fourier series, integral equations, Green's functions, etc.

There is no doubt that the introduction of so-called higher topics into secondary syllabuses is a recurring phenomenon and its inevitable consequence is to raise the level of training for secondary teachers. This is a feedback phenomenon to which we must pay great heed if we are not to run into disaster. In this connexion, Revuz has pointed out (OECD, 1964) that, even now, the first level of the Düsseldorf programme is inadequate as a proper grounding for the teaching of arithmetic and algebra according to the Dubrovnik programme (OECD, 1961), and that it is deficient in respect of probabilities.

So far we have considered only the strictly mathematical training of future teachers. If we wish the teacher to be able to show his pupils how useful mathematics is in society, he must himself know of interesting applications. For this reason the Unesco symposium at Budapest recommended that the training of all mathematics teachers should include courses in one (or two) science subjects (e.g. physics, chemistry, biology, mathematical economics, psychology).

Only in this way will the teacher be capable of personally presenting motivations and work regarding the applications of mathematics, and of co-operating with his colleagues in other sciences so that his teaching will not be arid and suffer from the absence of outside contacts. It is undeniable that, from this point of view, the reform movement in certain countries has been directed towards a broader theoretical structure and that so far not enough use has been made of mathematics as a tool in scientific investigation in secondary schools.

This situation may be due to several causes: (a) lack of interest or lack of attention shown by mathematics teachers with regard to the application of mathematics to science; (b) ignorance, on the part of science teachers, of the nature and value of modern mathematics as an instrument; (c) inadequacy of the level of the pupils' acquaintance with this instrument; (d) inadequate development of the quantitative and mathematical aspects of science teaching (for example, physics is presented from the aspect of qualitative phenomena, without using formulae, and the teacher does not make his pupils solve enough problems involving mathematics); (e) lack of co-ordination between mathematics and science courses. Mathematics and physics teachers should collaborate in setting their pupils real problems in which the formulation and data are taken from the laboratory; the outline of a solution is discussed with the physics teacher, and the numerical solution is done in the mathematics class.

It is during the initial training of mathematics and science teachers that the taste for application, and practical experience thereof, should be developed, so as to make people fully aware of the nature and role of mathematical models in the empirical sciences.

7.2.2   *Training in teaching methods*

A thorough knowledge of the subject to be taught is a necessary condition for being a good teacher, but is not sufficient in itself. There can be no real promotion of a subject without effective teaching methods.

Mathematicians often neglect the importance of teaching methods, although the scientists who have the greatest influence on the spread of mathematics are often outstanding teachers. Cases of brilliant mathematics students who have turned out to be equally brilliant teachers are often quoted, but alongside these fortunate examples of natural talent, there are many others who, lacking such gifts, are left at the mercy of their inexperience. The pupils then suffer from the trials and errors of the young teacher, who may never acquire an adequate knowledge of how to teach and blame his pupils for the results of his own lack of skill. There are few subjects where the influence of the teacher is so decisive as in mathematics.

Young pupils, in particular, are sensitive to the mode of teaching offered to or imposed upon them. The recent IEA survey carried out under the auspices of the Unesco Institute for Education, Hamburg showed that, in the first year of secondary school, the best results are obtained by open-minded teachers who encourage the personal work and personal expression of their pupils.

The pedagogical training of teachers should receive as much attention and be as up to date as their mathematical training. It was one of the merits of the Budapest International Symposium that it laid due emphasis on this point. It is not unusual to find two types of inadequately trained mathematics teachers. On the one hand, there are those who know mathematics but have only a rudimentary training in educational theory and methods, and, on the other hand, those who have a general training in education and are very nearly ignorant of mathematics.

(a) *Psychological training.* To strengthen the 'educational theory' side of teacher training, the most urgent need and the most profitable course is to get away from the usual general treatment of teaching methodology, theory and the history of education.

A proper training in educational psychology is essential and should cover three main points:

(i) Psycho-genetic development from childhood to adulthood including, for secondary teachers, sufficient data regarding adolescence to give them an understanding of the attitudes and resources of that age group.

(ii) Differential psychology of character and behaviour in order to enable the teacher to adapt his teaching to individual pupils rather than merely lecturing to an abstract 'pupil in general'; to handle a class efficiently, taking account of affinities in constituting working groups; to appreciate the psychological impact of his own reactions and, in particular, to assess the influence of his own personality in his relations – easy or difficult – with his pupils and his assessment of them. Certain tensions in the atmosphere of the mathematics class are due to failure to appreciate these points.

(iii) The psychology of intelligence, to understand the stages of learning in a rational subject like mathematics, and to make the teacher familiar with the means to be used to encourage learning and the precautions to be taken when moving from one mental level to the next.

In order to encourage an active approach in his pupils, the teacher should be aware of the various forms of motivation, and above all should realize the importance of the emotional aspects involved in learning, which are all the more vital since the subject is abstract and calls for the continuous active involvement of the learner if it is to be mastered.

The prospective teacher should be acquainted with the results of psychological research which are of significance for mathematics teaching. Much still remains to be done, but it is undoubtedly of advantage that teachers should be able to make the most of what is already known (see chapter 4) and that researchers should concentrate on the subjects requested by mathematics teachers.

At the Unesco symposium in Budapest the following recommendations were made as to subjects for research vital to modern mathematics teaching:

Besides a deeper investigation into the teaching of sets, vector spaces and connected topics, experiments should be continued on the presentation of the following subjects in the context of modern mathematics: elements of topology, elementary geometry, introductory statistics and probability, differential and integral calculus, mathematical logic. Each of these topics should be tried out with various age groups in different types of schools in order to find how early they can be introduced, and the methods to be used.

Research should be undertaken to show the motivations likely to induce the pupils to engage in true mathematical activity, according to their temperament and age: enjoyment of games, increases of interest through some individual choice of work, the many interesting applications of mathematics, the challenge of problem solving, satisfaction over success in solving a problem, spirit of competition (Olympiads), awareness of mathematical thought – its historical evolution, the beauty of the rational quality of mathematics.

There are various lines along which mathematics may be learned: practical and graphical work on a given topic, formal lessons given by the teacher, problem solving (individually or in groups), individual discovery work, discussion, reading of mathematical textbooks, films, study with the aid of teaching machines, television lessons. The respective pros and cons of these methods, for presenting various topics, should be studied with reference to levels of attainment and other circumstances.

In addition, suggestions were made as to subjects for research into the development of mathematical thought which would have a bearing on teaching: formation of concepts, proofs, role of problems, structured materials and games, use and role of diagrams and symbolization, etc.

It is also natural for mathematics students who have taken a course in probability and statistics to be introduced to the applications of these subjects in research on educational psychology. Mathematics teachers should be aware of the use made of mathematical methods applied to the social sciences.

(b) *Methodological training.* In addition to his psychological training, the future teacher should be given special training in teaching methods based on the new ideas.

There is a teacher-centred method of teaching, in which the teacher states the rules and makes the pupils learn them by heart and repeat them in application over and over again; or he states and proves theorems and then makes the pupils use them in exercises.

Modern active teaching methods are centred on the pupil who learns through what he does himself more than by any other means. Memorizing becomes functional; the pupil retains knowledge by repeating the same processes. Important concepts and properties are distinguished and fixed in the mind by being encountered repeatedly, and in varied and effective situations.

By adapting tasks to the pupils' abilities and progressively increasing the level of difficulty, it is possible to ensure repeated personal achievement, which provides one of the strongest emotional motivations.

Modern methods of mathematics teaching develop an approach similar to that employed by the users and creators of mathematics. It is obvious that mathematicians do not start with the statement of a problem, and even less with a theorem or definition. What they do first is to explore a situation, a state of affairs, concrete or abstract, which by its presence constitutes a challenge to their powers of discernment or invention. In the course of this exploration, ideas are clarified, some factors are recognized as important, while others are discarded. A scheme begins to take shape, whereby one or more problems are formulated and attempts are then made to solve them. The solution leads to establishing properties or accepting others as hypotheses or conjectures. Gradually a system of relations is built up, which must then be tested with all available means: intuitive models, logical deduction, counter-examples.

The young teacher must be trained in this methodology of situations, the importance of which was stressed by Gattegno (1958, 1963). It permits an heuristic approach to new topics and is to be recommended as a method of initiation at all levels, whatever the degree of abstraction (Van Hiele-Geldof, 1957). Many situations can be taken from real life, others are presented with mathematical material specially structured for the purpose. At the primary level, Dienes has devised a number of mathematical tales presenting effective learning situations.

Learning through discovery as a result of personal work is closely related to the situations method (Beberman, 1962). If it is used properly, it takes rather a long time, which may be incompatible with the length of syllabuses. In practice, a compromise is used, viz. guided or directed discovery, where the teacher does less teaching and speaking, and devotes himself more to encouraging and advising the pupil in his active learning.

At the start, the pupil is not bothered with problems of expression; he tackles the situation he is examining through action and reflection. Later, pupils engaged in the same type of investigation will exchange views and results. The need to express these in order to communicate them will provide a basis for using mathematical language.

With this method the teacher is no longer the sole repository of mathematical truth, which he dispenses by his words. His authority is no longer a barrier between the pupil and the object of study, for it is the latter which is the real objective reference and authority. (The idea of the barrier of the teacher's authority was introduced by Davis, 1964).

In the dialogue taking place in class, the teacher is no longer the person who answers all the questions; he holds back in order to encourage exchanges between pupils. Their mistakes, which are inevitable and salutary in the learning process, are no longer punished but are freely discussed so as to clarify the situation. If some pupils overshadow the others too much, they are made to speak last. Learners are thus encouraged to gain confidence in their own ability to cope with new situations.

To do something without understanding it is undoubtedly a blind and ineffectual way to proceed. This explains the mediocrity of a teaching system based on routine drill and forced learning by rote. Similarly, to understand something without doing it is an illusory gain, without any thorough assimilation. This is the cause of the low efficiency of the teacher whose abundant explanations deprive the pupil of the opportunity for reflection and practice.

Modern teaching methods seek to make the pupil do what he understands and understand what he is doing. In this way understanding and practice will contribute to the retention of knowledge.

Memory, of course, plays an extremely important part in mathematics when we have to seek and find ways of solving a problem or carrying out an algorithmic development accurately. What is needed as a basis is not purely mechanical rote learning, but organized memorizing, the effectiveness of which is assured through the mathematical links between the various elements. Thus, with the help of a few vital facts memorized in the new way, it is possible to evoke and find a whole arsenal hidden in the memory store.

That is why the structure of mathematical knowledge is just as important for its retention as for its comprehension. Thinking with the help of structures is more vigorous thinking. From this point of view, the axiomatic concept (chapter 3) may be seen as the summary of all that is necessary to ensure retention of a structure.

The organization of a theory can be better developed with the help of problems to which theorems correspond. It is of great educational importance that axioms and theorems should have a substantial content, so that knowledge can be anchored firmly to a few solid supports.

The exercises which contribute to the permanence of learning should be programmed in the modern sense, each exercise presenting a new difficulty which requires an effort of ingenuity. In this way, instead of settling down into the easy comfort of what he has already seen, the pupil gets practice in overcoming obstacles.

By means of a well-organized system of exercises and applications, it is possible to analyse in detail the systematic errors which so many pupils make. Such errors, well known to the teacher, are used by him as a reason for further explanations and remedial exercises designed to develop in the pupil the habit of checking and self-correction.

The future teacher must show the same open-minded and sympathetic attitude to all manifestations of mathematical thinking by young people, whether the results be mistakes or discoveries. With a knowledge of the psychology of learning, he is in the best position to ensure productivity in a happy classroom atmosphere.

'Education is and will remain an art; it will never become a science.' This statement is felt by some educationists to imply that education cannot attain to the method and objectivity which are peculiar to the sciences. Is the art of the doctor or the engineer devoid of method and objectivity and opposed, in some measure, to the science of the biologist or the physicist? Do not these arts – and education in particular – consist of making the most of the findings of science and integrating them into the practical, often complex, solutions of individual problems?

Educational theory cannot be identified with one of the forms in which it takes shape, viz. teaching method; this would merely reduce it to the level of vocational training. It must remain open to the general problems of methods, techniques and curricula, which are being so energetically reviewed and challenged today. In the study of these subjects, the prospective teacher must comprehend present-day mathematics in its logical organization and in its practical applications. He must see clearly what it can contribute to the thorough understanding of the subjects he has to teach. Psychology will provide him with data for understanding his pupils, their intellectual development and the processes of mathematics learning.

Teacher trainees should be instructed by highly competent teachers who display in their own teaching the qualities required of the future teacher. The methods by which he is taught should illustrate at a higher level what he should practise at a lower level: investigation, documentation, discussion, individual work or team work. Workshops and seminars should train his critical thinking and imagination and initiate him into experimental research on lessons, explanations, books, materials, syllabuses and evaluation methods relating to the various subjects taught in secondary school.

A fairly long period of teaching practice in schools, under the direction of the methodology teacher and with the guidance of serving teachers, should fit him to start teaching on his own with assurance and success.

The prospective teacher must be informed about the development of mathematics teaching, the attempts to improve it undertaken in various countries, the part he will have to play in its promotion, and his duty to keep himself up to date in his professional training in the future.

(c) *Present and future requirements.* The aim is to train good, even excellent, teachers to meet present and future requirements. It is essential to overcome the shortage of teachers not only in developing countries but, equally, in those countries anxious to maintain their level of development. Every teacher-training system has to solve the awkward problem of combining optimum quality and maximum quantity. Countries which set out, at all costs, to employ only properly qualified teachers who have had a long, thorough training, find themselves forced to give too many jobs to any teachers they can find.

Obviously, there is a threshold below which mathematical and pedagogical training would be permenently compromised. Training must ensure reasonable familiarity with the principles and the spirit of these disciplines. Additional training can come afterwards, but it is impossible to rectify a wrong grounding, and difficult to expand a foundation which is deficient from the beginning. Accepting this principle of the critical level, a prospective teacher need not be required to have the specialized training of a potential researcher. It would be regrettable to turn unduly advanced studies into a system of criteria of excellence of training.

The report of the Mathematical Association of the United Kingdom (1963) contains considerations full of prudent realism, including the following recommendations:

Grants should be made available for students who have been recommended by their university to repeat a year of their course. Grants should also be available for prospective teachers of mathematics who for academic reasons are not allowed to continue at university, so that they can transfer to other institutions where the academic pressure is more suited to their ability.

Universities should publicize more widely, preferably in attractively illustrated pamphlets, opportunities which exist for the study of mathematics at various levels at these institutions and for the many careers, including the teaching professions, which are open to mathematics graduates.

Universities should make still more places available for potential mathematicians.

Some universities *appear* to be more concerned with the very best students, who are less likely to teach in schools than the average student. They might well consider whether they should not make more effort to teach and help the slower students, and perhaps prevent them from giving up or changing subjects.

We shall add one factor whose importance increases with the rising competition of external demand: one of the causes of the shortage of teachers is the inadequate salaries paid in this profession.

7.3   Further training of teachers

7.3.1   *Responsibility for training*

In our rapidly evolving world, the further training of serving teachers is a necessity. Those in positions of leadership within the education system must understand that further training should be a regular part of the teacher's professional life, but should not be additional to their already very heavy school duties.

In countries active in teacher education, a variety of bodies assist in keeping teachers up to date: teachers' associations; specialized education centres and institutes; universities and higher educational establishments.

The following international organizations arrange meetings where mathematicians and teachers can pool their views and the results of their experience: the International Commission for the Teaching of Mathematics (ICTM); the International Commission for the Study and Improvement of the Teaching of Mathematics (ICSITM); Unesco and the Organization for Economic Co-operation and Development (OECD).

Mathematics teachers' associations take part spontaneously in the reform movement with more or less limited resources and sometimes without much support from the public authorities. This is an indication of how well teachers understand their responsibilities and how much reliance can be placed on the professional conscience and devotion of a large number of them. These are valuable contributions, for there is no doubt that serving teachers, well informed about the new ideas, are in the best position to carry out valid teaching experiments in sufficient numbers.

Mathematicians also share the responsibility for promoting mathematics education. It is not surprising that many of them, including some of the most eminent, provide teachers with essential basic information. Their support is a guarantee of the scientific quality of the reform.

Users of mathematics also have a contribution to make by specifying to teachers what are the requirements of science and technology. Their approach is of interest in that its pragmatism offsets the emphasis on theory on the part of pure mathematicians. If mathematics teachers are to have some idea of the present practical importance of their science and its new applications, they must be kept informed.

7.3.2 *Means employed in the advanced countries*

Serving teachers must acquire a new training in depth and this represents a long-term undertaking. However useful individual conferences may be in making teachers receptive to new ideas, opening up new prospects and giving them an over-all picture, it is essential to work on the new material for some considerable time. For this reason, various courses have been organized – weekly seminars, or repeated weekend meetings, or longer courses, during the holidays for instance.

Some countries have arranged television programmes for teachers or the general public. In this way it is possible to reach a very large audience, but the extreme brevity of the talks means that their content has to be very highly concentrated.

After a group initiation, teachers must get down to personal study if they are to acquire a sufficient mastery of the new basic ideas. Hence the need, stressed at the Unesco symposium at Budapest, for special manuals for teachers to acquaint them with the sense and importance of modern mathematical ideas and with the relevant methodology. Of similar importance is the distribution to teachers of documents on the international trends for reform, the particular situation in their country, the necessity of planned efforts, their personal responsibility to their pupils and the scientific value of the new ideas.

Educational news is also circulated by those experimenting with pilot classes. Teachers pay particular attention to articles explaining how to present a new subject in class, and follow with great interest practical lessons demonstrating modern teaching methods in action.

In recent years contacts have been established with other sciences and with industry, especially in countries anxious to develop an education which will have a practical relevance. In this way teachers are acquainted with the mathematical knowledge their pupils will need for careers or studies beyond secondary education.

Similarly, teachers must know what concepts may already be employed in secondary-school science. Contacts with teachers of physics, chemistry, biology, geography and economics are profitable, and should be established without delay to further one of the aims of the reform.

7.3.3   *Action in the developing countries*

In the developing countries acute problems of teacher training are encountered at two levels.

(a) Provision of competent staff and equipment for colleges of education. Here it is necessary to change both the curricula and the teachers' attitude towards their students.

(b) Application of reforms on a wide scale, for which a large number of teachers will have to be trained.

The training of a small number of teachers for the first task has been undertaken by consultants sent out under national or international aid programmes to give training courses. This system is inadequate for carrying out large-scale reform. A larger number of itinerant consultants would be necessary to give regular assistance for a year or more. However, these measures often do not affect those in positions of authority nor those best qualified academically. Too-great disparities in the training of the instructors taking part in the courses, and the fact that these are so short, militate against achieving adequate lasting results.

The solution might be, as found in the Republic of the Congo (Brazzaville), to bring together a group of well-qualified teachers for an intensive seminar providing them with ideas and means with which they can, on their own, continue the work started in a few special centres.

The reform must come from above. It would seem desirable for several countries to pool their most highly qualified teachers so that they can provide extremely concentrated instruction in a permanent institution where good consultants could give invaluable assistance.

Further efforts needed

Countries which started early enough in reforming mathematics teaching have already achieved significant and encouraging results. However, despite the efforts made, the teachers who have been equipped to apply a modern syllabus successfully represent only a fraction of the whole body of mathematics teachers. If all serving teachers are to be trained thoroughly, it will be necessary to commit much larger resources to the work. The progress of teaching is dependent on this.

One country where school organization shows great variety, the United Kingdom, has regrouped its forces in the Joint Mathematical Council of the United Kingdom. In its *Report on In-Service Training of Teachers of Mathematics*, the Council analysed the situation and recognized, *inter alia*:

that the numerous activities carried out to date have brought in only the most enthusiastic fraction of teachers;

that teachers were not only not obliged to participate but had to devote their free time to the work and would seldom do it for nothing;

that the organizers and their helpers, often unpaid, could not extend their activities owing to the lack of time and resources;

that the majority of mathematics teachers are not capable of coping with the situation unaided.

In order that the new training may be available to all, the Council recommended that the following bodies should be set up: local education authority mathematics centres, regional advisory units, a national committee, a national information centre.

An idea of their purpose can be gathered from the titles. The plan gives a detailed outline for the organization, role and cost of each of these parts of the machinery. This example shows how the training of serving teachers can be ensured by an organic system of institutions.

Countries already benefiting from the services of local centres and national bodies know that it is advisable to develop local activities and, at a higher level, to co-ordinate, guide and second their efforts. In fact, the promotion of mathematics teaching is not a mere matter of once-and-for-all reform, but must be the gradual result of a continuing development maintained by a complete organization provided for that purpose.

The reform movements will continue to encounter difficulties for some years, however much ground is gained. Teachers who have been outdistanced by the vanguard must be induced to bring themselves up to date. Owing to the shortage of teachers, it will scarcely be possible to grant leave for re-training and it will not be easy to find enough experienced persons for the task.

To overcome these obstacles, it will be increasingly necessary to share the intellectual wealth of mathematics in order to multiply it: teachers who have undergone the new training must act as instructors for fellow teachers attending re-training courses.

Similarly, countries must help each other more and more, pooling experience and exchanging teachers. This cross-fertilization must be fostered by national contributions and also by the international organizations which have been created for this purpose.

7.4 Teachers and parents

No drive for better mathematics teaching can be launched without the co-operation and goodwill of the mass of teachers responsible for giving it. As stressed in the previous section, the reform movement will require, to be effective, the further training of practising teachers, who must necessarily enlist support for their efforts on other levels, not only within the educational system but also in society at large.

Teachers should not neglect to obtain the support of a section of the public which is directly involved in the educational process – the parents of pupils. Parents are beginning to realize the disparity between the mathematics education they received and the mathematics now advocated and taught in schools. They must be informed and, if necessary, introduced to the new concepts and methods.

For the pupils drawn into the experimental curricula, the new mathematics takes on the charm of a creative activity in which the individual's own capacities for inquiry, ingenuity, discovery and invention can be enchantingly exercised. The ability to understand and make progress, formerly the lot of the few with the traditional 'bump of mathematics', is becoming accessible to larger numbers of pupils.

However, there are the parents – the people with ambitions for their children – who find themselves faced with exercise books, often cryptic and full of coloured graphs and esoteric symbols, where there is little trace of the good old mathematics of their own days. The reform movement need not fear resistance from the pupils, but may be hampered by the parents, especially, when without full knowledge, they give their views with conviction.

By way of example, here is the judgement of a father, which appeared in an article entitled 'Nous ne sommes plus au pays de Descartes' in the *Voix des Parents* of March 1962, quoted in Walusinski (n.d.).

It is obvious that the introduction of set symbolism into the primary syllabus brings us to the ultimate limit of absurdity; and yet is it not the logical conclusion of a succession of errors, of which one of the earliest and not the least, was the almost entire elimination of arithmetic teaching? Is it not madness that nowadays a pupil taking the class 1, or elementary mathematics course, should be incapable of solving the good old problems of proportion, net gain or loss, etc., without using xs and ys as crutches and without cranking up the blind mechanism of algebraic equations?

Walusinski goes on,

Obviously this extract is given in no spirit of mockery. We feel it to be helpful to draw the attention of *all* teachers to the unfortunately far from exceptional nature of such reactions. They come, clearly, from unsatisfactory information about the syllabuses as they now are . . ., about the reform proceeding, as they are and as they should be.

What are we to say when parents make sneering comments to their children as inept as they are ill-considered? Yet we must understand the parents' point of view.

Imagine their amazement and disappointment when they find in their children's exercise books notes on subjects which they themselves have never learnt, unknown symbols and problems they have difficulty in solving. It is disturbing and distressing for a father to admit to his twelve-year-old son that he knows nothing about a classroom problem or cannot solve it, particularly when the father in his time has had schooling at the same, or even a higher level. This is the explanation of the reaction cited above, which reveals the father's wish to be able to use his knowledge of standard problems – of proportions and the tap or train type of net gain or loss – the formative or practical value of which, it must be said, is limited.

This, in turn, produces two types of reactions which the author has frequently noted in the parents of pupils:

(a) A relocation of the alleged cause of a pupil's failure. Ill-informed parents no longer say, 'My son does not understand mathematics', but 'My son doesn't really grasp set theory.'

(b) Anxiety to bring themselves up to date: 'Where can I get a good book which explains all that better than the exercise book, where the notes are not explicit enough and where I'm not sure my son may not have made a mistake?'

In point of fact, good textbooks are necessary in two respects; they are as essential to the parents as to their children. It is on this account that some such books, like Papy's *Mathematique Moderne 1*, are written in colloquial style for adolescent or adult students.

The School Mathematics Study Group, like many other working groups, has realized how essential it is to inform parents and has prepared a fairly brief course for them, of which it says:

When students are placed in a new mathematics programme, their parents are often curious about the reasons for the new programme and the differences between that programme and the one they went through when they were in school. Some parents find it hard to see any change is needed. Others merely wish to have some information on the nature of the changes being made. In any case, many parents do have questions which rightfully deserve answers.

Some of these questions have already been answered in print (see especially *The Revolution in School Mathematics*, National Council for Teachers of Mathematics). There are, however, two kinds of questions often asked by parents which are not so easily answered. Typical of these are: 'What are the new topics in the new programmes and what good are they?', and 'What are the new ways of treating traditional mathematical topics?'

These questions cannot be answered by means of generalities.

The only way for a parent to understand a new mathematical topic, or a new way of presenting an old one, is to study it just as his children do in school.

For this reason, SMSG has prepared a small textbook for parents. Chapter 1 of this text deals with number bases other than ten, a topic relatively new to the school mathematics programme. The other chapter deals with a review of the whole numbers in which emphasis is put on concepts and structure, as well as computation.

The book is meant to be used as a text and to be studied carefully, rather than read superficially. Exercises are provided throughout each chapter, answers to which are supplied at the end of the text.

This last sentence underlines one of the real difficulties of the effective documentation of parents: assimilating the new ideas calls for work by them. Getting a grasp of present-day mathematics is not effort-free: indeed, it requires more effort from adults than from the young. The difference in the respective yields from the effort required today and from that required in the past is quite certainly that modern mathematics is more intelligible and that knowledge of it pays better through the deeper and broader operative power it confers. Parents who have really taken the trouble to work on the novel modern notions, like pupils in school, grasp their possibilities and become supporters of reform.

There remains those parents who cannot make the necessary effort for lack of time or lack of educational background. Even if they have not sufficient spare time for a real study of the subject, however, it is possible for them to get a fair idea of the intentions and purposes of the reform undertaken from short texts giving an understandable description of the essentials of the new ideas without mathematical development.

This is the nature of the booklet, *The Revolution in School Mathematics*, mentioned earlier, and of a recent publication by Revuz (1964), which discusses wrong ideas about mathematics, how present-day mathematics developed and the prospects for the future.

It is necessary that books or articles should seek not to impress the public with their learning, but to provide a simple and effective answer to the questions which interest their readership, namely the new subjects and the present-day methods. Though it may be desirable to put the accent on what is new, not only in regard to set theory, it is equally needful to drive home the point that the reform of mathematics is not a matter of throwing overboard everything old, but of pruning antiquated and useless topics to make more room for those items in the heritage from the past which are shown to be sound and important by the condition of things today.

Given the advance of science and man's ever growing creative ability, each future generation is bound to find that even young children must know subjects of which their parents never heard. In the final count, what should reassure parents is the child's superiority to themselves in mental agility and ingenuity where new things are concerned. To convince parents and mathematics teachers or users that the new mathematics teaching is on the right lines, there is no means more effective than to let them see for themselves the pleasure and liveliness with which children in class react to it.

References

BEBERMAN, M. (1962), *An Emerging Program of Secondary-School Mathematics*, Harvard University Press.

CAMBRIDGE CONFERENCE ON SCHOOL MATHEMATICS (1963), *Report*, Houghton Mifflin.

CUPM (1961/2), *Recommendations for the Training of Teachers of Mathematics: Course Guide for the Training of Junior High and Senior High School Mathematics*, Committee on the Undergraduate Program in Mathematics, Mathematical Association of America.

DAVIS, R. (1964), *Discovery in Mathematics*, teachers' edn, Addison-Wesley.

GATTEGNO, C. (1958), *Teaching Mathematics in an Expanding Economy: 1*, Reading: Cuisenaire.

GATTEGNO, C. (1963), *For the Teaching of Mathematics*, Reading: Educational Explorers.

JOINT MATHEMATICAL COUNCIL OF THE UNITED KINGDOM (1965), *Report on In-Service Training of Teachers of Mathematics*.

MATHEMATICAL ASSOCIATION OF AMERICA (1960), 'Recommendations for the training of teachers of mathematics', *American Mathematical Monthly*, December.

MATHEMATICAL ASSOCIATION OF THE UNITED KINGDOM (1963), *The Supply and Training of Teachers of Mathematics*, Bell.

OECD (1961), *Synopses for Modern Secondary School Mathematics*, Organization for Economic Co-operation and Development.

OECD (1964), *Mathematics Today*, Organization for Economic Co-operation and Development.

PIENE, K. (1963), 'Education of teachers for the various levels of mathematical instruction', *L'Enseignement Mathématique*, vol. 9, January/June.

REVUZ, A. (1964), *Mathématique moderne, Mathématique vivante*, OCDL.

VAN HIELE-GELDOF, D. (1957), *De didaktiek van de meetkunde in de eerste Klas van het VHMO*, Amsterdam: Meulenhoff.

WALUSINSKI, G. (n.d.), 'Les robinets de papa', *Bulletin de l'Association des Professeurs de Mathématiques de l'Enseignement public*, no. 222.

Appendix

Some Notions of the Basic Structures of Mathematics

Prepared by W. Servais

It is impossible to discuss the reform of mathematics curricula without referring to the new content, that is, to the basic structures which form the core of modern mathematics. This appendix presents some of these basic notions through definitions, examples and a few demonstrations.

The aim of this appendix is not to give a comprehensive introduction to the study of mathematics, a subject on which there are already numerous books addressed to various levels of learning, but rather to identify and explain a glossary of new terms and symbols. In this sense it is intended to serve as a reference for those involved in the planning and execution of modern mathematics curricula by providing them with a guide to the general concepts and specific terms and symbols employed throughout this book. In the Further Reading list the reader will find a short list of authors to be consulted for further reading on the topic discussed in each section.

The selection of topics represents a common core of a modern mathematics syllabus.* While the choice of topics and their sequence has meant adopting a particular point of view, it will be recognized from the sample syllabuses presented in chapter 5 that the pattern of presentation may vary considerably. In fact, experiments are still continuing in order to try out these topics with various age groups in different types of schools in order to determine how early they can be introduced and the methods to be used.

A.1 Logic

In modern mathematics teaching there is a tendency to make more explicit use of the concepts and symbols of logic.

A.1.1 *Expressions and terms*

In written language, use is made of graphic signs. In mathematics, assemblies of signs are used to represent *expressions.* For example, '1', '+', 'sin x',

---

*Due to lack of space, probability and statistics have been omitted, since they have not yet been accepted universally as part of the basic structure. Acknowledgement is made here to all those who, by their criticisms and comments, questions and encouragement, helped to define the aims of this section, particularly Mrs A. Z. Krygowska, G. Choquet, D. Gvozdenovic, G. Pickert, A. Revuz, S. Robinson, C. Roth, J. Sebastiao e Sylvia and M. Stone.

'$\int -du$', '$x+5 = 11$' and '7 is a prime number' are all signs or expressions used in mathematics. The inverted commas show that we are referring to the expression itself, not to what it symbolizes.

Some of the expressions, called *terms*, designate objects, which may be concrete or abstract, simple or complex. The terms '2', '$5-3$', 'Don Quixote', 'the moon', 'Humanity', designate objects precisely. These are *constant* terms. On the other hand, expressions such as '$1/x$', '$x-y$', 'the author of —', 'the planet round which — revolves' will only become designations of specific objects when appropriate constants are substituted for 'x', 'y', '—' respectively. These expressions are called *variable* terms. In particular, the unknowns used here are themselves variable, being called *free variables*, to indicate the possibility of substitution. The objects designated by the constants which replace the variables are called *values*.

A.1.2 Equality

The terms '2' and '$5-3$' designate the same object, the number two. This is denoted by the *equality*, $2 = 5-3$.

Let $T(x) \equiv x^3 - 6x - 10$. The result of replacing the variable x by the constant 2 will be called $T(2)$.

Then $$T(2) = 2^3 - 6 \times 2 - 10.$$
Similarly $$T(5-3) = (5-3)^3 - 6(5-3) - 10.$$

Since we have the equality $2 = 5-3$, we also have the equality $T(2) = T(5-3)$.

A.1.3 Propositions and conditions

A proposition is an expression making a factual statement which may be either *true* or *false*. For example, the propositions, 'Newton is a great mathematician', '$2 = 5-3$', 'the Earth moves round the moon', make factual statements of which the first two are true and the third false.

Principle of excluded middle. Every proposition is either true or false.

Principle of non-contradiction. No proposition is simultaneously true and false. Truth and falsity are the two opposite values of propositions in classical logic.

The expression 'x is a great mathematician' is not a proposition making a true or false statement. If we replace the variable 'x' by 'Henri Poincaré' or 'Carl Friedrich Gauss', we shall have true propositions, but if we replace it by the name 'Charlie Chaplin', the proposition will be false.

Similarly the equation $x = y-z$ is neither true nor false as long as we give no specific values to the variables 'x', 'y', 'z'. In substitution, variables are replaced by appropriate constants, giving a proposition – called a condition – which may be true or false. A condition is said to be *satisfied* or *verified* by the values of the variable or variables for which it becomes a true proposition. An *equation* is a condition having the form of an equality between two terms, at least one of which is variable, as $(x-3)(x+5) = 0$, or $x-y = 2(x+3y)$. A *solution* of an equation in a variable is a value of the variable for which the equation becomes true.

All the values which a variable may take constitute its *universe* or *domain* of variation. For example, in the condition

x is a great mathematician,

the universe of the variable may be taken as the set of men. When the condition contains several variables, each of them may have a universe.

A.1.4   Quantifiers

The expression '$\exists x$' is called the *existential quantifier* on the universe concerned. It is read 'there is at least one *x* such that'. For example, the existential proposition $\exists x (x^2 - x - 7 = 0)$ means that the equation $x^2 - x - 7 = 0$ has at least one real root, the set of real numbers being taken as universe.

The expression '$\forall x$' is called the *universal quantifier* on the universe concerned, and is read, 'for all *x*', or 'whatever *x* may be'. The proposition obtained is universal. In the universe of men we have $\forall x$ (*x* is mortal) which means, in ordinary language, all men are mortal.

We know that by convention in a substitution the same variable *x* must be replaced by the same constant, wherever it appears. Consequently, in a universe we have $\forall x : x = x$. This proposition expresses the *reflexivity* of the equality.

A.1.5   Equivalence

Given two conditions P and Q, their equivalence is denoted by $P \Leftrightarrow Q$, which is read, 'P is equivalent to Q'. It is true in every case where P and Q are either both true or both false; it is false in all other cases. This is summarized in Table 6, using the symbol '1' to denote true and '0' to denote false.

Table 6

P	Q	$P \Leftrightarrow Q$
1	1	1
1	0	0
0	1	0
0	0	1

Consider the equations

$3x - 4 = x$ and $x = 2$.

For all real values of '*x*', these two conditions are simultaneously true or simultaneously false. The equivalence $3x - 4 = x \Leftrightarrow x = 2$ is therefore true whatever the real value of *x*. This may be written $\forall x : 3x - 4 = x \Leftrightarrow x = 2$ on the set of real numbers. The conditions P and Q are said to be *equivalent*.

Any two true propositions, or any two false propositions, are equivalent. P ⟺ P, that is, any proposition is equivalent to itself.

Whatever the conditions P and Q may be, the equivalences P ⟺ Q and Q ⟺ P are in each case simultaneously true or simultaneously false, that is, there is true equivalence between them.

A.1.6 Negation

Every condition has its negation. It is written $\neg$P and read 'not-P'. It is true whenever P is false and false whenever P is true. Thus the negation of 'x is an even number' is 'x is not an even number'. The negation of $x = y$ is also written $x \neq y$. Whatever P may be, it is equivalent to its double negation $\neg(\neg P)$.

A.1.7 Contradiction

Two conditions, each of which is the negation of the other, are called contradictory. When one is true, the other is false. P ⟺ Q and P ⟺ ($\neg$Q) are contradictory, as are $\forall x : P$ and $\exists x : \neg P$.

A.1.8 Conjunction

The conjunction P and a condition Q (or P and Q) is written P ∧ Q. It is true whenever P and Q are both true, but false in all other cases. This may be tabulated as in Tables 7a and 7b.

Table 7a

P	Q	P ∧ Q
1	1	1
1	0	0
0	1	0
0	0	0

or

Table 7b

P	∧	Q
1	1	1
1	0	0
0	0	1
0	0	0

A system of two simultaneous equations (or inequalities) is their conjunction.

Whatever P may be, the conjunction P ∧ ($\neg$P) is false for all values of the variable, and its negation is true. This is the principle of non-contradiction.

The following equivalences are also true, whatever P, Q and R may be:

$$P \wedge P \Leftrightarrow P \qquad \text{(idempotence)},$$
$$P \wedge Q \Leftrightarrow Q \wedge P \qquad \text{(commutativity)},$$
$$(P \wedge Q) \wedge R \Leftrightarrow P \wedge (Q \wedge R) \qquad \text{(associativity)}.$$

A.1.9 Disjunction

The disjunction of P and Q is written P ∨ Q and read 'P or Q'. It is true in every case when at least one of the conditions P and Q is true, and false when P and Q are both false. It is summarized in Tables 8a and 8b.

Table 8a

P	Q	P ∨ Q
1	1	1
1	0	1
0	1	1
0	0	0

or

Table 8b

P	∨	Q
1	1	1
1	1	0
0	1	1
0	0	0

For example, the equation $(x^2 - x - 12)(x^2 - 16) = 0$ breaks down into the two equations $x^2 - x - 12 = 0$ and $x^2 - 16 = 0$. It is therefore satisfied for solutions of at least one of these equations, that is, to their disjunction

$$(x^2 - x - 12 = 0) \vee (x^2 - 16 = 0).$$

Whatever P may be, P ∨ (¬P) is true. This is the principle of the excluded middle.

Also $P \vee P \Leftrightarrow P$ (idempotence),
         $P \vee Q \Leftrightarrow Q \vee P$ (commutativity),
$(P \vee Q) \vee R \Leftrightarrow P \vee (Q \vee R)$ (associativity).

A.1.10   *Implication*

The implication of condition Q by condition P is written $P \Rightarrow Q$ and read 'if P then Q'. This is false in every case when P is true and Q false and is true in all other cases. This is summarized in Tables 9a and 9b.

Table 9a

P	Q	P ⇒ Q
1	1	1
1	0	0
0	1	1
0	0	1

Table 9b

P	⇒	Q
1	1	1
1	0	0
0	1	1
0	1	0

P is called the *antecedent* and Q the *consequent* of the implication. $Q \Rightarrow P$ is called the *reciprocal* of $P \Rightarrow Q$. When $P \Rightarrow Q$ is true in every substitution, we say that P implies Q or is a sufficient condition for Q, and that Q is a necessary condition for P.

For example, the equation $x = 2$ implies the equation $(x-2)(x+3) = 0$, since if the first equation is satisfied, so also is the second.

A.2   **Sets**

The idea of a set is the most fundamental in mathematics. Georg Cantor (1845-1918), the originator of set theory, expressed the idea as follows: 'A set M is a collection, as a single whole, of well-defined and distinct units of thought. These units are called the elements of M.'

It is easy to produce many examples of sets, of families, of classes, all synonymous from an elementary point of view; the pupils will themselves provide further and varied examples drawn from everyday life. Other sets, of a mathematical type, will soon become familiar to them: the set of integers, the set of multiples of three, the set of points in a plane, the set of points in a circle, the set of circles in a plane, etc.

To denote that an entity a is an element of the set E, or that a belongs to E, we write $a \in E$. We also say that E contains or includes a. If $b \notin E$, b is not contained in E.

To specify a set E, it is necessary and sufficient that for any given entity a, we have either that $a \in E$ or that $a \notin E$, with no ambiguity. The elements of a set E can be conveniently represented as points, round which a closed curve is drawn. This is called a Venn diagram (after John Venn, 1834–1923), an improvement on the circles of Euler.

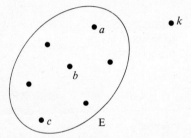

Figure 37 Venn diagram representing a set E containing elements a, b, c. . . . The element k is not included in the set E

To designate a set, the elements of which are represented by the symbols a, b, c, d, e, f, we use the notation $\{a, b, c, d, e, f\}$, placing the symbols between braces. Thus the expression $\{1, 2, 3, 4, 5\}$ represents the set of numbers one, two, three, four, five, and not merely the numerals which stand for them.

A set A is identical to set B if every element of A is an element of B and vice versa. In this case we write $A = B$. For example:

$\{1, 2, 3\} = \{2, 3, 1\}$,
$\{1, 2, 3\} = \{1, 2, 1, 3, 3\}$,
$\{1, 2, 3\} = \{1, 1+1, 1+2\}$.

For every object a there is a set $\{a\}$ which contains a as an element and no other. Such a set is called a *singleton*. Similarly, for every pair of entities a and b there is a set $\{a, b\}$ which contains each as an element and no other. Such a set is called a pair.

A.2.1 *Subsets*

Given a set A and a set B, it may happen that every element of A is also an element of B, as in the case when $A = \{1, 2\}$ and $B = \{1, 2, 4\}$ and also when

A = {4, 5} and B = {5, 4}. These are examples of inclusion, which is shown intuitively in Figure 38.

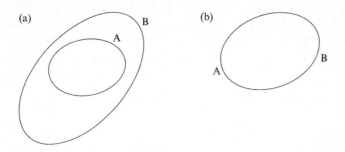

(a)   B   A   (b)   B   A

Figure 38 Venn diagrams representing the inclusion of set A in set B, written A ⊂ B : (a) A ≠ B, (b) A = B

Inclusion possesses the following properties.

(a) *Reflexiveness*. For all sets A, A ⊂ A.

(b) *Asymmetry*. For any sets A and B, if A ⊂ B and B ⊂ A, then A = B.

(c) *Transitivity*. For any sets A, B and C, if A ⊂ B and B ⊂ C, then A ⊂ C.

We begin with a set of entities $\mathscr{E}$. To determine a subset A of $\mathscr{E}$, a condition must be satisfied, or a property must be possessed by an element of $\mathscr{E}$ if and only if this element belongs to A. For example, in the set of positive integers $\mathbb{N} = \{0, 1, 2, 3, \ldots, n, \ldots\}$ we wish to specify the multiples of 5. This is the subset $\{x \mid x$ is a multiple of 5$\}$, which is read as 'the set of x such that x is a multiple of 5'. If we wish to make it quite clear that the basic set consists of the positive integers, we may write this more fully as

$\{x \mid x \in \mathbb{N} ; x$ is a multiple of 5$\}$.

In plane geometry, a locus defined by means of a condition imposed on its points is a subset of the plane which satisfies this condition.

For every set $\mathscr{E}$ and every condition $P(x)$ defined over $\mathscr{E}$, the elements of $\mathscr{E}$ for which $P(x)$ is true form a subset of $\mathscr{E}$, known as the truth set and denoted by $\{x \in \mathscr{E} \mid P(x)\}$ which is read, 'the set of elements x of $\mathscr{E}$ such that $P(x)$ is true'.

The set defined by $\{x \in \mathscr{E} \mid x \neq x\}$ cannot contain any elements, since, for all x, $x = x$. This is called the *empty set*, of which there can only be one. It is denoted by $\varnothing$ or by $\{\quad\}$. Every set contains the empty set as a subset.

If two conditions $P(x)$ and $Q(x)$, defined on a set $\mathscr{E}$, are such that, for each element in set $\mathscr{E}$, they are both simultaneously true or simultaneously false, the two conditions are said to be equivalent.

Examples. (a) In the study of geometrical loci, when a locus is defined by one property, we must find an equivalent property to enable us to recognize the locus.

(b) As $\{x \in \mathbb{N} \mid x^2 - 4 = 0\} = \{2\} = \{x \in \mathbb{N} \mid x - 2 = 0\}$,

the equations $x^2 - 4 = 0$ and $x - 2 = 0$ are equivalent on the set of positive integers $\mathbb{N}$, but they are not equivalent on the set of real numbers $\mathbb{R}$.

(c) In the set $\{2, 3, 5, 7, 8, 9, 12\}$, the conditions x is prime and $x < 8$ are equivalent, as they both determine the same set $\{2, 3, 5, 7\}$.

A.2.2   *Operations on sets*

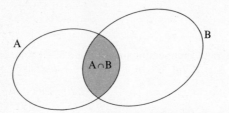

Figure 39 The intersection of set A and set B

Intersection. The *intersection* of set A and set B, written $A \cap B$, is made up of elements which belong at one and the same time to set A and set B,

$$A \cap B = \{x \mid (x \in A) \wedge (x \in B)\}.$$

When the sets A and B have no common element, they are said to be *disjoint* sets and we have $A \cap B = \varnothing$.

Examples. We are familiar with the intersection of geometrical figures, such as sets of points, lines or circles.

The intersection of the set of quadrilaterals and the set of regular polygons is the set of squares.

The intersection of the set of multiples of 6 and the set of multiples of 15 is the set of multiples of 30.

The solution set of a system of two simultaneous equations (or inequations) is the intersection of the solution sets of these equations (or inequations). When the intersection set is empty, the equations are inconsistent.

Union. The *union* of A and B is the set, written $A \cup B$, made up of the elements which belong to one or other, or both, of the sets A and B:

$$A \cup B = \{x \mid (x \in A) \vee (x \in B)\}.$$

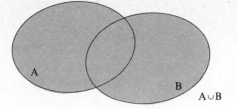

Figure 40 The union of set A and set B

Examples. The union of the divisors of 6 and the divisors of 10 is $\{1, 2, 3, 5, 6, 10\}$.

The equation $(x^2 - 9)(x^2 + 5x + 6) = 0$, which splits up into $x^2 - 9 = 0$ and $x^2 + 5x + 6 = 0$, has a solution set

$$\{x \in \mathbb{Z} \mid x^2 - 9 = 0\} \cup \{x \in \mathbb{Z} \mid x^2 + 5x + 6 = 0\}$$

or $\{-3, 3\} \cup \{-3, -2\} = \{-3, -2, 3\}$.

Difference. The *difference* A\B is the set made up of those elements which belong to A and do not belong to B.

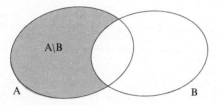

Figure 41 The difference A\B

Example. The difference between the set of integers $\mathbb{Z} = \{0, 1, -1, 2, -2, 3, -3, \ldots, n, -n, \ldots\}$ and the set of positive real numbers $\mathbb{R}^+$ is the set $\mathbb{Z} \setminus \mathbb{R}^+$ of negative integers and zero.

When set A is a subset of set B, the difference $A \setminus B = \varnothing$ and the difference $B \setminus A$ is called the *complement* of A with respect to B. In the set of natural numbers, for example, the set of odd numbers is the complement of the set of even numbers.

Symmetric difference. The *symmetric difference* $A \triangle B$ is the set made up of those elements which belong either to set A or to set B, but do not belong to both sets A and B.

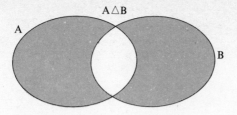

Figure 42 The symmetric difference A △ B

A.2.3 *Laws of the algebra of sets*

The operations, for given sets, which form their intersection, union or difference, are given the same names as the sets they produce. For any sets A, B and C, we have:

(a) *Idempotence* of intersection and union,

$$A \cap A = A \quad \text{and} \quad A \cup A = A.$$

(b) *Commutativity* of intersection and union,

$$A \cap B = B \cap A \quad \text{and} \quad A \cup B = B \cup A.$$

(c) *Associativity* of intersection and union,

$$(A \cap B) \cap C = A \cap (B \cap C) \quad \text{and} \quad (A \cup B) \cup C = A \cup (B \cup C).$$

(d) *Distributivity*,

$$(A \cap B) \cup C = (A \cup C) \cap (B \cup C) \quad \text{and} \quad (A \cup B) \cap C = (A \cap C) \cup (B \cap C).$$

(e) *Absorption*,

$$A \cap (A \cup B) = A \quad \text{and} \quad A \cup (A \cap B) = A.$$

(f) If A, B and C are subsets of the set $\mathscr{E}$, then $\mathscr{E}$ and the empty set $\varnothing$ are *neutral* or *identity* elements with respect to the operations of intersection and union respectively,

$$A \cap \mathscr{E} = \mathscr{E} \cap A = A \quad \text{and} \quad A \cup \varnothing = \varnothing \cup A = A.$$

(g) $\mathscr{E}$ and $\varnothing$ are also absorbing elements,

$$A \cap \varnothing = \varnothing \cap A = \varnothing \quad \text{and} \quad A \cup \mathscr{E} = \mathscr{E} \cup A = \mathscr{E}.$$

A.2.4 *Boolean algebra*

The operations on the subsets of a non-empty set are an example of a Boolean algebra (named after George Boole, 1815–64). A Boolean algebra consists of a non-empty set B of elements on which are defined two operations $\cap$ and $\cup$, which satisfy the following conditions: the operations must be everywhere defined, be associative, commutative and distributive, have at least one

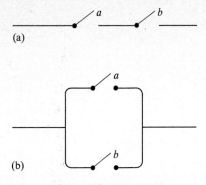

(a)

(b)

Figure 43 (a) Two switches a and b in series denoted by $a \cap b$; (b) two switches in parallel denoted by $a \cup b$

neutral element and at least one complementary element for each operation. An interesting application of this algebra is in electrical switching circuits. Two switches a and b, when connected in series are denoted by $a \cap b$, and when in parallel by $a \cup b$. The complement of an open switch a is closed and is represented by a'. 0 is a switch which is always open and 1 is a switch which is always closed. It follows that $a \cap a' = 0$ and $a \cup a' = 1$. By means of this system of algebra it is possible to reduce complicated circuit diagrams to simple or more difficult equations which can readily be solved.

A.3   Binary relations

Let $A = \{a_1, a_2, a_3, a_4\}$ be a set of cars and $B = \{b_1, b_2, b_3\}$, a set of drivers. To list all the possible cases of a car of A being driven by a driver of B, we must form all the couples of which the first element belongs to A and the second to B. These are shown in the Table 10.

Table 10

B \ A	a_1	a_2	a_3	a_4
b_1	(a_1, b_1)	(a_2, b_1)	(a_3, b_1)	(a_4, b_1)
b_2	(a_1, b_2)	(a_2, b_2)	(a_3, b_2)	(a_4, b_2)
b_3	(a_1, b_3)	(a_2, b_3)	(a_3, b_3)	(a_4, b_3)

    To indicate all the possible couples in set diagrams, each element of A is joined to each element of B, as in Figure 44. Alternatively, all the possible couples are represented by a rectangular array of points (Figure 45).

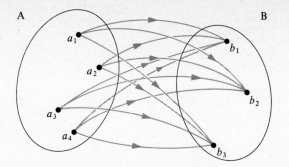

Figure 44 All the possible couples of which the first element belongs to set A and the second to set B are represented by the lines joining the elements of set A to those of set B

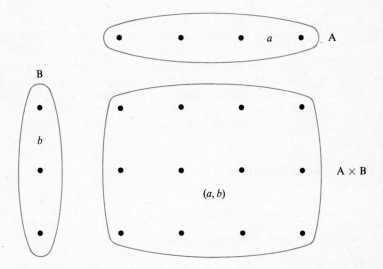

Figure 45 The couples of the Cartesian product A × B represented by a rectangular array

The set of all these couples is called the *Cartesian product* of A and B, and is denoted by A × B. The operation is called Cartesian multiplication. If A = B, the Cartesian product A × A is written A^2 (Figure 46) and is called the Cartesian square of A. For example, if we refer the coordinates of points in a plane to Cartesian axes Ox, Oy (Figure 47), the set of couples (x, y) of coordinates of the points is the Cartesian square $\mathbb{R}^2$ of the set $\mathbb{R}$ of real numbers. This is called the Cartesian plane $\mathbb{R}^2$.

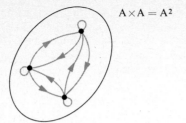

$$A \times A = A^2$$

Figure 46 The Cartesian square of set A : A × A or A²

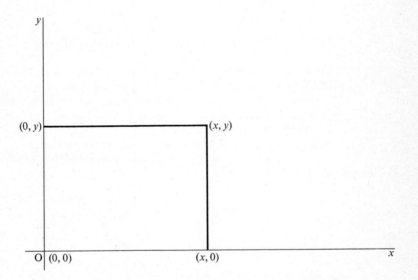

Figure 47 A point in a plane represented by a couple of coordinates (x, y). The set of couples of coordinates of all the points in a plane is the Cartesian square $\mathbb{R}^2$

Cartesian multiplication is distributive, but not commutative or associative. The Cartesian product can only be empty if at least one set is empty.

A *binary relation* is a set of couples. For example, the set {(Descartes, geometry), (Descartes, dioptrics), (Shakespeare, Hamlet), (Da Vinci, Mona Lisa)} is a binary relation. The idea may be extended to ternary relations, which are sets of triplets, and *n*-ary relations, which are sets of *n*-tuplets. Since a binary relation is a set, the usual laws of sets operate.

If $R = \{(1, 2), (1, 3), (2, 2), (2, 4), (3, 5)\}$, we may denote that a couple (x, y) belongs to this relation by writing xRy. The set made up of the first elements of the couples is called the *domain* of R; the set made up of the second elements is called the *range* or *image* of R. These are written as dom R and ima R respectively. To draw the graph of a relation R it is sufficient, in the set (dom R)∪(ima R) to represent each couple in R by drawing an arrow from the first element of the couple to the second. For example, the relation R = {(1, 2), (1, 3), (2, 2), (2, 4), (3, 5)} may be represented by the graph in Figure 48. A couple with identical elements, such as (2, 2) is represented by a loop.

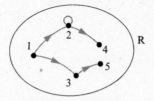

Figure 48 Graph of R = {(1, 2), (1, 3), (2, 2), (2, 4), (3, 5)}

A relation for which the couples start in A and end in B is called a relation of A to B, A being called the set of departure and B the set of arrival.

Instead of calling the set of couples a relation, as we have done here, some writers call a condition in (x, y) a binary relation, and the set determined by this condition on A × B its graph.

In the square A^2 of set A, the relation made up of all the couples (x, y) whose first element is the same as its second, is called the identity relation or the

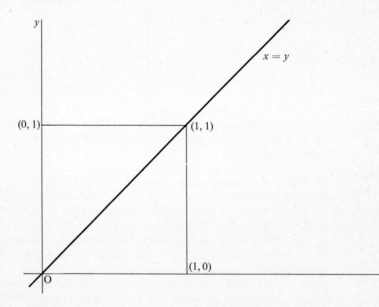

Figure 49 In the Cartesian plane $\mathbb{R}^2$ the identity relation $I_\mathbb{R}$ represents the line $x = y$ or the set of couples of equal numbers

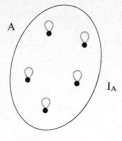

Figure 50 The identity relation I_A shown on a Venn diagram of set A as a loop at each point

identity determined by the condition $x = y$. When the set A is finite and we construct a table of A^2 in which the rows and columns are placed in the same order, the elements of the identity relation I_A will lie along the diagonal. For this reason I_A is described as the diagonal of A^2. In the Cartesian plane $\mathbb{R}^2$, the relation $I_{\mathbb{R}}$ is the Cartesian straight line $x = y$ (Figure 49) or the set of couples of equal numbers. Figure 50 is a Venn diagram in which the identity relation I_A on the set A is represented by a loop at each point.

In the set $A = \{1, 2, 3, 4, 6, 8\}$ the relation defined by the condition 'x is a divisor of y' is an example of a reflexive relation, since each number divides into itself. Consequently the couples $(1, 1)$, $(2, 2)$, $(3, 3)$, etc., belong to the relation, each being given a loop in the graph (Figure 51).

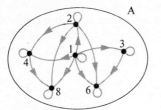

Figure 51 The relation defined by the condition 'x is a divisor of y' in the set $A = \{1, 2, 3, 4, 6, 8\}$ is a reflexive relation. There is a loop at each point in the Venn diagram

The relation obtained by interchanging the elements of each couple in R is called the *reciprocal* and written R^{-1}. The reciprocal of the relation $x < y$ is $y < x$. A relation which is identical with its reciprocal is called a *symmetrical* relation. In a set of persons, the relation x has the same forename as y, and the relation x was born in the same year as y, are each symmetrical. In a set of straight lines in a plane, the relation of parallelism is symmetrical, as is the relation of perpendicularity.

If R is a relation of set A to set B, and S is a relation of set B to set C, so that aRb and bSc, or the second element of a couple (a, b) of R is also the first element of a couple (b, c) of S, we say that the couple (a, c) belongs to the *composite* of R to S, written $R \circ S$ (Figure 52).

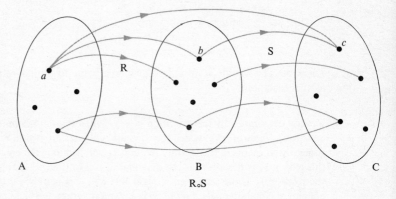

Figure 52 The composite relation $R \circ S$ of set A to set C, composed of the relation R of set A to set B and the relation S of set B to set C

For example, if A is a set of persons, B a set of books and C a set of towns, consider the relations R, of A to B (x has read y), and S, of B to C (y is published in z). Then the composite $R \circ S$ will be the relation of A to C determined by the condition that x has read a book y from B which is published in z. The graph is shown in Figure 53. Such a graph is clearer if three different colours are used.

Figure 53 Graph of the relation determined by the condition that x has read a book y published in town z

In the set of straight lines in a plane, using the signs $\perp$ to denote x perpendicular to y, and $/\!/$ to denote x parallel to y, we have

$$\perp \circ \perp = /\!/, \qquad \perp \circ /\!/ = \perp, \qquad /\!/ \circ \perp = \perp, \qquad /\!/ \circ /\!/ = /\!/.$$

It will be seen from this that it is possible to form a composite relation of R with itself, called $R^2 = R \circ R$.

The relation of parallelism has the important property that, as shown above, it is equal to its square.

The relation $x < y$ on the set $\{5, 6, 7\}$ is $\{(5, 6), (5, 7), (6, 7)\}$. Its square is $\{(5, 7)\}$. If, as in this case, the relation contains its own square, it is called a *transitive* relation.

Every relation R of a set $\mathscr{E}$, which is at one and the same time, reflexive, symmetric and transitive, is called a *relation of equivalence* on $\mathscr{E}$. For example, the relation of identity is clearly a relation of equivalence on every set. The relation of congruence modulo 5 (the remainders after numbers have been divided by 5 are equal) is also an equivalence relation. The equivalence of fractions, a/b and c/d, defined by the condition $ad = bc$, is also an equivalence relation in this sense.

In a set $\mathscr{E}$ of real numbers, consider the condition $x \leqslant y$. The relation so defined is reflexive, since x is equal to itself; transitive, since $x \leqslant y$ and $y \leqslant z$ it follows that $x \leqslant z$; and asymmetric. Such a relation, having these three properties, is called a *relation of order*, and the set is said to be *ordered*. It is the asymmetry which distinguishes a relation of order from a relation of equivalence.

A.4 Functions

Consider a relation in which each couple consists of one person and his birthday. The noteworthy features of this relation is that a person has only one

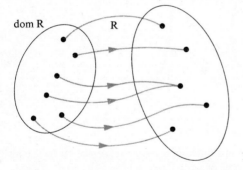

dom R   R

Figure 54 Relation in which each couple is a person and his birthday

birthday. Each element in the domain is the first term of one, and only one, couple belonging to the relation. In the graph, therefore, only one arrow will start from each of the points representing elements. This is the criterion of a *functional relation* or *function*. Expressed in symbols,

R is a function $\Leftrightarrow \forall x \in$ dom R $\exists (x, y) \in$ R.

We say that the function is *defined* in A and has its *values* in B. When the domain of the function is the whole of set A, we say that the function is defined *on* A, that it *maps* into B, or that it is a *mapping of* A *into* B (Figure 55).

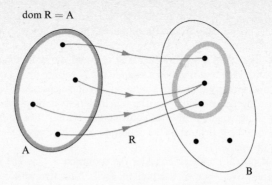

dom R = A

A

R

B

Figure 55 Graph of a function mapping set A *into* set B

When the image of the function is the whole of set B (Figure 56), we say that the function is *surjective* in relation to B, or a *surjection*. We say that it maps A *onto* B, as distinct from the incomplete use of B, which is mapping into.

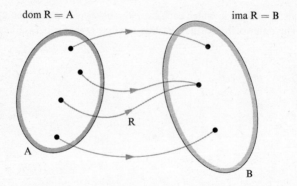

dom R = A

ima R = B

A

R

B

Figure 56 Graph of a function mapping set A *onto* set B. The image of the function is the whole of set B

A mapping of a set into itself is called a *transformation*.

The second term *y* of a couple (x, y) is called the *image* of *x* by that function. If the function is called F, the image of *x* is written $F(x)$, giving the condition $y = F(x)$. The function F, which is a set of couples, should not be confused with the equality $y = F(x)$, which is the condition fulfilled by the image *y* of an element *x* of dom F. Some authors do not distinguish between the function of A in B and the mapping of A into B, regarding the two concepts as synonymous.

Although each element of dom F is the first term of a single couple only,

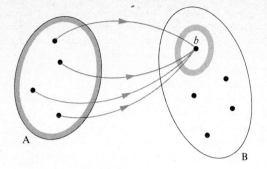

Figure 57 The mapping $A \times \{b\}$

there is nothing to prevent several elements of dom F having the same image. An extreme case is that in which all the elements of A have the same image, as shown in Figure 57. The mapping thus obtained is said to be *constant* on A. Its image is the singleton $\{b\}$. This constant mapping is the Cartesian product $A \times \{b\}$. It should be clearly distinguished from the element b.

A function is called *injective*, and the mapping called an *injection*, if and only if any two distinct elements in its domain have distinct images. A mapping which is both injective and surjective is called a *bijection*. In a bijection mapping A onto B, every element of A has as its image a specific element of B; and every element of B is the image of one and only one element of A. Thus the elements of A and B are in one-to-one or bijective correspondence. A bijection of a set A on itself is called a *permutation* of A. The special case of the permutation in which each element of A maps on itself is called the *identical transformation*.

Examples. There are many examples in daily life of functions in which one set A is mapped into another set B, by conditions like: 'y is the father of x', 'y is the mother of x', 'y is the name of x', 'y is the mass of x'. The definite article 'the' indicates the uniqueness of the image of x by the function in question.

Numerical functions which map a set of real numbers into or onto the set $\mathbb{R}$ of real numbers are well known. The practice of drawing up a table giving the value of $F(x)$ for each x is in accordance with the definition of a function.

In elementary work the notion of a function restricted to a mapping of $\mathbb{R}$ is often used and implied when we express functions by means of conditions like: $y = ax+b$, $y = ax^2+bx+c$, $y = 1/x$, $y = \sin x$, $y = a^x$, $y = \log_a x$.

A function may also be given by drawing its graph in Cartesian coordinates. The set of couples $(x, F(x))$ constituting F is displayed as a set of points with coordinates $(x, F(x))$. The set may consist of a single curve (which may be a straight line) or several curves, and may include isolated points.

Binary operations are functions defined on a set of couples.

Geometrical transformations which map part of a plane (or space) into the plane (or space) are functions. Translations, rotations, symmetries and enlarging transformations of the plane (or space) are permutations of it.

Measures which map a set of parts of a line, plane or space into a set $\mathbb{R}^+$ of non-negative reals are functions.

A real numerical sequence $u_1, u_2, u_3, \ldots, u_n, \ldots$, finite or infinite, is a mapping of the set of subscripts $\{1, 2, 3, \ldots, n, \ldots\}$ into the set $\mathbb{R}$ of real numbers, the image of n being u_n.

In classical logic the attribution of truth or falsity to the propositions of a given set determines a function on that set. The function is two-valued, true or false, and these values are usually denoted by 0 and 1.

If $y = F(x)$ the reciprocal image of y is the set, written $F^{-1}(y)$, of elements of A whose image is y by the function F. It is not, in general, a functional relation of B to A.

Examples:

If, in a set $\mathscr{E}$ of individuals, we establish a correspondence between each individual and his nationality, we obtain a mapping of $\mathscr{E}$ into the set of nationalities. This function determines in $\mathscr{E}$, as a reciprocal, a partition into classes, each presumed known, consisting of the set of all persons in $\mathscr{E}$ having a particular nationality. The same partition of $\mathscr{E}$ can be obtained from the equivalence condition, 'x is a compatriot of y'.

If we establish a correspondence between the integers and their remainders after division by 3, the result is a mapping of the set of integers $\mathbb{Z} = \{0, 1, -1, 2, -2, 3, -3, \ldots\}$ into the set of remainders $\{0, 1, 2\}$. To this mapping corresponds the partition of $\mathbb{Z}$ into three classes, the numbers which have one of the three forms $3n, 3n+1, 3n+2$, where $n \in \mathbb{Z}$.

If we project all points of a space $\mathscr{E}$ onto a plane P by rays parallel to a direction D, so that a point $x \in \mathscr{E}$ corresponds to its projection $p(x) \in P$; then if A is a straight line parallel to the direction D, all the points lying on A will be projected into the same point. The classes of partition of space are all the rays parallel to D and are determined by the equivalence $p(x) = p(y)$.

If $\mathscr{E}$ is a set of function of x whose derivatives with respect to x can be determined, a correspondence may be made between each function F and the derivative of F. This produces a mapping of $\mathscr{E}$ into the set of derivatives. The corresponding partition of $\mathscr{E}$ into classes of functions having the same derivative may also be obtained by the equivalence condition of the primitive functions $F(x) = G(x)+c$, where c is a constant.

Composite functions

If F is a function defined on A, with values in B, and G is a function defined on B with values in C, so that $y = F(x)$ and $z = G(y)$, then $z = G[F(x)]$, which may be written as a composite function $z = (G \circ F)(x)$ (Figure 58). The result produced by the composition of these two functions is a relation of A to C. It is defined on A and is functional, since an element x of A is the first term of at most one couple (x, z) belonging to the composite $G \circ F$, which is itself a mapping of A into C. The order of mapping is shown in the order of writing G and F. $G \circ F$ means that the first mapping is F and G follows. The composite of a bijection and its reciprocal is the identity mapping.

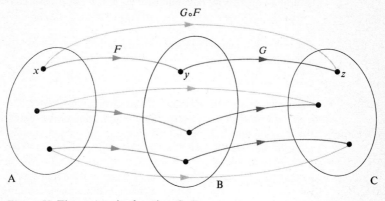

Figure 58 The composite function $G \circ F$

A.5 Cardinal numbers

The most primitive, and at the same time the most functional, way of determining the number of elements in a set of concrete objects is to establish a bijection between this set and a reference set of, for example, notches on a stick or knots on a string. This is the basis of counting. Two such sets, A and B, between which there exists a bijection, are said to be *equipotent*. This is written A $\sim$ B. The equipotence relation is an equivalence, which is (a) reflexive, since every set is equipotent with itself; (b) symmetrical, since if A is equipotent to B, B must be equipotent to A; and (c) transitive, since A $\sim$ B and B $\sim$ C $\Rightarrow$ A $\sim$ C, that is, the combined effect of the bijection between A and B and that between B and C is equivalent to a bijection between A and C.

When two sets A and B are equipotent, we say that they have the same *cardinal number* of elements and write

$\#A = \#B$ \quad (cardinal A equals cardinal B).

Some writers use the sign $|A|$, others write card A, for a cardinal. If we write $0 = \#\varnothing$, $1 = \#\{a\}$, $2 = \#\{a, b\}$, etc., the system of numerals develops.

All sets in the same equivalence have the same cardinal.

The sum of cardinal numbers is defined by means of disjoint sets. If $A \cap B = \varnothing$, that is, if the two sets are disjoint, the sum of $\#A$ and $\#B$ is the cardinal number of the union of A and B. The cardinal numbers 0, $0+1 = 1$, $1+1 = 2$, $2+1 = 3, \ldots$ form the sequence of natural numbers.

This set begins with 0. If the 0 is omitted and the series begins with 1, it is called the set of non-zero natural numbers. A set is finite and contains n elements if it is equipotent to $\{1, 2, 3, 4, \ldots, n\}$.

The addition of natural numbers is the function which brings a couple (a, b) into correspondence with the sum $a+b$. It follows that the addition of natural numbers is (a) commutative, $a+b = b+a$; (b) associative,

$$(a+b)+c = a+(b+c);$$

and (c) it has a neutral element 0, whose addition leaves the original number unchanged,

$$a+0 = 0+a = a.$$

The definition of the product of two cardinal numbers is derived from the Cartesian product of two sets. The multiplication of two natural numbers is the function which brings into correspondence with a couple (a, b) another number, the product $a \times b$. It follows that this multiplication is, like addition, (a) commutative, since $a \times b = b \times a$ and (b) associative, $(a \times b) \times c = a \times (b \times c)$, so that the order of multiplication of three or more numbers does not affect the result. It also has a neutral element 1, multiplication by which leaves a number unaltered, $a \times 1 = 1 \times a = a$, and an absorbing element 0, for which $a \times 0 = 0 \times a = 0$. Another property is that multiplication is distributive over addition,

$$(a+b) \times c = (a \times c)+(b \times c).$$

A.6 Groups

A function defined on a set of couples is called a *binary operation*. If this operation is defined for every couple in the set, it is said to be *everywhere defined*. If the operation maps the couples back into the original set, that is, if the result of the operation is to be found somewhere within the set, it is called an *internal operation*; this is the property of *closure*.

A set $\mathscr{E}$ which has an internal binary operation which is everywhere defined, is called a *groupoid* or *gruppoid*. If the operation is denoted by $*$, the groupoid is represented by the couple $(\mathscr{E}, *)$. If the operation is also associative it is called a monoid or demi-group.

If a set G has an internal operation $*$ everywhere defined, and also the following properties, it is called a *group*:

(a) The operation is associative,

$$\forall x, y, z \in G : (x*y)*z = x*(y*z).$$

(b) The set contains a neutral element $e \in G$,

$$\forall x \in G : x*e = e*x = x.$$

(c) Every element $x \in G$ has an inverse,

$$\forall x \in G \ \exists x^{-1} \in G : x * x^{-1} = x^{-1} * x = e.$$

The group here defined is written $(G, *)$. Every group must contain at least one element, the neutral element. The cardinal $\#G$ is the *order* of the group $(G, *)$, and according as the number $\#G$ is finite or not, the group is said to be finite or not. When the group operation is also commutative, the group is said to be an *Abelian* or *commutative group*.

Examples. The set of subsets of a set $\mathscr{E}$ forms a group with the operation $\triangle$ (symmetric difference). The group is Abelian.

The following are all Abelian groups: $(\mathbb{Z}, +)$, $(\mathbb{Q}, +)$, $(\mathbb{R}, +)$ and $(\mathbb{C}, +)$, where $\mathbb{Z}$ is the set of rational integers, $\mathbb{Q}$ is the set of rational numbers, $\mathbb{R}$ is the set of real numbers and $\mathbb{C}$ the set of complex numbers. These groups are sometimes called the additive groups.

The suffix reading non-zero, and $\mathbb{Q}$, $\mathbb{R}$ and $\mathbb{C}$ as in the previous example, $(\mathbb{Q}_0, .)$, $(\mathbb{R}_0, .)$, $(\mathbb{C}_0, .)$ are multiplicative Abelian groups.

In elementary geometry there are many examples of groups of transformations. The group of translations, the group of similitudes with a given centre in a plane or in space, the group of rotations in a plane or in space having the same centre or axis, are all commutative. Non-commutative are the groups of translations and rotational symmetries in a plane or in space, the group of dilatations in a plane or in space, the group of direct isometries in a plane, etc.

The set of polynomials in x with real coefficients, $\mathbb{R}[x]$, forms a commutative group with the operation $+$; so also does the additive group $(\mathbb{C}[x], +)$ of polynomials with complex coefficients.

The groups mentioned above are all infinite. We can also find many examples of finite groups.

The group of permutations of a pair of elements, one being the identity element I, the other the transposition T, which exchanges the elements, being the other, has a group operation table shown in Table 11.

Table 11

$\circ$	I	T
I	I	T
T	T	I

The identity transformation I and the symmetry S about a rectilinear axis form a group of order 2 with the group operation $\circ$ (composition) and the table is Table 12.

Table 12

$\circ$	I	S
I	I	S
S	S	I

The additive group of the residue classes, $\dot{0}$ and $\dot{1}$, modulo 2 yields Table 13.

Table 13

+	$\dot{0}$	$\dot{1}$
$\dot{0}$	$\dot{0}$	$\dot{1}$
$\dot{1}$	$\dot{1}$	$\dot{0}$

The multiplicative group of non-zero residue classes $\dot{1}$ and $\dot{2}$, modulo 3, has Table 14 as its group table.

Table 14

×	$\dot{1}$	$\dot{2}$
$\dot{1}$	$\dot{1}$	$\dot{2}$
$\dot{2}$	$\dot{2}$	$\dot{1}$

It is apparent that all these group tables of order 2 are identical in form. The reader should determine for himself, by checking the group axioms, whether Table 15, of order 3, defines a commutative group or not.

Table 15

*	e	a	b
e	e	a	b
a	a	b	e
b	b	e	a

Examples of such groups are the additive group of residue classes modulo 3, the rotation group which transforms a given equilateral triangle into itself, and the multiplicative group of the three complex roots of unity.

Groups of order 4, such as the additive group of residue classes modulo 4, the group of rotations which transforms a square into itself, the multiplicative group of non-zero residue classes modulo 5, and the multiplicative group of powers of the imaginary number $i - i^0$, i^1, i^2, i^3 – all have a table of the form of Table 16.

Table 16

*	e	a	b	c
e	e	a	b	c
a	a	b	c	e
b	b	c	e	a
c	c	e	a	b

In the group table it is impossible for an element to occur more than once in the same row or column.

A group in which the elements are all powers of one element is called a *cyclic* group. All cyclic groups are commutative.

Subgroups

A subgroup of a group $(G, *)$ is a subset of G which is also a group with the same operation $*$. In any subgroup $(S, *)$ of $(G, *)$, the neutral element of the subgroup is identical with that of the group and the symmetry of an element in the subgroup corresponds to that of the same element in the group.

In elementary geometry, either plane or in space, the subgroup of displacements is a subgroup of the isometries which is itself a subgroup of the similitudes. The group of translations is a subgroup of the group of displacements, of the group of translations and point symmetries, and of the group of translations and dilatations.

If in a group of permutations of a set $\mathscr{E}$ we take those permutations which remain unchanged, that is, which transform into themselves, these elements form a subgroup of the group. For example, in the group of isometries of space, we can form subgroups by taking (a) the isometries which leave a single point unchanged, (b) the isometries which leave two points unchanged or (c) those isometries which leave the vertices of a triangle unchanged.

When, in a group of permutations of a set $\mathscr{E}$, we take all those which leave a given subset invariant, that is, which transform the subset into itself, we obtain a subgroup of the original group. For example, we can obtain subgroups of the isometries of the plane or of space by taking those transformations which leave unchanged (a) an isosceles triangle, (b) an equilateral triangle, (c) a rectangle, (d) a square, (e) a regular polygon, (f) a circle. We may also obtain subgroups of the isometries of space by taking those transformations which leave unchanged (a) a tetrahedron, (b) a regular tetrahedron, (c) a regular pyramid, (d) a cube, (e) a regular polyhedron, (f) a sphere.

If $(S, *)$ is a subgroup of $(G, *)$, a *coset* is formed by taking every element $a \in G$ in turn, and forming the product, using the operation $*$ with every element of S. It is called a right-hand or left-hand coset, as the case may be, according to whether a lies to the right or left of the element of S in the product. These cosets are written $S * a$ and $a * S$ respectively.

The order of a subgroup of a finite group is a divisor of the order of the group itself. The only subgroups of a group whose order is a prime number are itself and the subgroup which has as its only element the neutral element. It is cyclic. Every group which is finite and of prime order is cyclic.

A.7 Rings and fields

The set of natural numbers $\mathbb{N}$, the set of integers $\mathbb{Z}$, the set of rational numbers $\mathbb{Q}$, the set of real numbers $\mathbb{R}$, the set of complex numbers $\mathbb{C}$, the set $\mathbb{R}[x]$ of polynomials of one unknown defined on $\mathbb{R}$, and the set $\mathbb{C}[x]$ of polynomials of one unknown defined on $\mathbb{C}$ – all these sets have two closed operations, defined throughout, namely addition ($+$) and multiplication (.). Any set which has these two operations can be written ($\mathscr{E}$, $+$, .).

A set (A, $+$, .) which has these two operations everywhere defined is called a *ring* if the following axioms hold:

(a) (i) Associativity,

$$\forall x, y, z \in A : (x+y)+z = x+(y+z).$$

(ii) There exists a neutral element $0 \in A$, such that

$$\forall x \in A : x+0 = 0+x = x.$$

(iii) Every element $x \in A$ has an inverse $\bar{x}$ for addition, such that

$$\forall x \in A \; \exists \bar{x} \in A : x+\bar{x} = \bar{x}+x = 0.$$

(iv) Addition is commutative,

$$\forall x, y \in A : x+y = y+x.$$

(b) (A, .) is a monoid,

$$\forall x, y, z \in A : (x.y).z = x.(y.z).$$

(c) Multiplication is distributive with respect to addition,

from the left $\quad \forall x, y, z \in A : x.(y+z) = (x.y)+(x.z),$

from the right $\quad \forall x, y, z \in A : (x+y).z = (x.z)+(y.z).$

When multiplication in a monoid is commutative, the ring is said to be commutative.

A *skew field* (K, $+$, .) is a ring in which multiplication determines a group in the set $K_0 = K \backslash \{0\}$. A skew field in which multiplication is commutative is called a *field*.

Examples. ($\mathbb{Z}$, $+$, .) is a commutative ring, as is also ($k\mathbb{Z}$, $+$, .), where $k\mathbb{Z}$ is the set obtained by multiplying the elements of $\mathbb{Z}$ by a fixed number $k \in \mathbb{Z}$.

($\mathbb{N}$, $+$, .) is not a ring.

($\mathbb{R}[x]$, $+$, .) and ($\mathbb{C}[x]$, $+$, .) are rings of polynomials.

($\mathbb{Q}$, $+$, .), ($\mathbb{R}$, $+$, .) and ($\mathbb{C}$, $+$, .) are fields.

The set of residue classes modulo m (where m is of course a whole number) with addition and multiplication mod m, is a commutative ring. When m is prime, the ring is a field.

The set of terminating decimal numbers, positive, zero or negative, is a commutative ring, but not a field, with addition and multiplication.

The set $\mathscr{P}(\mathscr{E})$ of subsets of $\mathscr{E}$, with the operations of symmetric difference $\triangle$ and intersection $\cap$ is a commutative ring ($\mathscr{P}(\mathscr{E}), \triangle, \cap$). Functions of real or complex values defined on a set $\mathscr{E}$ form a ring when addition is the addition of functions defined on $\mathscr{E}$ and with values in $\mathbb{R}$ or $\mathbb{C}$,

$$\forall x \in \mathscr{E} : (f+g)(x) = f(x)+g(x),$$

and multiplication is the multiplication of functions

$$\forall x \in \mathscr{E} : (f.g)(x) = f(x).g(x).$$

Matrices in a ring

Given a ring $(A, +, .)$, we can construct a *matrix* of m rows and n columns by forming a table written

$$\begin{bmatrix} a_{11} & a_{12} & \cdots & a_{1n} \\ a_{21} & a_{22} & \cdots & a_{2n} \\ \cdots & \cdots & \cdots & \cdots \\ a_{m1} & a_{m2} & \cdots & a_{mn} \end{bmatrix}.$$

The table is obtained by mapping the Cartesian product

$$\{1, 2, \ldots, n\} \times \{1, 2, \ldots, m\} = \begin{bmatrix} (1,1) & (1,2) & \cdots & (1,n) \\ (2,1) & (2,2) & \cdots & (2,n) \\ \cdots & \cdots & \cdots & \cdots \\ (m,1) & (m,2) & \cdots & (m,n) \end{bmatrix}$$

into A; that is, we make a correspondence between a number a and each of the elements of the product. Such matrices are then families of A indexed by this set of double indices. For this reason the set of matrices with m rows and n columns with values in the ring A is called $A^{m \times n}$. Matrices of the form $A^{1 \times n}$, having a single row, are called *row matrices*, and those of the form $A^{m \times 1}$, having a single column, are called *column matrices*. A matrix of the form $A^{m \times m}$, having the same number of rows as columns, is called a square matrix.

Matrices are equal when each element of the one is equal to the corresponding element of the other. The addition of matrices is the addition of corresponding elements, defined on a set,

$$(a+b)_{kl} = a_{kl}+b_{kl},$$

for all $k \in \{1, 2, \ldots, m\}$ and all $l \in \{1, 2, \ldots, n\}$.

From these definitions and the fact that $(A, +)$ is a commutative group, it follows that $(A^{m \times n}, +)$ is a commutative group for addition. The neutral element is the null matrix, when every element is equal to the neutral element 0 of $(A, +)$. The negative of a matrix is the matrix having each element the negative of the corresponding element of the first matrix.

Multiplication of matrices is defined only for the case of matrices in the form $A^{m \times p}$ and $A^{p \times n}$ (i.e. when the number of columns in the first is equal to the number of rows in the second), otherwise multiplication is not possible. Each term in the product matrix is obtained by multiplying each term in the appropriate row of the first matrix by each term in the appropriate column in the second matrix, and adding the products. When it is defined, matrix multiplication is associative and also distributive over addition, both from left and right. It is not, in general, commutative. $(A^{m \times m}, +, .)$ is a non-commutative ring. Square matrices of the form $A^{m \times m}$ have a neutral element for multiplication, the unit matrix

$$
\begin{bmatrix}
1 & 0 & \cdots & 0 \\
0 & 1 & \cdots & 0 \\
\cdots & \cdots & \cdots & \cdots \\
0 & 0 & \cdots & 1
\end{bmatrix}
$$

in which $a_{kl} = \begin{cases} 1 & \text{when } k = l, \\ 0 & \text{when } k \neq l. \end{cases}$

A square matrix in which all the non-zero elements lie on the leading diagonal, $a_{ij} = 0$ if $i \neq j$, is called a diagonal matrix:

$$
\begin{bmatrix}
a_{11} & 0 & \cdots & 0 \\
0 & a_{22} & \cdots & 0 \\
\cdots & \cdots & \cdots & \cdots \\
0 & 0 & \cdots & a_{mm}
\end{bmatrix}.
$$

A.8 Vector spaces

In elementary geometry, vectors of the plane or of space form a commutative group $(V, +)$ for addition. Multiplication of a vector by a rational or a real number results in a vector. If K is a field of numbers, the mapping

$K \times V \to V : (a, \mathbf{v}) \to a\mathbf{v}$

is called a scalar multiplication and has the following properties:

(a) $\forall \mathbf{v} \in V : 1\mathbf{v} = \mathbf{v}$.

The neutral element for multiplication in K, 1, is the neutral element for scalar multiplication, which is then a mapping of $K \times V$ onto V.

(b) $\forall \mathbf{v} \in V, \forall a, b \in K : a(b\mathbf{v}) = (ab)\mathbf{v}$.

Scalar multiplication is associative with multiplication in K. This is the mixed associative law.

(c) $\forall \mathbf{v} \in V, \forall a, b \in K : (a+b)\mathbf{v} = a\mathbf{v} + b\mathbf{v}$.

Scalar multiplication is distributive over addition in the group $(K, +)$.

(d) $\forall \mathbf{u}, \mathbf{v} \in V, \forall a \in K : a(\mathbf{u} + \mathbf{v}) = a\mathbf{u} + a\mathbf{v}$.

Scalar multiplication is distributive over addition in the group $(V, +)$.

If a commutative group $(V, +)$ has a scalar multiplication by the elements of a field K, and it has for its neutral element the neutral element of multiplication in K, and is also distributive over multiplication in both K and V, it is called a *vector space* on the field K, and is written $(K, V, +)$. If the scalars are real, the vector space is said to be real.

As we use the same notation for addition, $+$, in both K and V, it is convenient to use the same sign for multiplication in K and for scalar multiplication in the vector space. This does not lead to confusion if we use distinct symbols, such as bold type or superior arrows to denote vectors, as in geometry.

Examples. The additive group of vectors in a plane, or in space, together with multiplication by real numbers, form a vector space on the field of real numbers.

The plane, or space, with a fixed origin O is an Abelian group $(\Pi^0, +)$ when addition of points x, y, z is defined by

$$\forall x, y, z \in \Pi^0 : x + y = z \Leftrightarrow Ox + Oy = Oz.$$

If we introduce multiplication by reals, by the definition

$$\forall a \in \mathbb{R}, \forall x, y \in \Pi^0 : ax = y \Leftrightarrow a . Ox = Oy,$$

we obtain the vector space $(\mathbb{R}, \Pi^0, +)$.

Every field $(K, +, .)$ can be considered as a vector space on itself $(K, K, +)$, the module being $(K, +)$ and the scalar multiplication being multiplication in $(K, .)$. The fields $(\mathbb{Q}, +, .)$, $(\mathbb{R}, +, .)$, $(\mathbb{C}, +, .)$ can all be considered as vector spaces on themselves.

Every ring $(A, +, .)$ which has a subfield $(K, +, .)$ is a vector space $(K, A, +)$ on the latter. Also the field of complex numbers is a vector space on the field of real numbers and the field of real numbers is a vector space on the field of rational numbers.

The product of vector spaces (V_1, V_2) on the same field K is formed by constructing the Cartesian product $V_1 \times V_2$ and defining, for all $\mathbf{v} = (\mathbf{v}_1, \mathbf{v}_2)$, $\mathbf{v}_1 \in V_1, \mathbf{v}_2 \in V_2, \mathbf{u} = (\mathbf{u}_1, \mathbf{u}_2), \mathbf{u}_1 \in V_1, \mathbf{u}_2 \in V_2$,

the sum $\mathbf{u} + \mathbf{v} = (\mathbf{u}_1 + \mathbf{v}_1, \mathbf{u}_2 + \mathbf{v}_2)$,

and the product of $\mathbf{v}$ and $x \in K : x\mathbf{v} = (x\mathbf{v}_1, x\mathbf{v}_2)$.

The new vector space thus generated is called the product of a couple of vector spaces. Thus the vector space $(K, K^m, +)$ is the product of m identical spaces $(K, K, +)$.

A.9   Metric spaces

To a couple of real numbers (x, y) there corresponds a real, non-negative number $|x - y|$ called the distance between x and y, written $d(x, y)$. This determines a function:

$$\mathbb{R} \times \mathbb{R} \to \mathbb{R} : (x, y) \overset{d}{\to} d(x, y),$$

which has the following properties:

(a) $\forall x, y \in \mathbb{R} : d(x, y) \geqslant 0$,

(b) $\forall x, y \in \mathbb{R} : d(x, y) = 0 \Leftrightarrow x = y$,

(c) $\forall x, y \in \mathbb{R} : d(x, y) = d(y, x)$,

(d) $\forall x, y, z \in \mathbb{R} : d(x, y) \leqslant d(x, z) + d(z, y)$.

It will be seen that these properties fit in with, and are derived from the conventional idea of physical distance; here they are only a starting point.

If two numbers x and y are complex, we can define the distance between them as the absolute value $|x-y|$ which then determines the mapping

$$\mathbb{C} \times \mathbb{C} \to \mathbb{R} : (x, y) \overset{d}{\mapsto} d(x, y),$$

which has the same properties.

When a distance function d is defined on a set $\mathscr{E}$, the couple $(\mathscr{E}, d)$ is called a *metric space*.

Examples. Distance may be defined on any set $\mathscr{E}$. For instance, we may say that for every couple (x, y),

$$d(x, y) = \begin{cases} 0 & \text{if } x = y, \\ 1 & \text{if } x \neq y. \end{cases}$$

The distance thus defined is called the discrete distance on $\mathscr{E}$.

Many distances can be defined on any set. It is easy to see that if d is a distance on $\mathscr{E}$, and k is a positive real number, kd will also be a distance on $\mathscr{E}$.

In a plane, with rectangular axes of reference and equal units, the Euclidean distance between two points $x = (x_1, y_1)$ and $y = (x_2, y_2)$ is given by Pythagoras' theorem as

$$d(x, y) = \sqrt{\{(x_1 - x_2)^2 + (y_1 - y_2)^2\}},$$

which satisfies the axioms of distance. Distance on the real line and in the complex plane are similarly defined.

In the space $\mathbb{R}^n$, the Euclidean distance between points $x = (x_1, x_2, \ldots, x_n)$ and $y = (y_1, y_2, \ldots, y_n)$ is

$$d(x, y) = \sqrt{\left[\sum_{i=1}^{n} (x_i - y_i)^2 \right]}.$$

We can find a distance in the plane $\mathbb{R}^2$ by taking

$$d'(x, y) = \text{Max}(|x_1 - y_1|, |x_2 - y_2|)$$

or $\quad d''(x, y) = |x_1 - y_1| + |x_2 - y_2|$.

Let $(\mathscr{E}_1, d_1)$ and $(\mathscr{E}_2, d_2)$ be two metric spaces. For every couple

$$(x = (x_1, x_2), y = (y_1, y_2))$$

of the product $\mathscr{E}_1 \times \mathscr{E}_2$, let $d(x, y) = \text{Max}\,(d_1(x_1, y_1)\, d_2(x_2, y_2))$. We are thus defining a distance on the set $\mathscr{E}_1 \times \mathscr{E}_2$. The metric space $(\mathscr{E}_1 \times \mathscr{E}_2, d)$ is then the product of the couple of metric spaces $(\mathscr{E}_1, \mathscr{E}_2)$. Another definition of distance in the space product $\mathscr{E} \times \mathscr{E}$ is to take $d = \sqrt{(d_1^2 + d_2^2)}$. The definition can then be extended to a finite sequence of metric spaces.

In a metric space $(\mathscr{E}, d)$ a set of points of $\mathscr{E}$, $B(a, \rho)$ such that $d(x, a) < \rho$,

$$B(a, \rho) = \{x \in \mathscr{E} \,|\, d(x, a) < \rho\},$$

is an open ball of radius $\rho \geqslant 0$. The sphere centre $a \in \mathscr{E}$ and radius $\rho \geqslant 0$ is the set $S(a, \rho) = \{x \in \mathscr{E} \,|\, d(x, a) = \rho\}$. The union of these two, the open ball and the sphere, gives a closed ball. In a Euclidean three-dimensional space this corresponds to the Euclidean sphere, the open ball being its interior. In a Euclidean plane it gives a circle and an open or closed disc respectively.

Continuity

A function f on R is said to be *continuous* on the point $a \in \text{R}$ if, for all $\varepsilon > 0$ there exists a $\delta > 0$ such that $|x-a| < \delta$ implies $|f(x)-f(a)| < \varepsilon$. It is continuous over $A \subset \mathscr{E}$ if it is continuous at every point in A.

If $(\mathscr{E}, d)$ and $(\mathscr{F}, d)$ are two metric spaces, every constant function of $\mathscr{E}$ on $\mathscr{F}$ is continuous over $\mathscr{E}$.

In a metric space $(\mathscr{E}, d)$ we call a partition V of $\mathscr{E}$ which contains an open ball $B(a, \rho)$ of positive radius ρ and centre a, the neighbourhood of the point a. An open ball with positive radius is a neighbourhood for each of the points within it.

A.10   Topological spaces

If from the concept of metric spaces we remove the idea of distance, keeping only the open sets and their properties· we can still define neighbourhoods and continuity of functions. By doing so we arrive at the idea of *topological spaces*.

Given a non-empty set $\mathscr{E}$, we define a topology $\mathscr{T}$ on $\mathscr{E}$ as a family of partitions such that

$\mathscr{E} \in \mathscr{T}$;

$\varnothing \in \mathscr{T}$;

if $O_1, O_2, \ldots, O_n \in \mathscr{T}$ then $\bigcap_{i=1}^{n} O_i \in \mathscr{T}$;

if for all $i \in \text{J}, O_i \in \mathscr{T}$ then $\bigcup_{i \in J} O_i \in \mathscr{T}$.

The sets $O \in \mathscr{T}$ are called open sets of $\mathscr{E}$. The above conditions state that $\mathscr{E}$ and $\varnothing$ are open sets, that the intersection of a finite family of open sets is open, and that the union of such a family is open. These axioms are similar to those for open sets of a metric space. The couple $(\mathscr{E}, \mathscr{T})$, formed from a set $\mathscr{E}$ and a topology $\mathscr{T}$, is said to be a topological space defined on $\mathscr{E}$.

If $\mathscr{E}$ is a set on which there are defined two distances, d_1 and d_2, the two metric spaces thus obtained, $(\mathscr{E}, d_1)$ and $(\mathscr{E}, d_2)$, are said to be topologically equivalent if they generate the same topological space, that is, if the open sets of $(\mathscr{E}, d_1)$ and $(\mathscr{E}, d_2)$ are the same. A topological space is called separable if, given any two distinct points, there exist at least two disjoint open sets, each containing one of these points. Every space generated by a metric space is separable.

Examples. In a set $\mathscr{E} \neq \varnothing$, the set $\mathscr{T} = \{\varnothing, \mathscr{E}\}$ is clearly a topology and is contained in every topology of $\mathscr{E}$.

The set $\mathscr{P}(\mathscr{E})$ of partitions of a non-empty set $\mathscr{E}$ is a topology and $(\mathscr{E}, \mathscr{P}(\mathscr{E}))$ is a topological space. The topology $\mathscr{T}(\mathscr{E})$ of $\mathscr{E}$ contains every topology of $\mathscr{E}$.

Every space $\mathscr{E}$ which contains at least one pair $\{a, b\}$ has many topologies. For example, $\{\varnothing, \mathscr{E}\}$, $\{\varnothing, \{a\}, \mathscr{E}\}$, $\{\varnothing, \{a\}, \{b\}, \mathscr{E}\}$.

In a topological space $(\mathscr{E}, \mathscr{T})$, the neighbourhood V of a point a is a partition $V \subset \mathscr{E}$ which contains an open set $O \in \mathscr{T}$ to which a belongs.

Every open set is a neighbourhood of every point which it contains.

The complement of an open set is a closed set.

In every topological space the sets $\mathscr{E}$ and $\varnothing$ are at the same time both open and closed. When these are the only sets with this property, the space is said to be connected.

Further reading

For further recommended reading on the topics in this chapter, the reader is referred to books by the following authors listed in the Bibliography.

Logic
Allendorfer and Oakley (1959); Arnold (1962b); Behnke (1958); Dubisch (1963); Exner and Rosskopf (1959); Kemeny *et al.* (1959a, 1959b); Kirsch and Steiner (1966); Meschkowski (1964); Stolyar (1965); Suppes and Hill (1964).

Sets
Adler (1958); Allendorfer and Oakley (1959); Behnke (1958); Dupont (1965); Fletcher (1964); Kemeny *et al.* (1959a, 1959b); Kirsch and Steiner (1966); May (1959); Meschkowski (1964); Papy (1959, 1963); Rosenstiehl and Mothes (1965); Suppes *et al.* (1957).

Binary relations
Behnke (1958); Dupont (1965); Fletcher (1964); Kirsch and Steiner (1966); May (1959); Meschkowski (1964); Papy (1963).

Functions
Behnke (1958–65); Choquet (1964); Dupont (1965); Kirsch and Steiner (1966) ; Meschkowski (1964); Papy (1963).

Cardinal numbers

Behnke (1958–65); Dupont (1965); Kirsch and Steiner (1966); Meschkowski (1964); Papy (1963).

Groups

Adler (1958); Bachmann (1959); Behnke (1958); Dupont (1965); Fletcher (1964); Kemeny *et al.* (1959a, 1959b); Kirsch and Steiner (1966); May (1959); Meschkowski (1964); Papy (1961, 1963, 1964).

Rings and fields

Adler (1958); Behnke (1958); Dupont (1965); Fletcher (1964); Kirsch and Steiner (1966); Meschkowski (1964).

Vector spaces

Artin (1957); Behnke (1958); Choquet (1964); Dieudonné (1965); Kemeny *et al.* (1959a, 1959b); Kirsch and Steiner (1966); Papy (1959, 1963); Pedoe (1963); Yaglom and Boltyanski (1961).

Metric spaces

Artin (1957); Behnke (1958); Choquet (1964); Dieudonné (1965); Kirsch and Steiner (1966); Meschkowski (1964).

Topological spaces

Adler (1958); Arnold (1962a); Choquet (1964); Kirsch and Steiner (1966); Meschkowski (1964); Papy (1959).

Bibliography

Books

ADLER, I. (1958), *The New Mathematics*, John Day.

ADLER, I. (1966), *A New Look at Geometry*, John Day.

ALLENDORFER, C. B., and OAKLEY, C. O. (1959), *Fundamentals of Freshman Mathematics*, McGraw-Hill.

ALLENDORFER, C. B., and OAKLEY, C.O. (1963), *Principles of Mathematics*, 2nd edn, McGraw-Hill.

ARNOLD, B. H. (1962a), *Intuitive Concepts in Elementary Topology*, Prentice-Hall.

ARNOLD, B. H. (1962b), *Logic and Boolean Algebra*, Prentice-Hall.

ARTIN, E. (1957), *Geometric Algebra*, Interscience.

ASSOCIATION OF TEACHERS OF MATHEMATICS (1967), *Notes on Mathematics in Primary Schools*, Cambridge University Press.

ATHEN, H. (1960), *Vektorielle analytische Geometrie*, Hanover: Schroedel.

BACHMANN, F. (1959), *Aufbau der Geometrie aus dem Spiegelungsbegriff*, Springer.

BEBERMAN, M. (1958), *An Emerging Program of Secondary School Mathematics*, Harvard University Press.

BEBERMAN, M., and VAUGHAN, H. E. (1964-7), *High School Mathematics*, Courses 1-4, Heath.

BEHNKE, H. (ed.) (1958), *Der mathematische Unterricht für die 16–21 jährige Jugend in der Bundesrepublik Deutschland*, Göttingen: Vandenhoeck & Ruprecht.

BEHNKE, H., et al. (1958-65), *Grundzüge der Mathematik. Für Lehrer an Gymnasien sowie für Mathematiker in Industrie und Wirtschaft*, 4 vols., Göttingen: Vandenhoeck & Ruprecht.

BIRKHOFF, G. D., and BEATLEY, K. (1959), *Basic Geometry*, Chelsea Publishing.

BRUMFIEL, C. F., et al. (1960), *Geometry*, Addison-Wesley.

BRUMFIEL, C. F., et al. (1961), *Algebra*, vol. 1, Addison-Wesley.

BRUMFIEL, C. F., et al. (1963a), *Introduction to Mathematics*, Addison-Wesley.

BRUMFIEL, C. F., et al. (1963b), *Arithmetic: Concepts and Skills*, Addison-Wesley.

CALAME, A., and SUTER, N. (1965), *Mathématiques modernes*, Neuchâtel: Griffon.

CAMBRIDGE CONFERENCE ON SCHOOL MATHEMATICS (1963), *Report*, Houghton Mifflin.

CASTELNUEOVO, E. (1959), *Geometria intuitiva*, Florence: La Nuova Italia.

CASTELNUEOVO, E. (1962), *I Numeri, Aritmetica practica*, Florence: La Nuova Italia.

CASTELNUEOVO, E. (1963), *Didattica della Matematica*, Florence: La Nuova Italia.

CHOQUET, G. (1964), *L'enseignement de la géométrie*, Paris: Hermann.

CHRISTIANSEN, B. (1964), *Elementaer Kombinatorik og Sandsynlighedsregning,* Copenhagen: Munksgaard.

CHRISTIANSEN, B., LICHTENBERG, J., and PEDERSEN, J. (1964), *Almene Begreber fra Logik, Maengdelaere og Algebra,* Copenhagen: Munksgaard.

COHEN, D. (1967), *Inquiry in Mathematics via the Geo-Board. Teacher's Guide,* Walker.

COLLEGE ENTRANCE EXAMINATIONS BOARD. COMMISSION ON MATHEMATICS (1959), *Report, Program for College Preparatory Mathematics.*

CUNDY, H. M., and ROLLETT, A. P. (1961), *Mathematical Models,* 2nd edn, Clarendon Press.

DANTZIG, T. (1954), *Number. The Language of Science,* Doubleday.

DAVIS, R. B. (1964), *Discovery in Mathematics,* Addison-Wesley.

DAVIS, R. B. (1967), *Explorations in Mathematics,* Addison-Wesley.

DIENES, Z. P. (1960), *Building up Mathematics,* Hutchinson.

DIENES, Z. P. (1964a), *Mathematics in the Primary School,* MacMillan.

DIENES, Z. P. (1964b), *La Mathématique moderne dans l'enseignement primaire,* OCDL.

DIENES, Z. P. (1965), *Modern Mathematics for Young Children. A Teacher's Guide to the Introduction of Modern Mathematics to Children from 5 to 8,* Educational Supply Association.

DIENES, Z. P., and GOLDING, E. W. (1966a), *Explorations of Space and Practical Measurement,* Herder & Herder.

DIENES, Z. P., and GOLDING, E. W. (1966b), *Learning Logic, Logical Games,* Herder & Herder.

DIENES, Z. P., and GOLDING, E. W. (1966c), *Sets, Numbers and Powers,* Herder & Herder.

DIENES, Z. P., and GOLDING, E. W. (1967), *Geometry through Transformations,* Educational Supply Association – Hutchinson.

DIEUDONNÉ, J. (1965), *Algèbre linéaire et géometrie élémentaire,* Paris: Hermann.

DRENCKHAHN, F. (1958), *Der mathematische Unterricht fur die 6–15 jährige Jugend in der Bundesrepublik Deutschland,* Göttingen: Vandenhoeck & Ruprecht.

DUBISCH, R. (1963), *The Teaching of Mathematics. From Intermediate Algebra through First year Calculus,* Wiley.

DUPONT, E. (1965) *Apprentissage mathématique I. Ensembles, relations, nombres,* Paris: Sudel.

DYNKIN, E. B., and USPENSKII, V. A. (1963a), *Multicolor Problems,* Heath; Harrap.

DYNKIN, E. B., and USPENSKII, V. A. (1963b), *Problems in the Theory of Numbers,* Heath; Harrap.

DYNKIN, E. B., and USPENSKII, V. A. (1963c), *Random Walks,* Heath; Harrap.

EICHOLZ, R. E., MARTIN, E., *et al.* (1967), *Elementary School Mathematics. Number Readiness Books,* Addison-Wesley.

ENGEN, H. VAN, *et al.* (1962), *Seeing through Mathematics,* Books 1–2, Scott Foresman.

EXNER, R. M., and ROSSKOPF, M. F. (1959), *Logic in Elementary Mathematics,* McGraw-Hill.

FEHR, H. F. (ed.) (1962), *Mathematical Education in the Americas.* New York, Teachers College, Columbia University.

FEHR, H. F., CARNAHAN, W. H., and BEBERMAN, M. (1963), *Algebra with Trigonometry*, Heath.

FEHR, H. F., HUNT, L., and GROSSMAN, G. (1964), *An Introduction.to Sets, Probability and Hypotheses Testing*, Heath.

FEHR, H. F., and PHILLIPS, J. M. (1967), *Teaching Modern Mathematics in the Elementary School*, Addison-Wesley.

FELIX, L. (1957), *L'aspect moderne des mathématiques*, Paris: Blanchard.

FELIX, L. (1960), *Mathématiques modernes – enseignement élémentaire*, Paris: Blanchard.

FELIX, L. (1961), *The Modern Aspect of Mathematics*, Science Editions.

FELIX, L. (1962a), *Dans le jardin de Monsieur Fève (Introduction aux structures mathématiques)*, Paris: Blanchard.

FELIX, L. (1962b), *Exposé moderne des mathématiques élémentaires*, 2nd edn, Paris: Dunod.

FELIX, L. (1962c), *Les cent problèmes de petit Poucet*, Paris: Blanchard.

FELIX, L. (1966), *Modern Mathematics and the Teacher*, Cambridge University Press.

FLETCHER, T. J. (ed.) (1964), *Some Lessons in Mathematics*, Cambridge University Press.

FRENCH, P. (1964), *An Introduction to Calculating Machines for Schools*, MacMillan.

GATTEGNO, C. (1960), *Modern Mathematics with Numbers in Colour*, Reading: Educational Explorers.

GATTEGNO, C. (1962), *Eléments de mathématiques modernes par les nombres en couleurs. A l'usage du corps enseignant primaire*, Neuchâtel: Delachaux & Niestlé.

GATTEGNO, C. (1963), *For the Teaching of Mathematics*, 3 vols., Reading: Educational Explorers.

GATTEGNO, C., et al. (1965), *L'enseignement des mathématiques*, 3 vols., Neuchâtel: Delachaux & Niestlé.

GELFAND, M. B., and PAVLOVICH, V. S., *Vneklassnaya robota po matematike v 8-letney skole*, Moscow: Prosveščenija.

GOUTARD, M. (1963a), *Les mathématiques et les enfants*, Neuchâtel: Delachaux & Niestlé.

GOUTARD, M. (1963b), *Talks for Primary School Teachers*, Reading: Lamport Gilbert.

GOUTARD, M. (1964), *Mathematics and Children*, Reading: Lamport Gilbert.

HARTUNG, M. L., et al. (1958-63), *Seeing through Arithmetic*, books 1-6, Scott Foresman.

HAWLEY, N., and SUPPES, P. (1960), *Geometry for Primary Grades*, 2 vols., Holden-Day.

HERITAGE, R. S. (1965-71), *Learning Mathematics*, books 1-4, 3m and 4m, Penguin.

INTERNATIONAL SYMPOSIUM ON SCHOOL MATHEMATICS TEACHING (1962), *Report*, Budapest: Akadémiai Kiadó.

JEGER, M. (1964), *Konstruktive Abbildungsgeometrie*, 3rd edn, Lucerne: Rüber.

KEMENY, J. G., et al. (1959a), *Finite Mathematical Structures*, Prentice-Hall.

KEMENY, J. G., et al. (1959b), *Introduction to Finite Mathematics*, 4th edn, Prentice-Hall.

KEMENY, J. G., *et al.* (1962), *Finite Mathematics with Business Applications,* Prentice-Hall.

KIRSCH, A., and STEINER, H. G. (eds.) (1966) *Moderne Mathematik in elementarer Darstellung,* 5 vols., Göttingen: Vanderhoeck & Ruprecht.

KRISTENSEN, E., and RINDUNG, O. (1962–4), *Matematik 1, 2, 3,* Copenhagen: GEC Gads.

KRISTENSEN, E., and RINDUNG, O. (1965), *Sandsynlighedsregning,* Copenhagen: GEC Gads.

KRYGOWSKA, A. Z. (1965), *Geometria. Podstawowe wlasnosci plaszczgzny,* Warsaw: Panstwow Zaklady Wydawnictw Szkolnych.

LAND, F. (1963a), *The Language of Mathematics,* Doubleday.

LAND, F. (1963b), *New Approaches to Mathematics Teaching,* MacMillan.

LEHMAN, A. A., and BOLTYANSKIY, V. G. (1965), *Sbornik zadac moskovskih matematiceskih olimpiad,* Moscow: Prosveščenija.

LENZ, H. (1961), *Grundlagen der Elementarmathematik,* VEB Deutscher Verlag der Wissenschaften.

LIETZMANN, W., and STENDER, R. (1961) *Methodik des mathematischen Unterrichts,* Heidelberg: Quelle & Meyer.

MANSFIELD, D. E., and BRUCKHEIMER, M. (1965), *Major Topics in Modern Mathematics. Set and Group Theory,* Harcourt, Brace & World.

MANSFIELD, D. E., and THOMPSON, D. (1962–66), *Mathematics: A New Approach,* 5 vols., with teachers' guides, Chatto & Windus.

MAY, K. O. (1959), *Elements of Modern Mathematics,* Addison-Wesley.

MATTHEWS, G. (1964), *Calculus,* Murray.

MESCHKOWSKI, H. (1964), *Einführung in die moderne Mathematik,* Mannheim: Bibl. Inst.

MESCHKOWSKI, H. (1965), *Mathematik als Bildungsgrundlage,* Brunswick: Vieweg.

MIALARET, G. (ed.) (1964), *L'enseignement des mathématiques,* Presses Universitaires de France.

MIDLANDS MATHEMATICAL EXPERIMENT (1964), *O-Level,* 3 vols., Harrap.

MOISE, E. E. (1964), *Elementary Geometry from an Advanced Standpoint,* Addison-Wesley.

MOISE, E. E. (1967), *Calculus,* Addison-Wesley.

MOISE, E. E., and DOWNS, F. L. (1963), *Geometry,* Addison-Wesley.

MOSS, G. A. (1958), *Think of a Number,* 2 vols., Blackwell.

MOSS, G. A. (1960), *Geometry for Juniors,* 4 vols., Blackwell.

MOSTELLER, R., ROURKE, R. E. K., and THOMAS, G. B. (1961), *Probability: A First Course,* Addison-Wesley.

NESHKOV, K. I. (1963), *Matematika. Uchebnye materialy dlva IV klassa,* 3 vols., Moscow: APN.

NEWMAN, J. R. (1956), *The World of Mathematics,* 4 vols., Simon & Schuster.

OECD (1961a), *Mathématiques pour physiciens et ingénieurs,* Organization for Economic Co-operation and Development.

OECD (1961b), *New Thinking in School Mathematics,* Organization for Economic Co-operation and Development.

OECD (1961c), *Synopses for Modern Secondary School Mathematics,* Organization for Economic Co-operation and Development. Also published in French.

OECD (1964), *Mathematics Today,* Organization for Economic Co-operation and Development. Also published in French.

PAGE, D. A. (1964), *Number Lines, Functions, and Fundamental Topics. Mathematics for Elementary School Teachers,* Macmillan Inc.

PAPY, G. (1959), *Quinze leçons sur l'algèbre linéaire,* Brussels: Presses Universitaires.

PAPY, G. (1960), *Premiers éléments de mathématique moderne. Notes de cours rédigées à l'intention des élèves des écoles normales gardiennes,* Brussels: Presses Universitaires.

PAPY, G. (1961), *Groupes,* Brussels: Presses Universitaires; Paris: Dunod.

PAPY, G. (1963), *Mathématique moderne,* 6 vols., Didier.

PAPY, G. (1964), *Groups,* Macmillan.

PEDOE, D. (1958), *The Gentle Art of Mathematics,* English Universities Press, Penguin (1963).

PEDOE, D. (1963), *A Geometric Introduction to Linear Algebra,* Wiley.

PETER, M., and SCHAAF, W. (1965), *Mathematics: A Modern Approach,* 2 vols., Van Nostrand.

PÉTER, R. (1961), *Playing with Infinity,* Bell; Atheneum.

PICARD, N. (1966), *Des ensembles à la découverte du nombre,* OCDL.

PICARD, N. (1967), *A la conquête du nombre,* 4 vols., OCDL.

POLYA, G. (1954), *Mathematics and Plausible Reasoning,* 2 vols., Princeton University Press.

POLYA, G. (1958), *How to Solve It: A New Aspect of Mathematical Method,* Doubleday.

POLYA, G. (1962), *Mathematical Discovery: On Understanding, Learning, and Teaching Problem Solving,* 2 vols., Wiley.

PROBLEME DES MATHEMATIKUNTERRICHTS. Diskussionbeiträge sowjetischer Wissenschafter (1965), Berlin: Volk & Wissen.

RADE, L. (1965), *Sannolikhetslära och Statistik.* Gothenburg: NKI-skolan.

RENWICK, E. M. (1963), *Children Learning Mathematics,* Elms Court: Stockwell.

RÉNYI, A. (1965), *Dialógusok a matematikáról,* Budapest: Akadémiai Kiadó.

ROSENBLOOM, P., and SCHUSTER, S. (1966), *Prelude to Analysis,* Prentice-Hall.

ROSENSTIEHL, P., and MOTHES, J. (1965), *Mathématiques de l'action. Langage des ensembles, des statistiques et des aléas,* Dunod.

SAAD, L. G., and STORER, W. O. (1960), *Understanding in Mathematics,* Oliver & Boyd.

SAWYER, W. W. (1943), *Mathematician's Delight,* Penguin.

SAWYER, W. W. (1955), *Prelude to Mathematics,* Penguin.

SAWYER, W. W. (1959), *A Concrete Approach to Abstract Algebra,* San Francisco: Freeman.

SAWYER, W. W. (1964, 1966, 1970), *Introducing Mathematics,* 4 vols. (vol. 2 in press), Penguin.

SEALEY, L. G. W. (1960), *The Creative Use of Mathematics in the Junior Schools,* Blackwell.

SEALEY, L. G. W. (1961a), *Facts to Discover and Learn,* Blackwell.

SEALEY, L. G. W. (1961b), *Finding Mathematics around Us,* Blackwell.

SEALEY, L. G. W. (1961c), *Learning and Using Some Important Mathematical Ideas,* Blackwell.

SEALEY, L. G. W. (1961d), *Some Important Mathematical Ideas,* Blackwell.
SEALEY, L. G. W. (1962), *More Mathematical Ideas,* Blackwell.
SEALEY, L. G. W., and GIBBON, V. (1964), *Beginning Mathematics,* 4 vols., Blackwell.
SKEMP, R. R. (1964), *Understanding Mathematics,* 4 vols., University of London Press.
STABLER, B. R. (1953), *An Introduction to Mathematical Thought,* Addison-Wesley.
STEIN, S. K. (1963), *Mathematics, The Man-Made Universe,* San Francisco: Freeman.
STEINHAUS, H. G. (1964), *One Hundred Problems in Elementary Mathematics,* Basic Books.
STENDER, R. (1962), *Didaktische Themen aus der neueren Mathematik,* Heidelberg: Quelle & Meyer.
STERN, C. (1953), *Children Discover Arithmetic. An Introduction to Structural Arithmetic,* Harrap.
STOLYAR, A. A. (1965), *Logicheskie Problemy Prepodavaniya Matematiki,* Minsk: Vysshaya Skola.
SUPPES, P., *et al.* (1957), *Sets and Numbers,* Textbooks for kindergarten and grades 1 to 4, Singer.
SUPPES, P., and HILL, S. (1964), *First Course in Mathematical Logic,* Blaisdell.
THWAITES, B. (1961), *On Teaching Mathematics,* Pergamon.
TIETZE, H. (1965), *Famous Problems in Mathematics,* 2nd edn, Baltimore: Graylock.
TOEPLITZ, O. (1963), *The Calculus: A Genetic Approach,* Chicago University Press.
UNESCO (1967), *New Trends in Mathematics Teaching,* vol. 1, prepared by the International Commission of Mathematical Instruction, United Nations Educational, Scientific and Cultural Organization.
VAN HIELE, P. M. (1957), *De problematiek van het inzicht,* Amsterdam: Meulenhoff. Summary in English.
VAN HIELE-GELDOF, D. (1957), *De didaktik van de metkunde in de eerste klas van het VHMO,* Amsterdam: Meulenhoff. Summary in English.
VESSELO, I. R. (1962), *How to Read Statistics,* Harrap.
VISSIO, P., and ZADOU-NAISKY, G. (1963), *A la conquête de l'espace. Les structures algébriques de la géométrie euclidienne,* OCDL.
WAISMANN, F. (1959), *Introduction to Mathematical Thinking,* Harper & Row.
WALLIN, N. O. (1965), *Vektorer,* Lund: NKI-skolan.
WILLIAMS, J. D. (1954), *The Compleat Strategist,* McGraw-Hill, RAND Series.
WIRTZ, R. W., BOTEL, M., and SAWYER, W. W. (1961), *Math Workshop for Children,* Encyclopaedia Britannica.
WITTENBERG, A. I. (1963a), *Bildung und Mathematik. Mathematik als exemplarisches Gymnasialfach,* Stuttgart: Klett.
WITTENBERG, A. I. (1963b), *Redécouvrir les mathématiques. Exemples d'enseignement génétique,* Neuchâtel: Delachaux & Niestlé.
WITTMANN, J. (1952), *Ganzheitliches Rechnen,* 3rd edn, Dortmund: Gruwell.
WOLFF, G. (ed.), *Handbuch der Schulmathematik,* 8 vols., Hanover: Schroedel; Paderborn: Schöning.
YAGLOM, A. M., and YAGLOM, I. M. (1959), *Probabilité et information,* Dunod.

YAGLOM, A. M., and YAGLOM, I. M. (1964), *Challenging Mathematical Problems with Elementary Solutions*, Holden-Day.

YAGLOM, I. M. (1962), *Geometrical Transformations*, Random House.

YAGLOM, I. M., and BOLTYANSKI, V. G. (1961), *Convex Figures*, Holt, Rinehart & Winston.

Periodicals

American Mathematical Monthly (1894), 10/year. Mathematical Association of America, 1225 Connecticut Avenue, NW, Washington, DC.

Archimede, revista per gli insegnanti e i cultori di matematiche pure e applicate (1949), 6/year. Felice Le Monnier, Via S. Ammirato 100, Florence.

Archimedes, Anregungen und Aufgaben für Lehrer, Schüler und Freunde der Mathematik mit besonderer Pflege der Randbeziehungen zur Philosophie und zur Technik, 9/year. Verlag Josef Habbel, Gutenbergstrasse 17, Regensburg, G.F.R.

Arithmetic Teacher (1954), 8/year. National Council of Teachers of Mathematics, 1201 Sixteenth Street, NW, Washington, DC.

Australian Mathematics Teacher (1945), 3/year. The Mathematical Association (N.S.W. Branch), Sydney Teachers College, University Grounds, Sydney.

Bulletin de l'Association des Professeurs de Mathematiques de l'enseignement Publique (1910), 5/year. Association des Professeurs de Mathématiques de l'Enseignement Publique, 29 Rue d'Ulm, Paris 5ᵉ.

Bulletin of the International Study Group for Mathematics Learning (1962). International Study Group for Mathematics Learning, 200 California Avenue, Palo Alto, California 94306.

Elemente der Mathematik, Zeitschrift zur Pflege der Mathemarik und zur Förderung des mathematisch-physikalischen Unterrichts (1946), 2/month (English, French and German). Birkhäuser-Verlag, Basel, Switzerland.

Elementos, Revista de matematica para la enseñanza media (1963), 4/year. Ferdinández Blanco, 2045 Buenos Aires, Sucursal 31, Argentina.

L'Enseignement Mathématique, Revue internationale. Organe officiel de la Commission Internationale de l'Enseignement Mathématique (1899), quarterly. Institut de Mathématiques, Pavillon des Sciences, Bd. d'Yvoy, 1211 Genève.

Euclides, Monthly for the teaching of mathematics (1940). Chairman of the editorial staff: Dr. Joh. H. Wansink. Julianalaan 84, Arnhem.

Gazeta Matematică, Serie B. Publicatie lunařa pentru tineret (Monthly for youngsters) (1950). Societatea de Stiinte matematice din Republica Socialista Romania, Strada Academiei 14, Bucharest, Romania.

Középiskolai Matematikai Lapok (Mathematical Journal for Secondary Schools) (1894), monthly. Problems also in English and Russian. Posta Központi Hirlapiroda, Budapest V. József Nádor tér 1.

Matematic̆ko-Fizic̆ki List, Za ucenike srednjih škola (Journal of mathematics and physics for secondary-school pupils) (1951), 4/year. Društvo Matematic̆ara i Fizic̆ara N.R.H., Ilica 16/III, Zagreb, Yugoslavia.

Matematika i Fizika (1958), 6/year. Ministerstvo na Nar. Prosvetata. Boulevard Stamboliyski 18, Sofia, Bulgaria.

A Matematika Tanitása (1953), 6/year. Tankönyvkiadó Vállalat, Budapest V., Szalay utca 10–14.

Matematika ve Škole (1950), 10/year. Státni pedagogicke nakladelstvi, Jindřišská ul. Prague 1. Nové Město.

Matematika v Škole, Metodičeskij žurnal Ministerstva Prosveščenija RSFSR (1934), 6/year. Prosveščenie, Moscow, G.117, Pogodinskoya ul. Dom 8., USSR.

Matematyka, Czasopismo dla nauczycieli (1948), 4/year. Warsaw 2, pl. Dabrowskiego 8, Poland.

Mathematica et Pedagogīca (1953), 4/year (in French and Flemish). Société belge de professeurs de mathématiques, 143 rue des Trois Hurées, Jemappes, Belgium.

Mathematical Gazette, The Journal of the Mathematical Association (1894), quarterly. G. Bell & Sons Ltd, York House, Portugal Street, London, W.C.2.

Mathematical Log, official publication of the National High School and Junior College Mathematics Club, Mu Alpha Theta (1957), 3/year. Box 1127, University of Oklahoma, Norman, Oklahoma.

Mathematical Pie (1951), 3/year. Mathematical Pie Ltd, 100 Burman Road, Shirley, Solihull, Warwickshire, England.

Mathematics Magazine (1947), 5/year. Mathematical Association of America, 1225 Connecticut Avenue, NW, Washington, DC.

Mathematics Student Journal (1954), 4/year. National Council of Teachers of Mathematics, 1201 Sixteenth Street, NW, Washington, DC 20036.

The Mathematics Teacher (1908), 8/year. National Council of Teachers of Mathematics, 1201 Sixteenth Street, NW, Washington, DC, 20036.

Mathematics Teaching (1955), quarterly. Association of Teachers of Mathematics, Vine Street Chambers, Nelson, Lancashire.

Mathematik in der Schule (1963), monthly. Volk und Wissen Volkseigener Verlag, Berlin, W.8. Lindenstr. 54.

Der Mathematikunterricht, 5/year. Klett Verlag, Stuttgart.

Der Mathematische und Naturwissenschaftliche Unterricht (1948), 10/year. F. Dümmlers Verlag, Kaiserstr. 31/37, Bonn.

Mathematisch-Physikalische Semesterberichte, zur Pflege des Zusammenhangs von Schule und Universität (1963), 2/year. Vandenhoeck & Ruprecht, Göttingen.

Praxis der Mathematik, Monatschrift der Reinen und der angewandten Mathematik im unterricht (1958), monthly. Aulis Verlag Deubner, 5 Cologne, Antwerpenerstr. 6/12.

Pythagoras, Wiskundetijdschrift voor jongeren (1961), 6/year. Nederlandse Onderwijs Commissie van het Wiskunding Venootschap Machtiging 13, Groningen.

School Science and Mathematics, A journal for all science and mathematics teachers (1901), 9/year. Central Association of Science and Mathematics Teachers, Box 246, Bloomington, Indiana 47401.

Teaching Arithmetics, The British Journal of Elementary Mathematics (1963), 3/year. Pergamon, Oxford.

Series

The following list is intended as a general indication of teaching material available from educational publishers and organizations sponsoring publications in this field. For a complete list of titles and authors, the reader is advised to write to the addresses given.

Association des professeurs de mathématiques de l'enseignement public (APM), 29, rue d'Ulm, Paris 6ᵉ. *Les brochures de l'APM,* 1963-.

Authors: G. Choquet, A. Revuz, G. Revuz.
Association of Teachers of Mathematics, Vine Street Chambers, Nelson,
Lancashire, U.K. *Mathematics teaching pamphlets*, 1964–.
Authors: A. Bell, T. J. Fletcher, R. M. Fyfe.
Beihefte für den mathematischen Unterricht, 1954–, Braunschweig: Vieweg.
Authors: H. Meschkowski, E. Weber, K. Wellvitz.
Bibliotečka Fiziko-Matematičeskoj Školy, Matematika (Little Library of Physical-
Mathematical Schools: Mathematics), Moscow: Izdatelstvo 'Nauka'.
Authors: Y. Dynkin, S. I. Gelfand.
Biblioteka Matematičeskogo Kružka (The Library of the Mathematical Club),
1950–, Moscow: Gosizdat.
Authors: D. O. Shklyarskiy, I. M. Yaglom.
Cours de mathématiques pour l'enseignement des premier et second degrés, 1964–,
Dunod.
Authors: G. Brousseau, M. Dumont, L. Félix.
Exploring Mathematics, 1963–, The House of Grant.
Authors: P. French, R. J. Rickard.
Exploring Mathematics on your own, 1961–, Doubleday; Murray.
Authors: W. H. Glenn, D. A. Johnson, M. S. Norton.
Introductory Monographs in Mathematics, 1963–, Macmillan; St Martin's Press.
Authors: A. J. Moakes, W. Chellingsworth.
Mathematical Topics, 1964–, Hart-Davis.
Authors: A. G. Razell, K. G. O. Watts.
National Council of Teachers of Mathematics, *Yearbooks*. 1201 Sixteenth Street,
NW, Washington 6, DC.
Nuffield Foundation Mathematics Teaching Project. Project organizer:
Dr G. Matthews, 12 Upper Belgrave Street, London, S.W.1.
Textbooks and teachers' guides, 1967–, Murray.
Populyarnye lekcii po matematike (Popular lectures in mathematics), 1951–,
Moscow: Izdatelstvo 'Nauka'.
Popular Lectures in Mathematics. (Translation of *Populyarnye lekcii po matematike*),
Pergamon.
School Mathematics Project (SMP), The University, Southampton.
Textbooks, 1964–, Cambridge University Press.
Directors' reports, The University Bookshop, The University, Southampton.
Annually since 1962.
School Mathematics Study Group (SMSG). Director: Professor E. Begle, School
of Education, Cedar Hall, Stanford University, Stanford, California 94305.
Textbooks, 1960–, Yale University Press.
Monographs, 1961–, Random House, New Mathematical Library.
Conference reports, other publications: Studies in mathematics, study guides in
mathematics (annotated bibliographies), supplementary materials.
Scottish Mathematics Group
Edinburgh, W. and R. Chambers;
Glasgow, Blackie and Sons, 1965–.
Modern mathematics for schools. Books 1–5.
St. Dunstan's College Booklets, 1964–, Arnold.
Contemporary school mathematics.
Authors: C. A. R. Bailey, F. B. Lovis, G. Matthews, J. A. Reynolds, A. J. Sherlock.

Thinking with Mathematics, 1963–, Heath.
Authors: J. D. Bristol, A. L. Hess, R. Spreckelmeyer.
Topics in Mathematics (Translation of *Populyarnye lekcii po matematike*), 1963–, Heath.
Authors: A. S. Barsov, V. G. Boltyanskiy, Y. S. Dubnov, A. I. Markushevich, B. A. Trakhtenbrot, N. N. Varobyov.
Unterrichtshefte zur mathematik von Heute, Hannover: Schroedel; Paderborn: Schöning.
Author: H. Nickelsen.

Index